102 153 164 2

KT-416-838

Praise for *Willful Blindness*

SHORTLISTED FOR THE
FINANCIAL TIMES AND GOLDMAN SACHS
BUSINESS BOOK OF THE YEAR AWARD 2011

"Writing in clear, flowing prose . . . [*Willful Blindness*] made me think long and hard about how the pace and priorities of our daily lives can hinder our ability to live as decently and as truthfully as we can."
— *The New York Times*

"An important book that should be read by every MBA student, every lawyer and politician, every educator and everyone concerned about our future."
— *Guelph Mercury*

"[An] absorbing new book about why we choose to avert our gaze from wrongdoings or flaws or sad certainties we can't bring ourselves to confront. *Willful Blindness* cuts a broad swath across the fabric of our culture."
— *The Gazette* (Montreal)

"[A] riveting, important book. . . . [Heffernan] is an engaging writer able to marshal fascinating multi-disciplinary research into a narrative that traverses the quest for conformity, groupthink [and] how an overloaded mind leads to moral blindness. . . . Eye-opening."
— *Maclean's*

"A call to arms to any whistle-blowers who see what lies ahead and have the courage to speak up. . . . A sharp-eyed perspective on the ever-gathering storm."
— *Kirkus*

"A thoughtful and entertaining treatise on the seductiveness—and consequences—of ignoring what's right in front of our eyes . . . Heffernan's cogent, riveting look at how we behave at our worst encourages us to strive for our best."
— *Publishers Weekly*

OP Purchase

1 0 JUN 2016

Sheffield Hallam University
Learning and Information Services
Withdrawn From Stock

BY THE SAME AUTHOR

How She Does It: How Women Entrepreneurs Are Changing the Rules of Business Success

The Naked Truth: A Working Woman's Manifesto on Business and What Really Matters

OF Purchase
1 6 JUN 2016

WILLFUL BLINDNESS

Why We Ignore the Obvious at Our Peril

MARGARET HEFFERNAN

ANCHOR CANADA

SHEFFIELD HALLAM UNIVERSITY
WL
153.7
HE
COLLEGIATE LEARNING CENTRE

Copyright © 2011 Margaret Heffernan
Anchor Canada edition published 2012

All rights reserved. The use of any part of this publication, reproduced,
transmitted in any form or by any means electronic, mechanical, photocopying,
recording or otherwise, or stored in a retrieval system without the prior
written consent of the publisher—or in the case of photocopying or
other reprographic copying, license from the Canadian Copyright Licensing
Agency—is an infringement of the copyright law.

Anchor Canada is a registered trademark.

Library and Archives of Canada Cataloguing in Publication has been applied for.

ISBN: 978-0-385-66902-3

Cover design: adapted from an original by Nick Venables

Printed and bound in the USA

Published in Canada by Anchor Canada,
a division of Random House of Canada Limited

Visit Random House of Canada Limited's website: www.randomhouse.ca

10 9 8 7 6 5 4 3 2 1

For Pamela

CONTENTS

INTRODUCTION

Go, go, go, said the bird: human kind
Cannot bear very much reality.
—T. S. Eliot, *Four Quartets*

ON JULY 19, 2011, the British Member of Parliament Adrian Sanders asked James and Rupert Murdoch a question that temporarily silenced them both.

"Are you familiar with the term 'willful blindness'?

Reading from my blog on the subject, the member of the Select Committee on Culture, Media and Sport proceeded to explain what was, apparently, a highly uncomfortable idea for both Murdochs.

I had first encountered willful blindness when reading the transcript of the trial of Jeffrey Skilling and Kenneth Lay, CEO and Chairman of Enron. In his summing up, Judge Simeon Lake gave this instruction to the jury:

> You may find that a defendant had knowledge of a fact if you find that the defendant deliberately closed his eyes to what would otherwise have been obvious to him. Knowledge can be inferred if the defendant *deliberately blinded himself to the existence of a fact.*[1]

Judge Lake was applying the legal principle of willful blindness: you are responsible if you could have known, and should have known, something which instead you strove not to see. Skilling and Lay could have known, and had the opportunity to know, just how rotten their company was. Their claim not to know was no excuse under the law. Since they could have known, they were responsible.

Once the idea of willful blindness lodged in my mind, I started to see it everywhere: in the Catholic Church, Nazi Germany, at BP, in Iraq and Egypt, in our continuing failure meaningfully to reform the banking system. I was struck that so many, perhaps even most, of the greatest crimes had been committed not in the dark, hidden where no one could see them, but in full view of hundreds or thousands of people who simply chose not to look and not to question.

I noticed it in domestic lives too; in failing marriages, why had she never asked about all those business trips? In hospitals: Why had he skipped his check up? Why had she started smoking? At home, how could so many people have got themselves so deeply in debt? And why were skin cancers and obesity so intractable when everyone knows that suntanning and over-eating are dangerous?

When I mentioned willful blindness to friends and colleagues from any walk of life, their eyes lit up: they knew exactly what I was talking about. Doctors described unnecessary treatments their patients demanded and got. Lawyers recounted their struggles to forget information their clients should never have shared with them. Technologists expressed their amazement that Microsoft hadn't seen the Internet coming, while Google had been blindsided by social media. Intelligence chiefs confided that they had had no insight into the Arab spring while chief executives acknowledged that the hardest part of their job, even in a small company, was knowing what was going on. Almost everyone mentioned the Iraq War and global warming: big public blunders caused or exacerbated by a reluctance to confront uncomfortable facts.

Willful blindness had started life as a legal concept in the nineteenth century. A judge in *Regina v. Sleep* ruled that an accused could not be convicted for possession of government property unless the jury found that he either knew the goods came from government stores or had "willfully shut his eyes to the fact." Thereafter, English judicial authorities referred to the state of mind that accompanied one who "willfully shut his eyes" as "connivance" or "constructive knowledge."[2] Over time, lots of other phrases came into play – deliberate or willful ignorance, conscious avoidance and deliberate indifference. What they all have in common is the idea that there is an opportunity for knowledge, and a responsibility to be informed, but it is shirked. Nowadays, the law is most often applied in cases of money laundering and drug trafficking: if you've been paid a large amount of money to carry a suitcase, then you are being willfully blind if you don't check what is inside.

The law doesn't care *why* you remain ignorant, only that you do. But I am interested in why we choose to keep ourselves in the dark. What are the forces at work that make us deny the big threats that stare us in the face? What stops us from seeing that burying knowledge only makes it more powerful, and us so much more vulnerable? Why, after any major failure or calamity, do voices always emerge saying they'd seen the danger, warned about the risk — but their warnings went unheeded? And why, as individuals, companies and countries do we so regularly look in the mirror and howl: How could we have been so blind?

As I investigated the causes and patterns of willful blindness, from our daily lives to the boardrooms of global corporations, I could have confined myself to business alone; there's no shortage of material. But it struck me that one source of our blindness at work is the artificial divide between personal and working lives. Every workforce is a conglomeration of individuals whose behaviors and habits started well before they were hired. Individuals, singly and in groups, are equally susceptible to willful blindness; what makes organizations different is the scale of damage they can cause.

Whether individual or collective, willful blindness, doesn't have a single driver, but many. We can't notice and know everything: the cognitive limits of our brain simply won't let us. That means we have to filter or edit what we take in. So what we choose to let through and to leave out is crucial. We mostly admit the information that makes us feel great about ourselves, while conveniently filtering out whatever unsettles our fragile egos and most vital beliefs. It's a truism that love is blind; what's less obvious is just how much evidence it can ignore. Ideology and orthodoxies powerfully mask what, to the uncaptivated mind, is obvious, dangerous or absurd and there's much about how and even where we live that leaves us in the dark. Fear of conflict, fear of change keeps us that way: almost all employees believe their bosses do not want to hear the truth. An unconscious (and much denied) impulse to obey and conform shields us from confrontation and crowds provide friendly alibis for our inertia. And money has the power to blind us, even to our better selves.

Of course, willful blindness it isn't always disastrous. It oils the wheels of social intercourse when we don't see the spot on a silk tie, the girlfriend's acne or a neighbor's squalor. Ignoring political differences may contribute to office calm. In times of national emergency, blindness can be positively helpful. During the London Blitz, morale was better sustained by dancing and partygoing than by acknowledging a terrifying future. And it's far easier for all of us to maintain optimism and momentum by ignoring our own mortality.

Perhaps it is the sheer utility of willful blindness that sucks us into the habit in the first place. It seems innocuous and feels efficient. But the mechanisms that make us blind to the world also put us in peril. The children who grow up among abusive parents come to maturity feeling crazy, confused and anxious because their reality has been consistently denied. Ideologues, refusing to see data and events that challenge their theories, doom themselves to irrelevance. Fraudsters only succeed when they depend on our desire to blind ourselves to the questions that would expose their schemes. Companies full of compliant employees take on levels of risk beyond their ability to recover. And all the time that these perils go unacknowledged, they grow more powerful and more dangerous.

That willful blindness is so pervasive does not mean that it is inevitable. Some of the most inspiring people in this book are those who have had the courage to look, a fierce determination to see. That is what makes them remarkable. They aren't especially knowledgeable, powerful or talented. They're not heroes; they're human. But their courage in daring to see reveals a central truth about willful blindness: we may think being blind makes us safer, when in fact it leaves us crippled, vulnerable and powerless. But when we confront facts and fears, we achieve real power and unleash our capacity for change.

1

AFFINITY AND BEYOND

In life one and one don't make two;
One and one make one.
And I'm looking for that free ride to me:
I'm looking for you.
—The Who, "Bargain"

M EET REBECCA.
The first thing you will notice is that she is very tall—just under six feet. Mid-thirties. Healthy, wholesome—and even today, when she's had to bring her two children in to work with her, she has plenty of energy.

Meet Robert.

He's tall too—just over six feet. Mid-thirties. Handsome, clean-cut, and, despite some looming deadlines, unfailingly polite.

Meeting Rebecca and Robert together, you will notice what all their friends comment on: they look very alike. Not the same, of course; they're not twins. They're husband and wife. And their looks are not deceptive.

"Amazing similarities," Robert concedes. "Similarities in background that I didn't notice, but I like more and more. Not rich, not poor. Went to the same university, both Christian. But then there are more nuanced things, like the way we both think about family and friends and believing in hard work. And of course we work in the same industry and," he looks over at Rebecca and beams, "wear the unofficial uniform: neat jeans, crisp shirt." They both laugh.

Rebecca and Robert enjoy the fact that they are similar, because it makes them feel comfortable, safe, located within each other.

"It isn't that we like all the same things," says Rebecca when she's on her own. "I love going for walks—and Robert's had to learn to like them! But the skeleton of our lives, that's what we have in common. Very settled home lives, parents still together, parents who were always very encouraging. We didn't think consciously about these things when we started going out, but you look back and see these things, these patterns."

Rebecca and Robert enjoy the fact that they're so similar. They have very little sense that it limits them, narrows their perspective on life, or blinds them to a wide array of opinions, experiences, and different ways of thinking and being. But the fundamental human preference that they exemplify—for the familiar over the alien, the known over the unknown, and the comfortable over the dissonant—has insidious but important consequences. Embedded within our self-definition, we build relationships, institutions, cities, systems, and cultures that, in reaffirming our values, blind us to alternatives. This is where our willful blindness originates: in the innate human desire for familiarity, for likeness, that is fundamental to the ways our minds work.

Because for all that their similarities are so pronounced, in fact Rebecca and Robert are typical. Most people marry other people very like themselves: similar height, weight, age, background, IQ, nationality, ethnicity. We may think that opposites attract, but they don't get married. Sociologists and psychologists, who have studied this phenomenon for decades, call it "positive assortative mating"[1]—which really just means that we marry people like ourselves. When it comes to love, we don't scan a very broad horizon.

Gian Gonzaga used to work as a senior research scientist before leaving to join eHarmony, the online dating site. The "science of compatibility" that the site promotes argues that "compatibility is not enough! 29 Dimensions™ predict great relationships."

This is not romance, it's business. So eHarmony stands or falls on its success in finding people who really will like each other. In 2007, eHarmony claimed credit for 44,000 weddings, which amounted to 2 percent of all the marriages in America that year.[2] Today, they claim to average 236 marriages a day. What were all those people looking for?

"We know that people select for appearances, which is why you upload your picture. But our questionnaire goes a lot deeper and that's really based on what we know works. So we ask lots of questions about personality—how neat you are, how punctual—and about values: Do you value religion, altruism, volunteering? Values are the things you hold on to even in tough times and they are the things you most want validated by others. Of course interests count, too, but they change. You can learn to love walking, but values are really sticky."

Gonzaga and his wife, Heather Setrakian, don't just practice what they preach—they *are* what they preach. They met while working as academic researchers in UCLA's marriage lab; they're both in their thirties, dark-haired, and, according to their friends, brilliant, witty, and wise. The eHarmony system could have matched them, Gonzaga says, except that when his wife filled out her questionnaire she said she wanted someone two years younger.

That questionnaire certainly tests for patience and endurance. It takes at least a half hour to complete—longer if you're seriously committed to finding a mate. The questions are all designed to identify your key values and attitudes—those twenty-nine dimensions—and to match them up with someone else whose dimensions are as close to yours as possible. It may be software but it is, quite literally, matchmaking. It is not looking for opposites or quirky combinations.

"People may have an interest in people who are different from themselves," said Gonzaga. "But they don't marry them. They're looking for confirmation, for comfort."

Gonzaga bases his claims on data from twenty-five million questionnaires. What these tell him is that, whether we're using the wiring in our brains or the software underneath eHarmony's site, we go through life looking for people who make us comfortable because they're so much like us. We may be intrigued by difference—but ultimately, we reject it.

"For a while, I went out with women who looked different," Robert told me. "And women who really were different—sometimes very different indeed. But the turbulence of those relationships really drew me back to the center. You'd think it would widen the circle but it really didn't. I tried but I found I really didn't love Albanian women! Clearly some Albanian women are wonderful—I have nothing against the Albanians! But I think I learned that you're given a center of gravity that is immutable. You've been given a set of rules that you return to almost without thinking."

It isn't that Robert wasn't curious about other kinds of people and other cultures; he was. He wanted, more than many people, to explore beyond his own immediate knowledge and experience. But he rejected a difference that just felt too great. That puzzled him enough to make him think about it, but not enough to change his mind.

"I wonder if I might feel I am looking at myself when I look at Rebecca," Robert said. "Have I chosen myself?"

Robert and Rebecca are well educated and skeptical. They aren't inclined to take anything at face value. What makes them unusual is that they were prepared to analyze and talk about the powerful influence that their similarity has had on their relationship. They both acknowledge that it is a source of delight and comfort, but they worry that sticking to their own kind narrows their experience of life. By choosing to live and work among people like themselves, are they restricting what they see?

These findings—that we mostly marry and live with people very like ourselves—always annoy people. Confronted by the data, the most common response is a challenge: I'm not like that, my husband's not like that. Why are we so affronted? Because we all want to feel that we have made our own choices, that they weren't predictable, that we aren't so vain as to choose ourselves, and that we are freer spirits, with a broader, more eclectic range of taste than the data imply. We don't like to feel that we're blind to the allure of those who are not like us; we don't like to see how trapped we are inside our own identity.

But our minds operate somewhat like eHarmony's software: We go through life searching for good matches and, when we find one, it feels good. And that habit of mind pertains equally to things that really matter (like choosing a wife) and to things that don't matter at all. So when subjects in an experiment were led to believe that they shared a birthday with Rasputin, they were far more lenient in judging the antics of the mad monk than were those who had nothing in common with him. Just the thought that they shared a birthday made people like him more.

Even when it's something as trivial as our own initials, we stick to what we know best. A meta-analysis of the most severe hurricanes between 1998 and 2005 showed that people were more likely to donate to relief funds if the hurricane's name shared their first initial—so Kate and Katherine were more likely to donate to Hurricane Katrina relief than Zoe was.[3] I've always been baffled by monogrammed towels and shirts (do we really not know who owns the towels in our own homes?) but clearly these familiar letters mean a lot to us.

In other experiments, asked to choose a preferred letter from several pairs of letters, subjects tended, quite reliably, to opt for letters from their own names. What's so interesting about these findings is that the letters themselves are pretty meaningless—nothing will happen as a result of the choices made. Yet still the participants gravitate toward letters they see, and sign, every day. Even when it comes to the alphabet, we don't stray that far from home.

When you take this out of the lab and into the real world, the same pattern emerges. Carol, it seems, is more likely to drink Coke while Pete will choose Pepsi.[4] Leo likes Listerine but Tom likes Tom's of Maine—even if he's from Ohio. And while those choices may seem unimportant, it appears that life choices too may be influenced by those initials we love so much. Dentists are overrepresented by people whose names begin with "D" and there are more people named George than you should expect to find living in Georgia.

Familiarity, it turns out, does not breed contempt. It breeds comfort. In a series of experiments at the University of Michigan in the 1980s,[5] one group of sixty-four students was shown photographs of a male college student once a week for four weeks; the other group of sixty-four saw different faces each week. After the four weeks were up, the two groups were asked to assess how much they thought they would like the people whose faces they'd seen if they were to meet them in the future. They were also asked how far they believed those people to be similar to themselves.

The students who had seen the same face for four weeks believed more strongly that these were people they would like in real life. They also believed (on no evidence except the photograph) that those faces belonged to people who were similar to themselves. In other words, the familiar faces—with no supporting evidence—felt nicer. Women responded to the experiment in exactly the same way as men. A similar experiment, using irregular octagons, generated the same pattern of responses. The familiar makes us feel secure and comfortable.

This even pertains when we go looking for emotional experiences, as when we listen to music. It can be hard fully to enjoy a new piece the first time you listen to it; only after repeated hearings does it become a favorite. Part of that may be because if you're trying out, say, Mahler's Eighth Symphony for the first time, there is a lot to take in: two orchestras, two choirs, and eight soloists over eighty minutes won't create an instant impression. And listening to music is a hugely complex cognitive exercise.[6] Even the White Stripes' "Seven Nation Army" can take some getting used to. But once we've heard it a few times, we're used to it and like it. And then we don't want something different. We want more of the same.

"We score hundreds of attributes of every song," says Tim Westergren, the founder of Pandora Internet Radio. "And then we find the matches between those songs—and then that's what we recommend to you. Because we know that if you liked one piece of music, you are very, very likely to like another one that shares the same characteristics."

Westergren's business does for music what eHarmony does for dating. Each song is scored manually by musicians for some four hundred attributes; there are thirty for the voice alone, capturing everything from timbre to layers of the voice to vibrato. Then that "score" is matched to other songs that have scores that are as closely similar as possible. Pandora software is doing to music what we do when we meet people: looking for matches. And, when it finds them, people feel very happy.

"God, I love Pandora!" said Joe Clayton, a music fan in Boston. "I love it. I'm always finding new bands, new stuff that I just couldn't find otherwise—certainly not in any music store. And it's kinda creepy—but in a good way—because they almost never give me something I don't like. Almost never."

More than fifty million people use Pandora, and many are avid evangelists. But what Pandora can't do is come up with that serendipitous suggestion that introduces you to something completely different from anything you've ever heard before. I like Bruce Springsteen, Frank Zappa, and the White Stripes—but I also adore Handel. And given my first three preferences, Pandora wouldn't ever offer me Handel.

Westergren acknowledges that limitation. "We're never going to take you from rock and roll to baroque music. Pandora is about broadening your selection—but narrowing your taste. If you like jazz, you like more jazz. If you like hip-hop, you like more hip-hop. But Pandora is never going to take you from Springsteen to Handel."

All personalization software, whether eHarmony, Pandora, Amazon's book recommendations, or MyShape.com's clothing suggestions, does the same thing: makes our lives easier by reducing overwhelming choice. And software is doing it the same way that our brain does, by searching for matches. It's as though, online and off-line, our life is one gigantic game of Snap! This is immensely efficient: It means that the brain can take shortcuts because it is working with what it already knows, not having to start from scratch. When we find what we like, part of our pleasure is the joy of recognition.

But the flip side of that satisfaction is that we are rejecting a lot along the way. As Westergren says, we are narrowing our taste, reducing the music or books or clothes or people that might widen our horizons. Our brains aren't designed to draw us into experiences that are wild and different; there would be no advantage in doing something so risky. And so, by focusing in one direction and excluding others, we become blind to the experiences that don't match.

This is not to say that strange, serendipitous things never flow into our lives. Of course they do. You meet someone at work who introduces you to Handel and you develop a love of baroque music. Or—more likely—your son introduces you to Rammstein. But these encounters are random and risky. Remember Robert's problem with Albanian women.

There's a circle here: We like ourselves, not least because we are known and familiar to ourselves. So we like people similar to us—or that we just imagine might have some attributes in common with us. They feel familiar too, and safe. And those feelings of familiarity and security make us like ourselves more because we aren't anxious. We belong. Our self-esteem rises. We feel happy. Human beings want to feel good about themselves and to feel safe, and being surrounded by familiarity and similarity satisfies those needs very efficiently.

The problem with this is that everything outside that warm, safe circle is our blind spot.

Because not only are we rejecting music that doesn't match; we use these same processes to make important decisions in our everyday lives. When I had my first opportunity, as a producer at the BBC, to choose my own team, I hoped to hire people who would challenge me and each other and who would invest the entire project with intellec-tual richness and vigor. With all that firmly in mind, I selected liberal arts graduates who were all female, spoke several languages, and had birthdays within the same week in June. In other words, they were all like me.

Did I consciously intend to do that? Of course not. Like hiring managers the world over, I intended to hire only the best and the brightest and that's what I thought I was looking for. But did I also want people I'd feel comfortable working with, enjoy spending late hours with, people who shared the values of the project? Well, yes.

I was biased, in favor of those just like me. Everyone is biased. But just as we are affronted when told that we're likely to marry and associate with those very similar to ourselves, so most people vehemently reject the idea that they are biased: others may be, but not us. "And why beholdest thou the mote that is in thy brother's eye but considerest not the beam that is in thine own eye?" is how the Bible puts it.[7] Of course we consider the people who disagree with us to be the most biased of all.[8]

It's recently become easier to identify and measure biases with a suite of tests called the Implicit Association Test, or IAT for short. Designed by three psychologists, the computer-based tests examine thoughts and feelings that exist outside of our conscious awareness or control.[9] These may pertain to gender, age, race, or religion. In the test, participants are given two sets of images and two lists of words—one positive, one negative. Images and words appear randomly on the screen and you have to associate them with positives or negatives. You may link "male" with "intelligent" or "old" with "stupid." When making a link that isn't comfortable for us, we take longer. And that delay, say the researchers, is telling: it takes more time to overcome bias. The longer we take to accept a match, the greater our bias.

Since 1998, more than 4.5 million people have taken these tests and the researchers have found that bias is pervasive among all of us, whether we think we're biased or not. White physicians are friendlier toward anonymous white patients than toward black ones. Seventy percent of citizens in thirty-four countries associate science more with men than with women. More than 80 percent of us have a bias against the elderly. Ordinary people (including the researchers who direct the project) harbor negative associations in relation to various social groups even though they say they don't and often wish, quite earnestly, not to.

We see this play out in daily life everywhere. Go into any major corporation and look around. Despite decades of diversity campaigns and millions of dollars invested in programs to make recruitment and retention less biased and more equitable, the homogeneity of most companies is overwhelming. Look at the lists of where the graduates of Harvard Business School or Wharton go and you will see the same phenomenon: armies marching into banks, financial institutions, consulting firms, year after year.

This is one reason why, despite a great deal of goodwill and commitment and even, in some countries, equality legislation, it has proved so hard to shift women into top roles, shovel venture capital into ethnic businesses, or train a lot of male midwives. It isn't the only reason, of course, but the fact that we like people like ourselves, are unconsciously biased in their favor, makes a big impact. Stereotypes are energy-saving devices; they let us make shortcuts that feel just fine.[10] That's why they're so persistent.

The famous development of blind auditions for new symphony members provided graphic illustration of this point. Harvard economist Claudia Goldin and Princeton's Cecilia Rouse found that when musicians were allowed to audition behind screens, where their gender could not influence the evaluation of their music, women's chances of making it through the first round increased by 50 percent—and in the final rounds by *300* percent. Blind auditions have now become standard in the United States, with the result that the number of female players in major orchestras has increased from 5 percent to 36 percent.

In Europe, that practice is not ubiquitous—and many musicians argue that this perpetuates both gender and ethnic discrimination. Some of this bias isn't even implicit: The Vienna Philharmonic did not accept women until twelve years ago and even now only 2 percent of its 137 musicians are women. Moreover, despite the recent rise to prominence of many brilliant Asian musicians, the Philharmonic has never hired a visible "non-Aryan" because it feels that such individuals would "destroy the ensemble's image of Austrian authenticity."[11] Even white male musicians say that white male musicians prefer white male musicians.[12] Music may be a universal language but not, apparently, universally.[13]

The many voices arguing in favor of diversity in recent years have not been motivated only, or even primarily, by notions of social justice. The argument for diversity is that if you bring together lots

of different kinds of people, with a wide range of education and experience, they can identify more solutions, see more alternatives to
problems, than any single person or homogenous group ever could.
Groups have the potential, in other words, to be smarter than
individuals; that's the case put forward so compellingly by James
Surowiecki in his book, *The Wisdom of Crowds*. But the problem is
that, as our biases keep informing whom we hire and promote, we
weed out that diversity and are left with skyscrapers full of people
pretty much the same.

Just as we choose to work with people very like ourselves, we choose to
live among them also. The psychologist David Myers says that the way
we move around and build neighborhoods mirrors the way we choose
our spouses.

"Mobility enables the sociological equivalent of 'assortative mating,'"
he says. Now that we enjoy so much freedom to move around, choosing the jobs that we like, we can also choose the communities that we
like. And by and large we choose "those places and people that are
comfortably akin to ourselves."[14]

Across the United States, the journalist Bill Bishop studied this pattern and found that over the last thirty years, most Americans had been
engaged in moving toward more homogenous ways of living, "clustering in communities of like-mindedness." He calls this "the big sort"
and what strikes him is how well defended these communities can be.
When a lone Republican neighbor, living in a staunchly Democratic
part of Austin, Texas, dared to articulate his political opinion in a local
LISTSERV, the response he got was unambiguous: "I'm really not interested [in] being surprised by right-wing e-mail in my in box, no
matter what its guise. It makes me feel bad, and I don't like it."[15]

As we have either more freedom or less security in our work, we
move more. In 2008, thirty-four million people—11.9 percent of the
population—moved, and that was the lowest rate of migration since
1959.[16] And when people move, they mostly choose to live among
people who like the same coffee shops, bookstores, festivals, and politics.
When Bill Bishop went on to map this trend across the United States,
his data revealed that the preference people have for living with others
like themselves made a clear impact on the political map of the country.
Whereas in 1976, only 26 percent of people lived in landslide counties,
by 2000 45.3 percent did. That didn't make for a lot of argument outside the polling stations.

"The neighborhood where we live," Rebecca says, "is lovely. The neighbors are lovely. The family on the other side of us, Paul and Juliet—they *are* us! Mid-thirties, two boys. Slightly younger but exactly parallel. Juliet doesn't work, but I'm only part-time. The street is full of people like us. Each house is a carbon copy of the same kinds of people."

When Rebecca and Robert were house-hunting, she recalls that they were driven by price, proximity to work, and choice of schools. All her neighbors were using the same parameters, so perhaps it isn't so surprising that they'd all end up together.

"I guess you could say that," Rebecca concedes. "But there were other places that would have fit the bill. But when we came here, it was more than just functionality. We liked it here—we still like it here. It feels right for us."

Bishop argues that we have come to demand living arrangements that won't challenge us. We seek confirmation and validation from those around us, even if it is just a matter of our pastimes. Wesleyan College in Connecticut caters to this desire, by offering twenty-eight different dorms organized around themes, including one for "eclectic" students. (Apparently even dislike of themes is a theme.) Colgate College in New York has a dorm for the lovers of foreign films. Affinity is a big draw.

These dorms are merely mirroring what is happening in the communities from which these students come; real estate developers bank on it. They design neighborhoods such as Covenant Hills in Orange County for Christians so it boasts a Christian school. The more exotically named Terramor, on the other hand, aims to be one of the largest environmentally friendly developments in America, marketed to "cultural creatives" who want to send their children to its Montessori school.[17] As nice as they may be, what the dorms and developments also do is narrow the field of vision, providing environments in which the inhabitants can reside safe from challenge.

However, living in communities that look different may not deliver real social diversity. Years ago, my family and I lived in the North End of Boston, the colorful Italian district of the city. After living in Europe, we'd chosen it because we were used to, and enjoyed, hearing Italian spoken on the streets and liked the aroma of garlic in the evenings. But we didn't have any Italian friends. We had an Italian longshoreman as a neighbor but we knew Louis only well enough to say "ciao."

Who were the people we spent time with? People like us: educated white professionals with young kids.

Living in London wasn't so different. Yes, we lived in Stockwell, which real estate agents would call "a mixed area"—meaning an ethnically diverse and sometimes volatile combination of elegant early Victorian terraces and 1960s public housing. But you didn't see much traffic between those two architectures, not a lot of cups of sugar being borrowed. Teachers, professors, businesspeople, and TV producers lived in elegant stucco homes; single, often teenage parents lived across from them. At least we could see each other but that was about as far as it ever went.

By following our instincts to cluster together in like-minded communities, we reduce our exposure to different people, values, and experiences. But we also slowly but surely focus on what we know, losing sight of everything else. We may have more choices than ever before but our tastes are more narrow than ever, too.

Media companies understand this perfectly. They know that when we buy a newspaper or a magazine, we aren't looking for a fight. The Fox News fan does not buy the *New York Times*. My Italian neighbor might read the *Boston Herald* but I would never see the *Boston Globe* on his doorstep. We select our media knowingly, rejecting the programs, newspapers, and TV stations that we don't agree with because we feel comfortable sticking to the same groove. The search for what is familiar and comfortable underlies our media consumption habits in just the same way as it makes us yearn for Mom's mac 'n' cheese.

This is natural but it isn't neutral. In what he calls the "group polarization effect," legal scholar Cass Sunstein found that when groups of like-minded people get together, they make each other's views more extreme.[18] (It is worth noting that Sunstein, a professor at Harvard, is married to Samantha Power, also a professor at Harvard, and they both are currently on leave serving the Obama administration. Even people who write about this behavior can't escape it.) Just as Pandora narrows your taste, like-minded people have the same impact on your opinions.

In 2005, Sunstein got together with some of his colleagues to conduct an experiment. They brought together two groups of like-minded people: liberals from Boulder, Colorado, and conservatives from

Colorado Springs. In their respective groups, each was asked to deliberate on three topics: civil unions, affirmative action, and climate change. But before the discussions began, individual participants recorded their private opinions on each topic. Then the groups were mixed up and encouraged to discuss their views.

The group deliberations were consistently respectful, engaged, and substantive, but when they were finished, almost every member ended up with more extreme positions than they had held at the start. Conservatives from Colorado Springs who had been neutral on a climate-change treaty now opposed it. Boulder liberals who had felt somewhat positive about civil unions became firmly convinced of their merit. What small diversity each group might have had at the outset was, says Sunstein, "squelched," while the rift between them had grown larger.

Even when presented with a wide range of data and arguments, Sunstein's work with groups demonstrated that when individuals read, they focus on the information that supports their current opinion, paying less attention to information that challenges their views. Overall, people are about twice as likely to seek information that supports their own point of view as they are to consider an opposing idea.[19] Rather than broadening their attitudes, the very process of discussion renders them blind to alternatives. We stop looking at places or jobs or information or people that will prove too uncomfortable, too tumultuous for our closely held beliefs. We may think we want to be challenged, but we really don't. Our intellectual homes are just as self-selected and exclusive as our physical homes.

In theory, the Internet was going to change all of this. Access to the world's store of knowledge was supposed to liberate us from the confines of the people we knew and the institutions to which we belonged. After all, online you can meet anyone from anywhere. But while it's true that all of us now have access to more information than ever before in history, for the most part we don't use it. Just like newspapers, we read the blogs that we agree with—but there we encounter a virtually infinite echo chamber, as 85 percent of blogs link to other blogs with the same political inclination.[20]

In fact, the great strength of the Internet lies in this ability to develop and connect affinity groups. It goes beyond connecting Tea Party members with other Tea Party members, and jihadists with jihadists. Wherever you live, whatever your age, whether you love or-chids, aikido, or ideology, you can find and connect to like-minded enthusiasts. Why do you want to do that? Because in doing so, you gain access to shortcuts: information from people like you that you believe to be reliable. If you don't know how to lift and split your orchids, the community of orchid aficionados will save you a lot of money and grief. Off-line or online, what's the advantage of clustering in strongly defined communities of like-minded people? You believe the advice or recommendations your neighbors give you. If they like a school or a restaurant or a movie, well then you will probably like it too; you don't have to try them all or read all the reviews. We cling together because it feels comfortable and safe but also because it's highly efficient. We don't have to learn everything ourselves, the hard, slow way.

Shortcuts do make us smarter and more efficient and they reward us in many ways—until they lead us astray. Which is what happened when Bernie Madoff tapped into a community of investors, all very much alike and eager to pass on what they knew.

"I inherited my account from my dad," said Irvin Stalbe.

We spoke in Stalbe's modest apartment in Pampano Beach, Florida. He retired there when he was fifty-five but had continued to work part-time in a bank, just for the companionship. The money he made from his Madoff account was for extras—vacations, a little gambling—and to pay for his grandchildren's education.

"I didn't know much about it. I got it when my parents died. They weren't wealthy, they just put a little aside every year. I'd tried invest-ing for myself but I wasn't that good at it, and I just thought: it's steady and it works.

"When I brought the paperwork to my accountant and he saw the income, he said he'd like to add money to it. So we worked out a way we'd issue 1099s to anyone who put money in. In the end, I had forty friends and family in the account."

Did the accountant, did anyone, do any research before they joined? I wondered.

"No, not really. We were in it for twenty-five years, my parents twenty years before me! Over the years, we brought in friends, grand-kids, all under my name. For many years, it was wonderful. Of course what I realize now is I should have remembered the golden rule: Never put all your money in one place. But at the time, I mean, everyone was in it. We didn't have to worry."

Madoff's was an affinity crime, preying on people like him who knew people like themselves, who didn't ask questions because their level of comfort with each other was so high that they felt they could take shortcuts. Sitting with Stalbe and his family in their Florida sitting room, I sensed that these aren't greedy people. They just wanted the safety of a reliable return and they believed they'd found that in an investment vehicle that they all validated for one another. It is something we all do every day, but few of us pay such a high price for it.

"I'm okay," Stalbe says. "I still have some income and I work at my son's take-out restaurant, cleaning tables, working behind the counter. I like to talk to people. But my sister, she's devastated, she has nothing. My sister-in-law, the same thing: 90 percent of her money was in there. Because of me."

What distresses Stalbe most isn't his own loss, but the fact that he drew so many others in. He's angry with himself because his confidence is what gave them confidence. Everyone felt so comfortable with each other, they all had so much in common, that no one ever asked any questions. It's that affinity that allowed Madoff's fraud to reach such astronomic proportions.

Shortcuts can be very pragmatic, but when you take them, you miss a lot along the way: that's what shortcuts are for. Living, working, and making decisions with people like ourselves brings us comfort and efficiencies, but it also makes us far narrower in how we think and what we see. The more tightly we focus, the more we leave out.

These blind spots have a physical reality in the brain. Robert Burton is former chief of neurology at Mount Zion–UCSF Hospital. He has a restless mind and is always looking for ways to understand and to challenge the certainty that our biases give us. He's very aware that, in its endless search for matches, our brain rejects information that might broaden our outlook, widen our gaze, or make us just a little less certain.

"Neural networks," said Burton, "don't give you a direct route from, say, a flash of light straight to your consciousness. There are all kinds of committees that vote along the way, whether that flash of light is going to go straight to your consciousness or not. And if there are enough 'yes' votes, then yes you can see it. If there aren't, you could miss it.

"But here's the thing: What does your brain like? What gets the 'yes' vote? It likes the stuff it already recognizes. It likes what is familiar. So you will see the familiar stuff right away. The other stuff may take longer, or it may never impinge on your consciousness. You just won't see it."

We were talking on a beautiful morning in Sausalito, overlooking the harbor. It was early, there weren't many people about, but there were a few. Even before his first coffee, Burton eagerly scanned the horizon.

"I'm aware of people moving around, the town starting to wake up," Burton continued. "But it's a kind of fuzzy background, it doesn't get much attention from me. But if someone I knew walked across the street, I'd see that at once. Zip—straight in to my consciousness, 'yes' votes all the way. A perfect match."

Burton is very wary of our love for matches and craving for certainty. It goes right against the spirit of inquiry that, as a scientist, he loves. But mostly he's suspicious of it because he thinks it stops us seeing so much. He likens the development of the neural networks in our brain to the creation of a riverbed.

"Imagine the gradual formation of a riverbed. The initial flow of water might be completely random—there are no preferred routes in the beginning. But once a creek is formed, water is more likely to follow this newly created path of least resistance. As the water continues, the creek deepens and a river develops."

It's a beautiful metaphor, and a useful one too. The longer we live, and the more we accumulate similar experiences, friends, and ideas, the faster and more easily the water flows. There's less and less resistance. That absence of resistance produces a sense of ease, of comfort, of certainty. Yet, at the same time, the sides of the riverbed grow higher. As we pursue like-minded people, in like-minded communities, doing similar jobs in homogeneous corporate cultures, the riverbed sinks deeper and deeper, its sides become steeper and steeper. It feels good; the flow is efficient and unimpeded. You just can't see anything.

This is how willful blindness begins, not in conscious, deliberate choices to be blind, but in a skein of decisions that slowly but surely restrict our view. We don't sense our perspective closing in and most would prefer that it stay broad and rich. But our blindness grows out of the small, daily decisions that we make, which embed us more snugly inside our affirming thoughts and values. And what's most frightening about this process is that as we see less and less, we feel more comfort and greater certainty. We think we see more—even as the landscape shrinks.

2

LOVE IS BLIND

Love to faults is always blind,
Always is to joy inclin'd.
—William Blake, *Poems (1791–1793)*

THE VACCINE FOR German measles was first introduced in 1970 but, in the years before that, getting measles when pregnant was dangerous for the mother and the baby. Michael's mother knew this—there were so many doctors in the family—but there was nothing she could do. So Michael was born with a congenital heart defect.

Growing up, he was frail and was not allowed to play sports. But as though he knew that his future must depend on brain not brawn, he was so very clever. All his Jesuit teachers knew he was a student to cherish, bound to do well on exams and get into a top university, maybe even become a priest himself. They were disappointed in the last ambition but Michael grew up to be one of those individuals you knew, almost at first sight, was electrifyingly brilliant. That he was also very funny was a necessary saving grace.

After graduating from college, he worked in broadcasting, first in radio and then in television. But TV was too stressful and his time there coincided with his first heart valve replacement. Typically, he confronted the event with bravura that masked fear. Open-heart surgery wasn't something most men in their twenties had to contemplate. Afterward, when kids in a swimming pool marveled at the thick red scar that ran down his chest, he would impress them—and intimidate

them a little—by explaining he was a bionic man, with just one little
piece of clicking plastic keeping him alive.

Like tuberculars in the nineteenth century, the closeness of death
made Michael more alive than other people. Each experience was so
vivid, every encounter so vital. When the plastic valve started to fail
and another operation was needed, he wasn't so afraid because he
knew the drill. Sitting by his hospital bed while Michael regaled
friends with tales of the long-fingered, Porsche-loving heart surgeon
Magdi Yakoub was one of the best social scenes in town. But it was
becoming clear that, as far as marriage and a family went, Michael
wasn't a great proposition. However much women might find him
charismatic, attentive, and insightful, he was a bad bet. By the third
operation, his girlfriend of nine years' standing, Leslie, decided it was
time to move on. She took him to tea to explain that, however much
she might love him, she had a long life to consider. Walking back to
work after their conversation, he thought about the different ways a
heart can fail.

But a few years later, back in radio, he fell in love with a colleague,
got married, and for a time had everything he had ever dreamed of: a
good marriage, a stimulating job that earned him respect, and the
company of writers, artists, and musicians who all enjoyed his courage and his wit. He began to think of starting a family, but then became ill again. This time he would need a heart transplant, but before
it could be arranged, Michael died at the age of thirty-eight.

Was I willfully blind when I married Michael? Of course I was. I
knew about his heart condition—everyone did. But I fell in love with
him and decided it didn't matter. We were going to live forever, somehow. Now I know that the fact that we had the same initials, were both
expatriates, had gone to the same university, and were of medium build
made the relationship highly determined. But I might have done the
research and discovered his short life expectancy or talked to psychologists about the pain of grieving or read books about the sadness of
widowhood. But I didn't do any of those things. I looked away from
those sad certainties and pretended that they weren't there.

Love is blind, not, as in mythology, because Cupid's arrows are random but because, once struck by them, we are left blind. When we
love someone, we see them as smarter, wittier, prettier, stronger than
anyone else sees them. To us, a beloved parent, partner, or child has
endlessly more talent, potential, and virtue than mere strangers can

ever discern. Being loved, when we are born, keeps us alive; without love for her child, how could any new mother manage or any child survive? And if we grow up surrounded by love, we feel secure in the knowledge that others believe in us, will champion and defend us. That confidence—that we are loved and therefore lovable—is an essential building block of our identity and self-confidence. We believe in ourselves, at least in part, because others believe in us and we depend mightily on their belief.

As human beings, we are highly driven to find and to protect the relationships that make us feel good about ourselves and that make us feel safe. That's why we marry people like us, live in neighborhoods full of people like us, and work with people like us: Each one of those mirrors confirms our sense of self-worth. Love does the same thing but with infinitely more passion and drive. We think well of ourselves because we are loved and we will fight fiercely to protect the key relationships on which our esteem depends. And that seems to be just as true even if our love is based on illusion. Indeed, there seems to be some evidence not only that all love is based on illusion—but that love positively requires illusion in order to endure.

When psychologists studied young dating couples, they analyzed each partner's view of his or her beloved, and then compared that with the beloved's own view or him- or herself. They found that not only was there a big disconnect—the lover thought better of her beloved than he did of himself—but the relationships in which that idealization occurred were the ones that were more likely to persist. Individuals were more satisfied in their relationships when they saw virtues in their partners that their partners did not see in themselves. In other words, idealizing the loved one helped the relationship endure. In fact, "systematic inaccuracies, in the form of positive illusions, predicted greater, concurrent happiness among both dating and married couples . . . Despite the rigors of time, married intimates were happier when they idealized one another, not when they more accurately understood each other."[1]

The beneficial effect of these positive illusions went even further. When you love someone, he or she may even start to adapt to your illusion of him or her. So there is a kind of virtuous circle: you think better of your beloved who starts to live up to your illusions and so you love him or her more. It sounds a little like a fairy tale, but kissing frogs may make them act like princes or princesses. It is indeed a

kind of magic, illusions transforming reality. We don't have to love
people for who they are but for who we think they are, or need them
to be.

So I married a man whom I did not think of as an invalid, and one
reason we were happy together was because we lived as though there
was nothing wrong with him. This was a benign blindness, without
which the relationship stood no chance. And even when it isn't a matter of life and death, this is something everyone does: overlook the
flaws, discount the disappointments, focus on what works. Our love
for each other allows us, even compels us, to see the best in each other.

This doesn't mean we don't have doubts; of course we do. But such
doubts tend to surface only after we have already invested a great deal
in a relationship. And that investment—although it sounds very cold-
blooded to say so—is like our other investments: as the behavioral
economists Kahneman and Tversky found, losses loom very much
larger than corresponding gains.[2] When you apply that principle to
love life (instead of the stock market) it means that when a relationship starts to sour, our fear of losing it may far outweigh any hopes we
might cherish of freedom and release. If things go wrong in a relationship, we hang on, trying hard to adapt, or to trivialize our worries. We find excuses (he's had a horrible day, or a horrible childhood),
we weave alternative interpretations (she didn't really mean it, I must
have misunderstood), or we may just trivialize the disappointment (it's
not a big birthday). We use considerable ingenuity to sustain our illusions, blind ourselves to inconvenient or painful facts. We protect our
life with our illusions.

Because our identity and security depend so much on our loved
ones, we don't want to see anything that threatens them. So, most of
the time that I was married to Michael, I didn't think about his frailty
or his heart. We went on walking trips and swam a great deal. I might
rationalize that, in keeping him fit, I was keeping him healthy, and
perhaps I was. But I was also acting as though my husband were just
as strong and fit as anyone else my age. I had to believe that.

Mine was perhaps an extreme case of love masking all physical realities. But even the most educated and rational can be amazed by how
little impact rational understanding makes when love is involved.

"I remember my mother calling me up and explaining about the
pains she was having in her arm and her stomach that had lasted about
twenty minutes," Andrew Dick told me one evening. Dick is a highly

experienced, level-headed physician not known for pulling his punches. Like many doctors, he loves the intellectual puzzle of diagnosis and isn't easily second-guessed. "And she said to me perhaps it was something she ate. And I said, instantly, yes, it must have been something you ate. And I put the phone down."

As he tells this story, Dick's wife, Lindsey, looks on, bemused. She is also a doctor, but it isn't her parents we're talking about.

"So I hung up the phone and told Lindsey about the conversation and she looks at me and says, 'No, it isn't what she ate. She's having a heart attack.' And of course she was right! So I was straight back on the phone to her."

Dick tells his story with wry amusement that he could have got something so simple so wrong. But of course that is why physicians aren't supposed to treat family members—because love blinds them to the realities of the case. This doesn't, unfortunately, stop family members from asking for advice and even, on occasion, free care. And it has proved impossible for professional organizations to prevent doctors treating their own families. The dangers are twofold: a tendency either to underplay the problem (I love you and can't bear for you to be ill) or to overplay the problem (I couldn't bear to lose you so will treat the tiniest symptom). Every doctor I've met has experienced one of those responses; they know they can't do a proper diagnosis and they also know that that isn't a reflection of their clinical expertise.

Our identity depends critically on the people we love, and a central function of family life is to preserve our positive illusions about one another. That is what families are for. The fictional poster child for love blindness in families must be Carmela Soprano, who hovers between knowing and not knowing that her husband is a murderous, adulterous gangster. How can she acknowledge the truth? It would destroy everything she loves: her family, her home, her children, her sense of herself as a good person. For the children, Meadow and Anthony Junior, facing facts is easier; they did not choose their father and don't feel their identity depends on his. But Carmela chose Tony, so for her the cost of facing what she has condoned is too high: not just Catholic guilt but responsibility for "terrible acts" that she cannot bring herself to imagine. She so desperately wants Tony to be a good father, for her family to be the archetypal American happy family that most of her physical and psychic energy is devoted to maintaining the illusions that make her life worth living. She is blind to Tony's criminal activity because she has to be.

Carmela's dilemma is extreme but it is also something everyone can relate to; that's why it's great television. So many couples find themselves in predicaments in which they fear something bad is happening but prefer not to know. As in Carmela's situation, it feels easier to turn a blind eye and act as if everything is normal. For few of us is the dark secret likely to be murder and criminality but, for 30 to 60 percent of Americans, it could be infidelity.[3]

"In couples when someone is having an affair, nobody really wants to know," says Emily Brown. Brown is a marriage therapist whose deep knowledge and study of marital infidelity doesn't seem to have damaged her optimism. In her mid-fifties, she dresses in warm but vibrant colors; an office crammed with books and artwork overlooks a stunning view of the Arlington hills. Only a pottery jar labeled COGNITIVE OVERLOAD hints that sometimes knowledge can be a burden.

In her professional practice, Brown works with couples and individuals whose marriages are threatened by affairs. By the time her clients come to her, the affair has usually been discovered and part of what she sees is the rage that betrayed spouses feel at not having noticed what was going on.

"They may have had their suspicions," says Brown. "But even in marriages where one spouse has suspicions, how can you ask and have things remain the same? If the other partner is not having an affair, you've created doubt and hostility. If the other partner is having an affair and denies it, now he or she has been rumbled. If the other partner is having an affair and admits it, everything starts to fall apart. So there is no way to ask and have things remain the same."

That state—of knowing and not knowing—is extremely painful and can last for months. The sheer routine of daily life makes blindness easier, less dramatic, less traumatic.

"So I see people thinking, I should ask. I won't ask. It's self-protection. Many of my clients have grown up in families where no one ever talked about risky topics—there's plenty of polite conversation but nothing meaningful—so they don't know how to have the conversation in the first place. But then they think, if we're talking about it that means it could be real. So they try to make it disappear by not saying anything."

In Brown's experience, the blindness is on both sides: The unfaithful spouse is blind to the possibility of being found out, refusing to see what the consequences might be and preferring to maintain the illusion that no one will get hurt. This isn't stupidity; it's a genuine desire that the affair and the family can peacefully coexist. And on the other side, the betrayed spouse resolutely refuses to connect the dots because as long as they're just dots, nothing is happening, nothing has to change, and love remains.

"I had one case," Brown recalled, "where the husband had had an affair and his wife hadn't guessed. And his wife had got a sexually transmitted disease and had gone to the doctor about it. When she told her husband, he just brushed it off, saying, 'You must have got that when you were camping with the kids.' So she thought no more about it."

"Ten years later, she's at the hairdresser's and she's reading a magazine article about STDs and she figures it out! And only then did she confront her husband. Now in that case, there was a double blindness: He was blind to being caught and she was blind to what was going on."

Most people, according to Brown, do intuit that something is amiss. One reason these marriages are so hard to repair is that betrayed spouses feel so angry, not just with their partners but with themselves. How could I not have known? each asks, feeling so stupid, so naïve. Suddenly they feel like they are watching a jigsaw puzzle self-assemble: All the pieces snap together, creating a hideous picture that no one wants to see. Self-esteem, that precious self-worth that has been fed by the illusions that sustain love, is destroyed as the truth emerges.

That we will fight so hard to protect our self-esteem is a universal. It doesn't matter how successful or wealthy people are. They all need to feel that they're good people, even—or especially—when they're bad.

"I knew my actions were wrong but I convinced myself normal rules didn't apply. I thought I could get away with whatever I wanted to." Even Tiger Woods was willfully blind when it came to his own marriage.[4]

"Success confers its own blindness," says Brown. "Successful people believe they can get away with it. I talked once to a group of men who'd all become millionaires before the age of forty and who'd had affairs. They don't even see the danger! It isn't a love of risk. They think, the wives will never know, so where's the harm? Everything else in their lives has worked out, so they think they have some kind of magic, that their success has meant that they can have everything they want and they're invulnerable. And they were completely blind to the harm that they had done. They just couldn't conceive that, as good men, they'd done something bad."

Brown says she feels like a veteran, her consulting room a battlefield where wives and husbands have waged titanic battles to preserve their self-respect. Blindness helps them do that, she says. And where children are involved, adulterous spouses can be especially blind. They convince themselves that kids, of any age, know nothing, notice nothing, that just by dint of being children they couldn't have any insight into the lives of grown-ups. It's a comforting fallacy often bolstered by the kids themselves who say nothing because they are trying so hard to keep the family together. Everyone colludes in the collective fantasy that the family is fine.

"One couple I've worked with, they're semi-separated," Brown recalls. "They had a lot of fights in front of their kids and the husband moved out into an apartment that was above the garage. And they got together for one of the kids' birthdays. But both the husband and the wife said they thought the kids didn't suspect a thing. Well their kids are thirteen and ten and Dad isn't living at home anymore . . ."

Talking to Brown, it's clear that this kind of blindness is so common that it no longer surprises her. But she also thinks that the blindness that accompanies affairs often started very much earlier. One of the many downsides of living in communities in which we are always surrounded by people like ourselves is that we experience very little conflict. That means we don't develop the tools we need to manage conflict and we lack confidence in our ability to do so. We persuade ourselves that the absence of conflict is the same as happiness, but that trade-off leaves us strangely powerless.

"In many cases, affairs start because people are conflict averse or intimacy averse. People stay away from stuff that needs to be dealt with; they think that they mustn't ever say anything negative—they don't know how to articulate criticism or doubts in a way that won't feel like an attack. So then when they finally articulate their discomfort, via the affair, it does come out as an attack and provokes more attacks. A lot of this derives from not dealing with emotions, not understanding one's own feelings. It feels easier to be blind than to deal with uncomfortable feelings."

Running throughout Brown's conversation, and the experience she's had in her practice, is a belief that we become blind because we are so afraid of what we might see and what we might feel. Our identity and sense of self-worth depend on the people we love, to the extent that we cling to them even though they do us harm.

"We want our parents to love us and one way to do that is to be what they want us to be," recalled Louise Miller, who has been coming to Brown for advice and therapy after years of an abusive marriage in which she had worked hard not to notice what was going on around her. Miller was so eager to please the people she loved, she says, that she never really dared to question anything.

"I got married in my early twenties—I really didn't want to but I thought that was what you do. I was dating, I was the right age to get married, I got married. Then in my thirties, I had kids and I thought: I'll have this perfect life according to my parents' thinking. I had a beautiful huge colonial home with a big yard in a nice neighborhood and I thought: now I will have my nice life. I didn't see *me* until I was forty. All those years I was trying to do what my parents wanted, what my husband wanted. I thought if they were happy, I'd be happy. But I was just blind to myself!"

So desperate was Louise to secure the approval and love of her parents and her husband, by sticking to her "cookie-cutter" idea of what happiness and family life should look like, that she never dared to ask any serious questions about what was going on around her.

"When I was growing up, there was never any alcohol in the house— not even for cooking. So when I met my husband, I had no way of knowing he was an alcoholic. I met him in college and when he was a little wild, I just thought that was party behavior and he'd grow out of it. But he never did. And I'd complain but he couldn't stop. Then one day his father said to me, 'Do you know you're married to an alcoholic?' I was in my forties! How can you be in a relationship with an alcoholic and never even see it?"

In a desperate attempt to break free from everyone else's expectations for her, Louise had an affair with a colleague at work.

"I never thought anything would happen. I became very depressed and guilty and one night I told my husband. I thought that once I told him, we could reconnect and fall in love again! And that's when we went to see Emily. I really hoped she would know the end of the story and everything would be all right. It took me a long time to see that I had choices. And that it was my life."

As Louise tells me her story, it feels as though layers and layers of blinders are being removed, one at a time—her love for her parents, the love she had for her husband, the love she has for her children. She had struggled so hard to cling to these because for years she simply did not believe that she was anybody without them. Emily says how amazed she is by Louise's personal growth, by how far she has come. But it is a journey she could never have made without daring to confront the truth about herself and her marriage.

Tales of marital blindness are legion, the stuff of high drama and low comedy alike. From Othello to Pierre Bezukhov to *Mad Men*'s Betty Draper, we can identify with characters who won't see the truth because they let us explore our deepest fears, that we might be wrong about each other or wrong about ourselves. We laugh with relief because it isn't us, and we weep because it so easily could be.

Nowhere is that drama more intense or more threatening than in families damaged by child abuse. Although we are all so conscious of "stranger danger" and go to great lengths to ensure that our children keep well away from anyone unknown or suspicious, it remains the case that most child abuse occurs within families or involves perpetrators known to the children.

In the UK, according to the National Society for the Prevention of Cruelty to Children (NSPCC), fully 16 percent of children experience sexual abuse before they reach 16 years of age. With numbers like those, you have to wonder: How can abuse go unnoticed within such a small unit as a family?

"In the majority of cases of child abuse, it is family members or friends who are responsible," says Chris Cloke, Head of Child Protection Awareness for the NSPCC. "It's often very hard to see because there's often a great deal of love—for the family, for the child—which just doesn't want to acknowledge what's going on. Lots of people don't even want to acknowledge that child abuse exists at all—and they'd far prefer to think of stranger danger, than of the fact that it mostly occurs within families."

Felicity Wilkinson works on the NSPCC's front line—its Helpline. She says: "You often find a situation where a mum is in a relationship with a man who is abusing her kids. That is someone she is in love with and the last thing she wants to think about is that they would do that kind of thing. It can take a long time for it to sink in, even where there are certain signs."

This pattern is certainly borne out by the Public Health Agency of Canada's study into child abuse, which (unlike US and UK studies) finds that the majority of sexual abuse is caused by a stepfather/ common law partner or other family relative.[5]

"One case that springs to mind," says Wilkinson, "is a woman who was saying that she was aware her partner had a conviction from the past for sex abuse. She was trying to convince herself that that didn't matter now because it had all happened such a long time ago, so he must have changed. She was really calling to ask for confirmation— hoping against hope that I would say it was so long ago that she need not worry. She was in love with this man and he was doing a lot for her and looking after her kids. She just didn't want to think that her kids were at risk."

Wasn't it hard, I asked Felicity, for parents to acknowledge that there might be danger in their own family?

"It is always hard. So hard. When I worked as a social worker for a local authority, the parents always struggled with this. And it was very hard for the parents to acknowledge that their own behavior might contribute to the problem. They loved their kids and hoped that that was enough. And it's also hard because if they give us, at the NSPCC, information that indicates the child truly is at risk, we are obliged to contact Children's Services. So they don't want to acknowledge what is going on—and they're afraid to start that whole process."

"It isn't necessarily that they are unconscious," says Eliana Gil, "but that they are unable or unwilling to face up to what is happening."

Dr. Gil is director of clinical services for the nonprofit organization Childhelp Children's Services of Virginia, one of the largest child welfare services in the United States. She has had years of experience watching families make the painful transition from being blind to finally seeing what is happening around them. And she says that there is a pattern to the revelation.

"It is as if someone has been invited to attend something. They turn up, the door is opened, and they see it is a surprise birthday party for them. In that moment of shock, they suddenly understand—that's why there was a ribbon on the bed this morning and that's why my brother canceled dinner tonight and that's why Jane's been acting so strangely. Suddenly all these little pieces of information, which have been stored in memory without meaning, get retrieved in context and have a whole new meaning.

"That is my experience with the moms. When someone says your child has been abused by the father—suddenly they remember: that's why I found her walking around the room at night and that's why her clothes were in my bedroom . . . All those details, stored without meaning, suddenly acquire meaning.[6]

"That kind of response—of seeing and not seeing—helps to explain how these things go on for such a long time. It doesn't explain why the abuse itself happens in the first place, of course. But it explains how it can continue for such a long time inside the family. If you maintain an illusion, you don't have to make the hard choices. Life just goes on. But if you accept reality, it forces a huge decision and many people want to avoid that."

According to Dr. Gil, it is often several fears together that conspire to keep unwanted knowledge from a parent's mind. If the abusing father is the major breadwinner, the mother's fear of losing support and income may suppress her knowledge. Fear of shame and social exclusion are powerful forces, too. But underlying all of these threats is a more existential fear, a sense that acknowledging the abuse would destroy everything.

"It's just too dangerous to acknowledge the idea—it's the last thing anyone wants to imagine. Moms feel that just to ask the question is to be questioning their own reality. And especially mothers who themselves come from unhappy families, they are so idealistic about their own parenting that they don't want to acknowledge anything could be wrong. They think they're protecting the child by maintaining a front. In putting together that illusion and protecting it, they just cannot break through the barrier to explore the possibility that something is wrong."

Protecting herself and her illusions becomes so critical to the mother's sense of her own worth that her doubts have to be quashed.

"For many of the moms I've worked with, their identity is so tied into the role of being a good mother or a good wife that they have very little sense of self. Putting on an identity like a coat becomes very important to them. And they cannot take that coat off, it would leave them too vulnerable. It is like they've invested themselves in this role and they simply cannot afford to challenge their illusion. It is such an invested process. So when it turns out that it was an illusion, they often feel that they have absolutely nothing left."

For someone navigating such painful issues, Dr. Gil is remarkably positive, utterly determined that out of this family wreckage, real gains can come—but only by recognizing what has occurred. She's a passionate believer that if willful blindness perpetuates abuse, it is only facing facts that can end it.

"I've been working with a woman who has four children. Her husband was arrested for having a lot of child pornography on his computer and I started working with the mother, and her kids, because they were just in shock when this happened. And at first, the kids seemed okay except that they'd been photographed by him in rather unusual poses. As I started working with the mother, helping her to learn how to get along without her husband, other things started to surface. The couple had had no sex for two years, and she thought that was odd but then she figured they were older, maybe it was not a big deal. Then she realized he did have a special relationship with their ten-year-old little girl. And a little part of her was happy for the child—that he had such a strong attachment—but she also started wondering. 'I wondered if I should have been concerned'—that was just how she phrased it. 'I wondered if I should have been concerned.'"

After working with the mother and her children for about nine months, Dr. Gil became concerned that the ten-year-old had behaviors compatible with a child who has been abused. So she asked the mother about that.

"And she says, 'Well I guess there was one time I walked in and they were in bed together cuddling and I could see he had an erection.' So I asked her if she had talked to him about it and all she said was, 'I mentioned it and he denied it so I thought I must have been seeing things.'"

For all her experience, even Dr. Gil was amazed that so much could have happened and not been seen. Over the next few months, Dr. Gil was impressed as the mother gradually developed the courage to put the picture together.

"Gradually things are becoming more clear in her mind but at the time they were just too threatening to consider. She is very resilient pulling herself up; she has come a long way from the depressed state we found her in, to a person coming into her own. Her eyes are brighter and it is like she has a new sense of herself. But at the time, she couldn't compromise that sense of identity because she couldn't see possibilities for herself. Her daughter paid the price for that, because her mother couldn't see what was in front of her face, and she was not willing to do anything because she was afraid."

This is the true cost of blindness: as long as it feels safer to do and say nothing, as long as keeping the peace feels more benign, abuse can continue. Our desire to protect our self-worth results in others paying a very high price.

Emerging brain science lends a physical reality to the emotional turmoil experienced by the victims of romantic and maternal love alike. A team of neuroscientists at the University of London have spent years studying brain activity in romantic couples and in mothers. They knew that love itself has an evolutionary advantage; we fall in love, mate, and look after our children because that is how the species perpetuates itself. But they wanted to understand which areas of the brain are active in response to love and which areas are not.

They found, not so surprisingly, that love activates those areas of the brain associated with reward; the cells that respond to food, drink, money, or cocaine respond to love, too. That's why it feels so good to love and to be loved. Moreover, there appears to be some evidence that love may even reduce our fear of death.[7] While it would be inaccurate to conclude that we are addicted to love, it is the case that we need it.[8]

Even more illuminating than the areas activated by love were the areas of the brain that were deactivated. As volunteers lay in fMRI (functional MRI) scanners thinking of their children or their partners, two particular parts of their brains were not engaged. The first is the area responsible for attention, memory, and negative emotions; the second was associated with negative emotions and social judgment, the ability to distinguish other people's feelings and intentions. In other words, the chemical processes of our brain that are stimulated by love disable much of our critical thinking about the loved one. Our illusions persist because our brains don't challenge them. Like much neuroscience, this gives a concrete reality to what the poets have always known: love does not judge.

The neuroscience is a helpful reminder that blind love isn't stupidity or ignorance. It is a physical reality of a kind that doesn't distinguish between rich and poor, educated or otherwise. We develop and protect illusions around the people we love because we are made to do so, because we feel our very lives depend on it. What is impressive, though, is that when men and women who have suffered in abusive, unhappy relationships successfully overcome their blindness, and insist on facing the truth, they have surmounted very real and daunting obstacles.

Such obstacles are even more formidable when they are reinforced by institutional, social, and political support. That is what happened in the child abuse scandals that have ripped through churches in England, Ireland, Canada, Australia, and the United States. Love of church, love of parents, love of tradition all conspired to keep whole communities blind to what they somehow always knew.

"For so long, everyone pretended these things weren't happening. So sad. So ridiculous. If we acknowledge these things, we can address them. But for years, everyone knew. And no one knew. You just couldn't say anything."

Colm O'Gorman runs Amnesty International in Ireland. He's a powerful force in the land these days, well known and highly respected, organized, efficient, and bold. But he wasn't always that way. In the 1970s, growing up in Wexford, he was regularly abused for two and a half years by a local priest, Sean Fortune. O'Gorman was trapped between his love for his father and his mother, and their love of the Church. At the time, he was just a child, with a very fragile sense of identity. The one thing he felt certain of was that his family would be destroyed if the priest told O'Gorman's family what he had done with the boy.

"Panic raced through me and the world started to spin. I wanted to escape, jump from the car, anything to get away from that awful moment. My father . . . it would kill him to know what I'd done, what I was. He would die of shame . . . I knew I could not stay alive if everyone knew, especially if my father knew."[9]

O'Gorman felt that everything his life depended on would be destroyed if anyone knew that the priest was abusing him. So he kept silent, while the abuse continued and for many years afterward. His experience, tragically, was far from unique. The 2005 Ferns Inquiry unearthed 100 complaints against 21 priests in O'Gorman's diocese alone. A year later, the Murphy Report examined the history of 46 priests, picked from a sample of 102 against whom complaints had been lodged. Just those 46 priests surfaced allegations from more than 320 children. "One priest admitted to sexually abusing over 100 children, while another accepted that he had abused on a fortnightly basis during his ministry which lasted for over 25 years," the report said. "The total number of documented complaints recorded against those two priests is only just over 70." And that was just in Dublin.

At this level, nothing can quite be a secret. It was, O'Gorman says, the scandal that everyone knew about but no one would admit. In his own village, children told their friends about the priests that should be avoided when you were on your own, the ones you shouldn't go to the graveyard with. Parents had distinct preferences about which priests were better choices for confirmation classes. Likewise, the Gardaí—Irish police— would, informally, mention that certain priests shouldn't be left too long with children. Widespread knowledge and widespread blindness coexisted; as Gorman puts it, "They'd tell you but they hadn't told you."

Eventually, O'Gorman left home and wandered, frequently unemployed and homeless, through the streets of Dublin and London, an outcast who belonged nowhere. It was only many years later that he had the confidence he needed to acknowledge what had been done to him. When he finally confided in his parents, they did not reject him and his life could begin again. He brought a lawsuit against Sean Fortune and he established a help line for victims of child abuse.

"What silences the child," says O'Gorman, "is the fear that the family will be broken up. Family is the only source of love and security that the kid knows. How can he hurt his parents, whom he loves and might also fear? What would he have left? I couldn't prevent what was happening to me and I couldn't escape it, so I just refused to allow it to be true. I would just look at a spot on the ceiling and split myself off from what was happening. In that place, denial kept me sane. I didn't go mad. Finding the spot on the wall meant I wasn't in the room."

The fact that O'Gorman's wasn't a solitary case, and that abuse was so pervasive, meant that it wasn't only O'Gorman's family that was threatened. Ireland at the time was a highly theocratic culture. The Church ran most of the major institutions and was largely left to do so by the government. Any attack on the Church, therefore, challenged its dominance, threatened its role in the social and political life of the nation. To dare to question the moral authority of the most powerful institution in the land might make anyone hesitate.

"If one has a strong sense of or connection with the Church, then the destruction of that is terrifying," says O'Gorman. "It really is unthinkable. Unthinkable. It is a loss of security. It makes you wonder whether any security is real. Suddenly everything is at risk. My acceptability within my institution and by God is because I am acceptable to the faith. If I name all that, accuse all that, do I lose my connection with God? Never mind the power of the institution . . ."

The blind intransigence of the institution has stunned even some of its most faithful adherents. The pope's envoy to Ireland refused to testify before Irish lawmakers, while none of the bishops who failed to report pedophile priests has been fired. O'Gorman was appropriately daunted.

"Ireland was a country in denial," says O'Gorman. "If a whole society is in denial, you are really in trouble—because you believe your survival depends on turning a blind eye to the truth. So the thing that we feared most as a society—that our sense of self would come crashing down—that turned out to be valid.

"But what we didn't question at the time was whether that might be a good thing. We had had a sense of ourselves as a good pure Catholic society, where good exists and always wears a collar. But when we finally understood the cost of that illusion, then we had to let it go. The cost was just so high, the damage so great."

Sean Fortune, O'Gorman's abuser, committed suicide before his trial concluded. Other priests and bishops retired or disappeared. The Church itself, when it learned of the scale of the abuse, had taken out insurance policies against the cost of future lawsuits. But some clergy felt let down by their own hierarchy, which left them ignorant and inexperienced in dealing with these cases.

"I knew of the existence of child abuse certainly but less about recidivism in the offender and the long-terms effects in the life of the victim," one churchman confided to me.

Not surprisingly, he insisted on remaining anonymous. Sitting in the lobby of an elegant Dublin hotel, he would, years ago, have been the center of attention, a man of power, accustomed to deference. Now our conversation was muted, his presence shrunken, almost furtive. He described to me how rumors of abuse would reach him but he never quite knew what to do about them.

"What I still find quite remarkable and almost unbelievable twenty years later is that not a single person among the legal, medical, and counseling profession whom I consulted on innumerable occasions advised me either to report an offense to the Gardaí or to remove a priest from ministry except for a very short period of time," he said. "I knew that this problem had surfaced in the USA and was being dealt with by numerous U.S. bishops but their approach offered no great insights into the problem. In fact, they seem to have made all the mistakes that we in Ireland were to make about a decade later. On the home front, we showed a marked reluctance to discuss the problem, hoping, I suppose, that if we didn't discuss it, it would go away."

That hope—if we don't talk about it, it will go away—persisted for decades. In the end, it was not the Church but the courage of victims like O'Gorman that finally brought priests into court and the clergy's disgrace out into the open. That was the moment when many priests might have sided with the abused, but instead most of them just slunk away. If the problem would not disappear, they would.

Moreover, the Church has continued to protect the identity of abusing clergy, which means they can't and won't be brought to trial. For O'Gorman, this has been their ultimate failure: not to have sided with the truth once it was out there.

"For fear of the worst of ourselves, what we do or people close to us do or institutions do, is we deny the best of ourselves—which is our capacity to respond," O'Gorman says. "We make ourselves powerless by pretending we don't know."

As O'Gorman and I discussed the profound impact the scandals have had on the whole of Irish social and political life, I was struck by the sympathy and breadth of his argument. He seemed to be arguing that while the greatest harm was that done to children by priests, further harm still was caused by the Church's moral failure to support their victims. The crisis offered an opportunity for the Church, and its priests, to dig deep and find the best in themselves. But they lacked the vision and courage to seize it. Today, a third of the Irish population has no trust "at all" in the Church; the police, the supermarkets, and the media enjoy higher levels of public confidence.[10] When I contrast my conversation with O'Gorman and my earlier one with the priest, it is O'Gorman who, despite years of suffering, confusion, poverty, and personal vilification, has led the richer life. The priest has enjoyed comfort and respect but today he is left still embroiled in a battle, between himself and the truth, trying to decide who gets the upper hand.

Some less thoughtful critics might dispute this interpretation, saying the priest just doesn't care, that his apologies and explanations are just an easy way of making sure he gets to live as he's always lived, without having to change. That is certainly what many said of Albert Speer, Hitler's chief architect and, after 1942, the second most powerful man in the Reich. One of the few of the Nazi elite not to be hanged following the Nuremberg trials, he was outspoken about the criminality of Hitler's regime and determined to accept responsibility for what he had done as a member of the government. In some ways, that decision was Speer's simplest; he believed in collective responsibility. The hard part for Speer was seeing what it was that he took responsibility for.

"Speer didn't see anything he didn't want to see," says Gitta Sereny, Speer's biographer. "I think he would have liked to have that capacity, but he just didn't. Speer was in fact a highly talented man, highly intelligent, but studied obliviousness was his defense. And the defense was there because he somehow knew there was something wrong."[11]

Sereny saw Speer at Nuremberg but she got to know him when, in

1978, she began a conversation with him—almost an interrogation—that would continue right up until his death in 1981. In her book *Albert Speer: His Battle with Truth,* she meticulously chronicles Speer's torturous negotiation with himself, and then with her, as he tries to see, but also wiggle out of seeing, the full horror of what he did as a Nazi. Sereny's is a masterful confrontation, obsessive about detail, challenging Speer's facts, and constantly blocking ethical escape routes. What makes their duel so dramatic is that Speer is even more desperate to know the truth than Sereny; she wants to know but he needs to know. The obstacle they both wrestle with is his lifetime of abnegation and blindness. That blindness, according to Sereny, was profoundly motivated by Speer's love for Hitler.

"In the early years, Speer is very hung up on Hitler—and in a very personal way," she said. "It's something quite apart from politics. It is more of a father-son feeling. Speer found that difficult to give up; he depended on it. He needed it to feel whole."[12]

Indeed, when Speer described to Sereny his first meeting with Hitler in 1933, his account came dangerously close to the purple prose of romantic fiction.

"Can you imagine this," said Speer. "Here I was, young, unknown, and totally unimportant, and this great man, for whose attention—just for one glance—our whole world competed, said to me, 'Come and have lunch.' I thought I'd faint."

Because Speer, an architect, had visited a building site prior to his meeting with Hitler, his jacket was dusty and Hitler lent him one of his own.

"Can you conceive what I felt?" Speer asked again. "Here I was, twenty-eight years old, totally insignificant in my own eyes, sitting next to him at lunch, wearing his clothes and elected—at least that day—as virtually his sole conversation partner. I was dizzy with excitement."[13]

It isn't only Hitler's power that so bedazzled Speer. Hitler saw in the young, mediocre architect far more than Speer saw in himself. When Speer was given tremendous commissions for the new Reich, it was clear that Hitler believed him to be talented, important, and artistic— all those things Speer longed to be and that his own parents had signally failed to see in him. Hitler, as Speer said later, became his life.[14]

"He saw himself as Hitler's son," said Sereny. "All his chances, his opportunities came to him through Hitler. He liked Hitler and he loved Hitler—and it was reciprocated. Hitler really loved Speer and Speer grew to love Hitler. The thing is: people around Hitler became what he wanted them to be."[15]

Speer's reciprocated love for Hitler, and the political climate around the führer, was for Speer a deadly combination. With his own identity so entirely dependent, nothing critical of Hitler could ever be allowed to impinge on Speer's consciousness. He saw pools of blood near one of his building sites. One of the architects in his practice resigned after Kristallnacht. But, says Speer, "my mind was on other things."[16] When the evacuation of Jews from Berlin began in 1941, Speer wrote about "a feeling of unease, a foreboding of dark events," but Sereny challenged him, thinking him evasive. How, she wondered, could he have been uneasy if he knew nothing?

"By that time," Sereny wrote, "I was very familiar with that sudden sharp look from under those thick black eyebrows when he sensed disbelief. It was not only his look which became both hooded and guarded; his voice on the whole invariably quiet could also suddenly change. 'I was blind by choice,' he said coldly, 'but I was not ignorant.'"

In 1942, when Speer was made minister of armaments and war production, blindness and ignorance became increasingly difficult to preserve. Speer was no longer designing rallies and memorials for the thousand-year Reich; now he was in charge of arming Germany and ensuring that the war machine had the labor it needed. In appointing him to this position, Hitler had identified Speer's true genius, which was not as an architect but as a manager and administrator. But just as Speer discovered his true talents, they embroiled him in atrocities. Now he was spending more time with Hitler's inner circle, privy to conversations about the Jews.

"This is when I should have begun to realize what was happening," Speer said. "This was the point, I now think, when, had I *wanted* to, I could have detected hints."

Sereny asked Speer what he would have done if he had known about the Final Solution.

"Don't you know that this is the question I have asked myself a million times, continuously hoping that I would be able to give myself an answer I could live with?" He rested his head in his hands. "My answer to myself is always the same," he said, his voice dark and a little hoarse. "I would somehow have gone on trying to help that man win his war."

Speer's moral corruption, Sereny says, "had its seed in his emotional attachment to Hitler—he likened it to Faust's fatal bargain with Mephistopheles. Achievement and success rooting it ever deeper over the years, he lived—almost addictively—in an increasingly vicious cycle of need and dependence."[17]

He carefully avoided visiting any labor or concentration camps. His one visit—to Mauthausen, in Austria—carefully kept him away from anything he might find shocking. But Speer's new role brought him closer and closer to the evil that his ministry perpetrated. In August 1943, he visited Dora, the underground labor camp deep in the Harz mountains where Wernher von Braun's V-2 rockets were being produced. There, slave laborers worked eighteen hours a day with their bare hands, sleeping in tunnels they had hollowed out, more than a thousand prisoners on four levels that stretched for a hundred yards. Without heat, ventilation, or water to drink or wash with, the cold and filth and dysentery killed thirty thousand men.

"I was entirely unprepared," Speer told Sereny. "It was the worst place I have ever seen . . . I saw dead men . . . they couldn't hide the truth. And those that were alive were skeletons."[18]

Three months later, the regional Nazi party leaders and paramilitaries (*Reichsleiter*) were assembled to learn about the Final Solution in order that they all be implicated. An unresolved debate still rages over whether Speer was in attendance for Heinrich Himmler's speech about the extermination of the Jews. Speer believed he had left before Himmler spoke, but both Sereny and Speer himself doubted his memory. But whether or not he was actually present for Himmler's speech, he would undoubtedly have learned of its contents.

In January 1944, Speer was losing ground in power struggles with others in Hitler's circle. He also now had unavoidable knowledge of Hitler's genocidal program. It was too much. Everything on which his identity depended was undermined: Speer's love of Hitler, and Speer's love for the Speer that Hitler had created, became untenable. Studied obliviousness failed. Speer had a breakdown. The bond between them had snapped. When he returned to work three months later, everything had changed.

"Meeting Hitler again was a shock. I stood up as he entered the room. He came up to me very quickly holding out his hand. But even as I stretched out mine, I had an extraordinary sense of unfamiliarity. Of course I hadn't seen him for almost ten weeks, but that wasn't it. It was his face: I looked at it and thought: 'My God how could I have not seen how ugly he is? This broad nose, this sallow skin. Who is this man?'"

The spell was broken; Speer could see the evidence of Hitler's criminality all around. He started secretly to ignore orders, to undermine command, to resist Hitler's scorched-earth plan. When he was arrested and tried by the Allies, Speer accepted "coresponsibility"—but not guilt. In prison and after his release, Speer waged a titanic battle with himself, not wanting to believe he was a bad man, but well aware he wasn't stupid, either. Like a lover awakening from a dream, he could not quite make sense of what had happened or of what he had become.

"He had loved Hitler, he thought Hitler loved Germany and that was enough," Sereny told me. "But once he had seen that his ambitions were wrong, he couldn't feel the same way, about Hitler, about Germany, about himself. Speer's tragedy was that, after Dora, he really wanted to die. But his will to live was too strong. And so he really spent the rest of his life struggling, trying to become a different man."

Sereny's account of Speer's life after the war describes an epic struggle between what Speer knew and what he must have known. That debate continues to this day, with some historians still skeptical of what they see as Speer's disingenuousness. Sereny, although she clearly liked Speer, is no apologist for him. She was impressed by how hard he was finally prepared to work in order to see clearly. She is drawn to his battle because it is so intensely human.

"Not knowing, that's fine. Ignorance is easy. Knowing can be hard but at least it is real, it is the truth. The worst is when you don't want to know—because then it must be something very bad. Otherwise you wouldn't have so much difficulty knowing."

To some degree, Speer's postwar struggle with the truth was Germany's: the desire not to know, coupled with an awareness that confronting the truth was the only way to construct a meaningful future. While he still loved the image of himself that Hitler had constructed, Speer could not become a different man, just as, while it was still in love with the past, Germany could not become a different nation. The pain of that struggle is in all of us, particularly when we are in love and there are truths we don't want to acknowledge. You don't have to be a war criminal to have closets you would prefer not to open.

Nations, institutions, individuals can all be blinded by love, by the need to believe themselves good and worthy and valued. We simply could not function if we believed ourselves to be otherwise. But when we are blind to the flaws and failings of what we love, we aren't effective either. As Colm O'Gorman said, we make ourselves powerless when we pretend we don't know. That's the paradox of blindness: We think it will make us safe even as it puts us in danger.

3

DANGEROUS CONVICTIONS

Ideology is a conceptual framework, it's the way people deal with reality.
Everyone has one. You have to. To exist, you need an ideology.
—Alan Greenspan, October 23, 2008

IT'S AS EASY to fall in love with an idea as with a person. Big ideas
are especially alluring. They bring order to the world, give meaning
to life. When we join political parties or churches or governments, we
find soul mates with the same worldview, the same values—and life
feels complete. We may even talk of being "wedded" to our ideas.
Much of our identity is defined by what we believe and we actively
seek confirmation of those beliefs. Actually, we go even further: Our
brains treat differently any information that might challenge our closely
held beliefs.

In 2004, a team of cognitive neuroscientists set out to see what this
process actually looks like. Drew Westen, at Emory University, was
interested in what psychologists call "motivated reasoning" and what
Freud called defense mechanisms: the processes by which people adjust what they know to avoid bad feelings such as anxiety and guilt.
He theorized that the brain's neural networks would try to satisfy two
kinds of constraints: cognitive constraints—we want to put information together in a way that feels rational—and emotional constraints,
meaning we want to feel good about the information we take in.

To test his theories, Westen and his team recruited fifteen committed Democrats and fifteen committed Republicans to submit to

fMRI scans of their brains while reading political material. As they lay in the scanner, they read pairs of quotes attributed either to President George W. Bush or to presidential candidate John Kerry. In each pair, one statement was entirely compatible with the candidate's position, but one statement was contradictory. Westen wanted to find out whether the brain would treat the contradictions of the preferred candidate in the same way as it would treat the contradictions of a disliked candidate.

The experiment found that the partisan participants gave a far rougher ride to the contradictions that came from the candidate they opposed.

"They had no trouble seeing the contradictions for the opposition candidate," Westen wrote. "But when confronted with potentially troubling political information, a network of neurons becomes active that produces distress. Not only did the brain manage to shut down distress through faulty reasoning—but it did so quickly. The neural circuits charged with regulation of emotional states seemed to recruit beliefs that eliminated the distress and conflict."[1]

But, said Westen, the brain didn't stop at eliminating the uncomfortable contradictions. It worked overtime "to feel good, activating reward circuits that give partisans a jolt of positive reinforcement for their biased 'reasoning.'"[2]

In Westen's experiment, the reward circuits the brain was using were the same that are activated when a junkie gets a fix. In other words, when we find the thoughts we agree with, or are able to eliminate the ones that make us uncomfortable, we feel that same kind of euphoria and reassurance that an addict feels when reunited with his drug of choice: all is right with the world. At least for a while.

The brain doesn't like conflict and works hard to resolve it. This may be one reason why, when we gather with like-minded people, we are more likely to seek out common ground than areas of difference: quite literally, it feels better. But it also feels rational, even when it isn't. Which means that when we work hard to defend our core beliefs, we risk becoming blind to the evidence that could tell us we're wrong.

Alice Stewart arrived in Oxford, England, in 1941 to work as a resident physician at the Radcliffe Infirmary. She was, by all accounts, an outstanding doctor, the youngest woman at the time to enter the Royal

College of Physicians. Her colleagues considered her to be a wonderful teacher and an outstanding diagnostician, full of boundless energy, with an appetite for big challenges and hard problems. Doctors were much needed during the war and the fact that, as a mother with two small children, she couldn't be called up for military service made her even more valuable, while her failing marriage meant she was willing and able to go wherever she was needed.

While in Oxford, Stewart treated patients but also led a number of research projects into problematic, puzzling disease patterns. One of them involved trying to figure out why munitions workers filling shells with TNT seemed so susceptible to jaundice and anemia. In wartime, the munitions factory was staffed by "the ragtag of the popu-lation,"[3] which posed the question: Were they getting ill because they were vulnerable anyway, or was TNT the culprit? What originally started as a laboratory study soon became a field study: By persuading her healthy medical students to work in the plant and emulate the lives of the factory workers, Alice was able to prove that the diseases were not a consequence of their weaker health but of their exposure to TNT. Subsequent projects—investigating high turnover among laborers working with carbon tetrachloride, and another into miners suffering from lung disease—meant that, without having deliberately chosen to do so, Alice found herself working in the field of social medicine and epidemiology. It was an emerging discipline awash with hard problems.

Growing concern about the connection between high rates of illness and low social status led to the creation in 1942 of Oxford's Institute of Social Medicine. Why did poorer people suffer approximately twice the rate of infant mortality; ear, mastoid, and respiratory illnesses; ul-cers; and heart disease? What was the relationship between poverty and illness and what, in the light of the newly formed National Health Service, could be done about it? Stewart was recruited to the institute by one of the founding fathers of epidemiology, John Ryle, and she brought to her work all the indignant energy that was her hallmark.

"Practicing medicine without asking these larger questions is like sell-ing groceries across the counter," she said. "You go in with an illness; the doctor sells you a pill. It's no more responsible than that. Nobody goes out and asks, 'Who didn't come in because he was too sick to come? Why are so many people coming in with this, and so few with that?'"[4] But when Ryle died in 1950, Stewart's progress ground to a halt.

His institute was demoted to the "Social Medicine Unit" and Stewart lost her mentor and her status.

Abandoned by the Oxford establishment, and left with a tiny salary but no building, no funding, and no work, in a field that commanded little respect and few kudos, Alice found that the only way she could make her mark was by identifying—and solving—a hard problem. The burning issues of the day—lung cancer, cardiovascular disease, and polio—were crowded. This left just one: leukemia. Incidence of the disease was on the increase, at a rate that made it look like an epidemic, but the number of patients was still so small that the field was difficult to study using statistics, the traditional tool of epidemiology. Two anomalies caught Alice Stewart's eye. Leukemia was affecting children aged two to four. That was odd because typically by that age children are healthy: they've survived infancy and haven't yet started school. And the children dying from leukemia weren't poor: In fact, they came from counties with better medical care and lower overall death rates. How could that be? Stewart decided to interview the mothers of leukemia victims to see if she could find anything in their lives that might account for this pattern. She didn't know what she was looking for, so her questions started with conception.

"It was a needle-in-a-haystack search," says Gayle Greene, who first met Alice Stewart in 1992. Even at the age of eighty-six, Stewart was so dazzling that Greene was inspired to write her biography.

"Alice didn't know what she was looking for, so she asked questions about everything: exposure to infection, inoculation, cats, dogs, hens, shop-fried fish and chips, highly colored drinks, colored sweets, and have you had an X-ray?"[5]

Stewart proposed interviewing all of the mothers of children who had died of leukemia and other forms of cancer between 1953 and 1955. But she couldn't get mainstream funding for her work. A mere £1,000 was found, from the Lady Tata Memorial Fund for Leukemia Research, to pay for Alice's pioneering study. With such minimal resources, she had to be inventive. She designed her questionnaire and took it in person to all the medical officers in 203 county health departments in the country. With characteristic tenacity, she persuaded them to use their own people and local records to answer all the questions on her survey. Her tiny grant was all spent on train fares as she went up and down the country, laden with carbon paper and manila envelopes.

"When the Americans tried to do a study like ours," Alice later re-called, "they gave up because it cost too much. But it cost us so little because I was making use of existing records."[6]

Her study compared five hundred leukemia deaths, plus five hun-dred deaths from other forms of cancer, with one thousand live chil-dren of the same age, sex, and region. When the surveys started to come back, the results leapt out. The common denominator wasn't the colored sweets, the pets, or even the fish and chips.

" 'Yes' was turning up three times for every dead child to one for every live child, for the question, 'Had you had an obstetric X-ray?' *Yes was running three to one.* It was a shocker. They were as like as two peas in a pod, the living and the dead. They were alike in all respects except on that one score. And the dose was very small, very brief, a single diagnostic X-ray, a tiny fraction of the radiation exposure con-sidered safe. And it was enough to almost double risk of an early cancer death."

The recognition that X-raying pregnant mothers so dramatically increased the chances of childhood cancer was the kind of finding epidemiologists dream of: a hard problem with good data pointing to a clear solution. But, like the thorough scientist she was, when her excitement died down, Stewart questioned her results over and over again and she asked colleagues to check them before she published them. When her article, "Preliminary Communication: Malignant Diseases in Childhood and Diagnostic Irradiation In-Utero," appeared in *The Lancet* in 1956, it caused a stir. The Nobel Prize was mentioned and Alice was asked to repeat her survey in Scotland. Over the next eighteen months, Stewart and her team continued to collect data. Within a three-year period they had traced 80 percent of *all* childhood cancer deaths in England between 1953 and 1955. Publishing a full re-port in the *British Medical Journal* in 1958, they were able to conclude definitively that a fetus exposed to an X-ray was twice as likely to de-velop cancer within the next ten years as was a fetus that had not been exposed.

"We reckoned that a child a week was dying from this practice. We thought that doctors would stop X-raying on the mere suspicion that we were right and we felt that we must hurry to cover all the deaths that occurred in the next ten years, because once they stopped X-raying, there would be no further cases."

To the contrary, doctors carried on X-raying pregnant mothers for the next twenty-five years. Not until 1980 did major American medical organizations finally recommend that the practice be abandoned. The United Kingdom followed suit a year later.

Why did it take so long? How could so many doctors, the world over, have been so blind? Stewart's findings were clear, her data voluminous and, initially, greeted with acclaim. To us now, and to Alice at the time, it seemed obvious that the practice of X-raying pregnant women should stop immediately. What happened?

Many like to lay the blame on a personality clash with fellow epidemiologist Richard Doll.

"Doll was really influential and he was on the Medical Research Council and he truly did not want to let her into the story," argues Gayle Greene. "I think he knew that she was a better scientist than he and I think she had principles that he did not have and he could not forgive her for that."

Doll rushed out a paper refuting Stewart's paper—a tiny, quick study that he later acknowledged was "not very good" and the results of which he later described as "unreliable." But Doll was a dominant figure in the British medical establishment and his voice carried a long way. Alice Stewart's daughter, Anne Marshall, remembered the impact Doll's opposition had on her mother.

"I don't know if Mum was upset by Doll but he certainly made her think again and again. And then she'd settle down and do the work—and she knew she was right. She didn't enjoy a fight but, if she felt strongly about something, she was very good at having one."[7]

It didn't help that Stewart was an unconventional scientist; she was a divorced mother with two children, at a time when there were few women—and even fewer mothers—in science and when divorce was still not entirely respectable. Looking after her children alone didn't leave Alice much time to network, build alliances, or seek out support.

"She wasn't a political person," says Gayle Greene. "She was doing her research, raising her family, and that took thirty-two hours of the day! Compare that to Doll who was such a schmoozer, such a political creature. So smooth! When I met him, I thought: this is a guy who's done a lot of PR! You would never say that meeting Alice. She was authentic, genuine, a very disarming person—I mean everybody loved her, but she was not playing the game."

Doll was a major obstacle. But personality alone doesn't explain why, worldwide, the practice of X-raying unborn children persisted. At the Harvard School of Public Health, Brian MacMahon also set out to refute Stewart's findings—but he found exactly what she had found: Cancer mortality was 40 percent higher among children whose mothers had been X-rayed. In the early 1960s, one of the largest radiation studies examined six million X-ray subjects in New York, Maryland, and Minnesota; that too confirmed Alice's findings. New statistical methods and the advent of computers all served to make collecting and analyzing data easier and more accurate—but all the subsequent studies did, over and over again, was show that Alice Stewart, with her paper surveys and carbon paper, had been right all along. So why did doctors continue a practice that study after study showed to be so dangerous? How could they be so blind to all the data?

In part, the sexiness of X-rays was to blame. Ever since their discovery in 1895, X-rays had developed an aura of mastery and mystique. They were used as an exquisite and expensive form of portraiture in the 1890s and even were used as the ultimate tool for finding a ring that had been mistakenly baked into a cake.[8] Shoe stores boasted of X-ray machines that ensured a perfect fit: "The salesman, the purchaser and even a purchaser's advisory friend can visually know exactly how well a shoe is fitting, both under pressure and otherwise," claimed the 1927 patent for the "shoe fluoroscope." "With this apparatus in his shop, a shoe merchant can positively assure his customers that they need never wear ill-fitting boots and shoes; that parents can visually assure themselves as to whether they are buying shoes for their boys and girls which will not injure and deform the sensitive bone joints."[9]

With so much investment in it, neither shoe salesmen nor doctors wanted to hear that there might be any risks associated with the new technology. They were wedded to it.

"No one likes to be told they've been doing something wrong all their lives!" That's how Anne Marshall explains the reaction to her mother's findings. "That's what the radiologists and obstetricians took from Mum's work—that they'd been doing something wrong. There were lots of them and they liked what they were doing and wanted to keep on doing it."

"Doctors' enthusiasm about radiology was so enormous that medical centers had invested in all kinds of X-ray equipment," explains Gayle Greene. "They didn't like being told that they were not only *not* helping their patients—but they were actually killing them! People are very resistant to changing what they know how to do, what they have expertise in and certainly what they have economic investment in."

But Alice Stewart's survey of childhood cancers did something even more radical and provocative than question standard medical practice. Her findings struck at the heart of a Big Idea central to scientific thinking at the time. Threshold theory maintained that, while a large dose of something like radiation would be dangerous, there was always a point—a threshold—beyond which it was safe. (That point is what, today, we might call a tipping point.) But Alice Stewart was arguing that in this case, there was *no* acceptable level of radiation that was safe for fetuses. It wasn't just shoe shops and medical centers; a cornerstone of scientific orthodoxy was under attack.

She had to be wrong. If she was right, too many other assumptions had to be reexamined. What Alice Stewart had provoked in her scientific colleagues was cognitive dissonance: the mental turmoil that is evoked when the mind tries to hold two entirely incompatible views. It could not be true that threshold theory was right—but also that such tiny doses of radiation caused cancers. It could not be true that radiation was both a new wonder tool—and that it also killed children. It could not be true that doctors cured patients—and made them sick. The dissonance produced by mutually exclusive beliefs is tremendously painful, even unbearable. The easiest way to reduce the pain—the dissonance—is to eliminate one of the beliefs, rendering dissonance consonant. It was easier for scientists to cling to their beliefs: in threshold theory, in the benevolence of X-rays, and in the idea of doctors as authoritative, smart, good people. Alice Stewart and her findings were sacrificed to preserve the Big Idea. Dissonance is eliminated when we blind ourselves to contradictory propositions. And we are prepared to pay a very high price to preserve our most cherished ideas.

The theory of cognitive dissonance was initially developed by Leon Festinger around the same time that Alice Stewart was studying childhood cancers. He had developed much of his theory studying the religious millenarian movements in the nineteenth century, but he yearned for a live, modern case study to test his ideas. In September 1954, he found his opportunity in a newspaper story.

PROPHECY FROM PLANET. CLARION CALL TO CITY: FLEE THAT FLOOD.
IT'LL SWAMP US ON DEC. 21, OUTER SPACE TELLS SUBORDINATE.

The story described a suburban housewife, Marian Keech, who believed, on the basis of automatic writing, that the earth would be flooded on December 21. The fact that Mrs. Keech and her adherents held such a specific belief about an event destined to occur on a specific date made this a perfect test case for Festinger's research: What would happen when a deeply help belief—a Big Idea—was disconfirmed by events? That the end of the world was due in months, and not years, made his research practical, too. When, as Festinger predicted, the flood failed to take place, would Mrs. Keech surrender her belief in the light of experience? Festinger's theory suggested that she would continue in her faith but also, crucially, that it would become stronger than ever.

Even more unconventional in his research methods than Alice Stewart, Festinger and a few of his colleagues from the University of Minnesota set out to infiltrate Mrs. Keech's community. For two months, they monitored the beliefs and varying levels of commitment among a small group with whom Mrs. Keech had shared the automatic writing, which she believed came to her via extraterrestrial messengers. Dr. Thomas Armstrong, a physician at Eastern Teachers College in Collegeville, and his wife, Daisy, became Keech's devoted followers and they, in turn, recruited numerous students until there was a core of some fifteen devotees.

Mrs. Keech's messages described an apocalyptic vision, according to which Lucifer had returned to Earth in disguise and was leading scientists to build ever greater weapons of destruction. Their work would culminate in the Earth falling apart and the disruption of the entire solar system. While forces of light struggled to reclaim humanity, man's only hope was that enough people would be open to the light to escape another explosion.

Festinger went out of his way to point out that Keech and the Armstrongs weren't crazy and weren't psychotic. "True, Mrs. Keech put together a rather unusual combination of ideas—a combination peculiarly well adapted to our contemporary, anxious age," Festinger wrote. "But scarcely a single one of her ideas can be said to be unique, novel or lacking in popular support."[10] There was nothing in her belief system that people haven't believed before—or since.

Central to these beliefs was the prediction Mrs. Keech received that the world would end with an enormous flood on December 21. Only true believers would be saved. "The Supreme Being is going to clean house by sinking all of the land masses as we know them now and raising the land masses now under the sea. There will be a washing of the world with water. Some will be saved by being taken off the earth in spacecraft."[11]

The messages were so bizarre and the belief system so open to ridicule that Festinger took pains to document just how serious and how real the group's commitment was. These were not a bunch of kids pretending. One particularly devout member, Kitty O'Donnell, quit her job, quit school, lived off her small savings, and moved into an expensive apartment because she did not expect to need what little remained of her cash. Two members—Fred Burden and Laura Brooks—gave up their college studies; Laura Brooks threw away many of her personal possessions. Dr. Armstrong was eventually asked to resign his college position; the amount of time he spent talking to students about flying saucers had caused a flurry of parental complaints. But he was not dismayed, considering this merely "part of the plan."[12] His wife chose not to bother getting her dishwasher repaired: "It isn't worth it, because the time is so short now."[13] And when Mrs. Keech received a call from a salesman of cemetery lots, she calmly explained that burial was "the least of my worries."[14] However ludicrous the prophesies may seem to us, this group lived their lives in the sincere belief that the flood was imminent.

Mrs. Keech and her followers confidently expected flying saucers to transport them to other planets before the cataclysm occurred. Several false alarms, when messages seemed to promise the arrival of spacemen who failed to arrive, tested their faith. But on each occasion, the group either reinterpreted the messages to fit events or blamed themselves for faulty understanding. On the eve of the promised flood, the group spent the day together in "peaceful idleness" confidently awaiting their rescue. Arthur Bergen, a teenage member of the group, complained that his mother had threatened to call the police if he weren't home by two the next morning. "The believers smilingly assured him that he need not worry—by that time they would all be aboard a saucer."[15] Warned not to wear metal of any kind, they fastidiously eliminated it from their clothing—zippers, snaps, belt buckles, bra clips—and removed foil from chewing gum, watches from wrists.

The last ten minutes were tense. When one clock said 12:05, a chorus of people pointed out that a slower clock was more accurate. But even when the slower clock confirmed midnight, no one appeared and nothing happened. No flood, no flying saucers. Mrs. Keech continued to receive long, confusing messages from "the Creator" but by two A.M. Arthur Bergen had to take a cab home to his mother. By four thirty A.M., the group was distraught, close to tears, and some were beginning to show signs of doubt. How would they handle the disconfirmation of their passionately held beliefs? This was the gist of Festinger's two-month study.

At four forty-five A.M. Mrs. Keech received a new message. "Not since the beginning of time upon this Earth has there been such a force of Good and light as now floods this room and that which has been loosed within this room now floods the entire Earth."[16] The goodness of the group had saved the world from flood.

The group was jubilant: the belief system was intact. But a greater change overcame Mrs. Keech. Previously highly reticent, now she was more eager than ever to call the local newspaper and share her good news. Another member of the group insisted the news go farther, to the Associated Press; the Creator surely wouldn't want the story to be an exclusive. Despite—or because of—the initial challenge to their belief, their faith now was stronger than ever and the believers more energetic in their proselytizing. Evidence had not upset belief. Just as Festinger had hypothesized, disconfirmation had actually made their belief stronger.

And they never lost it. While Mrs. Keech eventually left Lake City, she continued to receive automatic messages that she relayed to the faithful. The Armstrongs were as devout as ever, their faith "boundless and their resistance to disconfirmation sublime." Of the eleven members of the Lake City group, each of whom had witnessed unequivocal disconfirmation firsthand, only two completely gave up their belief in Mrs. Keech's writings—and they were the two who had been least committed from the outset.

Festinger's academic account of this episode can't resist some of the humor implicit in it, but the thrust of his argument is deadly serious. He and subsequent psychologists argued that we all strive to preserve an image of ourselves as consistent, stable, competent, and good. Our most cherished beliefs are a vital and central part of who we are—in our own eyes and the eyes of our friends and colleagues. Anything or anyone that threatens that sense of self produces pain that feels just as dangerous and unpleasant as hunger or thirst. A challenge to our big ideas feels life-threatening. And so we strive mightily to reduce the pain, either by ignoring the evidence that proves we are wrong, or by reinterpreting evidence to support us.

Psychologist Anthony Greenwald called this phenomenon the "totalitarian ego."[17] It operates, he said, just like a police state: locking away threatening or incompatible ideas, suppressing evidence, and rewriting history, all in the service of a central idea or self-image. Marian Keech's followers would reinterpret events to fit their expectations, because not to have done so threatened to destroy their sense of who they were in the world. If doctors and scientists who read Alice Stewart's research believed it, and acted upon it, then they would have had to accept that they had harmed patients. But doctors don't like to think of themselves as sources of harm; they go into medicine to be, and do, good. Scientists embracing Alice's findings would have had at least to question the big idea of threshold theory, but scientists like big ideas, organizing principles, perhaps more than the rest of us do. They're what hold the data together, in just the same way that our beliefs and values hold our sense of self together. Acknowledging error, in these areas that are so vital for our self-definition, feels far too costly. Even as late as 1977, the National Council of Radiation Protection argued that doctors must have X-rayed only those fetuses that were destined to get cancer. How they could have known which these were the council never explained. But that scientists should have developed so convoluted an argument illustrates how hard the mind will work to defend its most cherished and defining beliefs.

Festinger argued that, as individuals, we are all highly driven to make sense of the world and of our place in it. And we do so by gathering around us the ideas but also the people that verify our story, so to speak. The work that Drew Westen and other scientists have done more recently has served to illustrate that cognitive dissonance is not just a theory; it has a physical reality in the way the brain handles information that we like—and the way that it handles the information that causes us distress. The fact that, as we already know, we're drawn to people similar to ourselves merely reinforces this process. Mrs. Keech and her followers would have had difficulty maintaining their faith if they had been isolated and alone: confirmation of each other by each other kept their commitment secure. In just the same way, the medical profession stuck together, led by the socially adroit Richard Doll, holding out against Alice Stewart's findings.

Social support makes it easier to do things, or believe in ideas, that would feel a lot more uncomfortable if we were on our own. That so-cial support always comes in the form of family, friends, or colleagues who share, and act on, the big ideas that bring them together. But insti-tutional power is a particularly seductive form of social support. After all, if you are in a position of tremendous institutional or political power, then not only are you hugely confirmed by the colleagues who share your beliefs, but questioning them would threaten everything: job, position, reputation, future career.

There's an exquisite moment in Errol Morris's film about Robert McNamara, *The Fog of War*, when McNamara talks about meeting North Vietnamese former foreign minister Nguyen Co Thach years after the ending of the Vietnam War. As U.S. secretary of defense from 1961 to 1968, McNamara had been as convinced a Cold Warrior as any of his cabinet colleagues. His job, as he saw it then, was not to question the war but to prosecute it effectively. His passion, both for the ideology of the administration and for the success of his career, he later saw, had blinded him to any understanding of his enemy.

"Mr. McNamara, you must never have read a history book," McNa-mara recalled Thach saying to him. "If you had, you'd know we weren't pawns of the Chinese or the Russians. McNamara, didn't you know that? Don't you understand that we have been fighting the Chinese for a thousand years? We were fighting for our independence. And we would fight to the last man. And we were determined to do so. And no amount of bombing, no amount of U.S. pressure would ever have stopped us."

Cold War ideology had blinded McNamara and his colleagues to the fundamental, primary motivation of the Vietnamese. They weren't fighting to become part of a greater communist bloc. They were fight-ing to become free from *all* imperial powers. But for anyone to have questioned Cold War orthodoxy within the Johnson administration at the time would have jeopardized status, reputation, and position. Mc-Namara's blindness doomed him to failure; he could not win the war because he did not understand his opponent. Far from making sense of events, the big idea left him powerless to understand them. And so, ultimately, he lost everything he had striven so hard to protect.

Economic models work in ways very similar to such ideologies: pulling in and integrating the information that fits the model, leaving out what can't be accommodated. The economist and Nobel laureate

Paul Krugman compared such models to ancient maps. At first, they were wildly misleading but did incorporate a lot of information: secondhand travelers' reports, guesses, and anecdotes. As the standard for accuracy rose, much of that information wasn't deemed good enough so it got left out—with the result that by the eighteenth century, most of Africa went blank. But Krugman, whose reputation for beautiful models has brought him such fame, recognizes how incomplete they can be.

"I think there's a pretty good case to be made that the stuff that I stressed in the models is a less important story than the things I left out because I couldn't model them, like spillovers of information and social networks."[18]

The problem with models, in other words, is that they imply that whatever does not fit into them isn't relevant—when it may be the most relevant information of all. But we treasure our models and personal big ideas because they help us to make decisions about what to do with our lives, whom to befriend, and what we stand for. A profound and innate part of who we are, they become so deeply entwined in all aspects of our lives that we may forget how profoundly they filter what we see, absorb, and remember. As our brains give our preferred ideas a smooth, easy flow, impeding distressing contradictions, the riverbed of our beliefs gets deeper and its sides grow higher.

In the case of someone like Mrs. Keech, it was very obvious (to everyone but her) just how peculiar her ideas were. But when ideas are widely held, they don't stand out as much; they can even become the norm. We may not see them as ideology and we don't see their proponents as zealots. But appearances can be deceptive.

"Greenspan's willful blindness was incredible," says Frank Partnoy, professor of law and finance at the University of San Diego. "He had a highly simplistic view of how markets behaved. He believed in the core of his soul that markets would self-correct and that financial models could forecast risk effectively." Partnoy doesn't criticize the former chairman of the Federal Reserve Bank lightly or from the lofty perch of someone observing financial shenanigans from a safe distance. He sold derivatives on Wall Street from 1993 to 1995 and knew, firsthand, in gritty detail, just how convoluted, disingenuous, obscure, and risky they were. He eventually left the industry, utterly disillusioned by how fraudulent it was. But his years on Wall Street had shown him, up close and personal, what the derivatives market was all about. And he watched with mounting frustration and disbelief as the so-called Maestro Greenspan failed to do anything about it.

"There was just so much happening in markets that Greenspan didn't understand—because it was inconsistent with his worldview," says Partnoy. "It really illustrates the dangers of having a particular fixed view of the world and not being open to evidence that your worldview is wrong until it is too late."

Greenspan's worldview was significantly developed when, in his late twenties and early thirties, he became a devoted acolyte of Ayn Rand. At this time, Greenspan had given up on his career playing bebop with a big touring band and turned to economics. He dropped out of Columbia's Ph.D. program to form a consulting firm while developing a close personal relationship, and passionate intellectual relationship, with Rand and her fellow Objectivists. Rand's attraction to men remains somewhat mysterious: an adulterous, failed screenwriter who'd emigrated from revolutionary Russia, she seems an unlikely muse for corporate titans and gurus of economic theory. Her understanding of how markets worked derived from the traumatic experience of having lived through the Russian Revolution, during which her family lost everything. But she had never trained as an economist, had never run a business, and wrote extraordinarily hideous, often impenetrable prose that purported to be philosophy. Nevertheless, Greenspan was smitten, springing to Rand's defense when her second novel, *Atlas Shrugged*, received an unfavorable critical review. Defending the book in 1957, he wrote to the *New York Times*: "Justice is unrelenting. Creative individuals and undeviating purpose and rationality achieve joy and fulfillment. Parasites who persistently avoid either purpose or reason perish as they should." Greenspan could not conceive that a book with such properties might have its flaws.

What Greenspan admired in Rand, and what he embraced with evangelical fervor, was the belief that, if he were only liberated from the regulations and constraints imposed by government, man would attain ever greater heights of freedom, creativity, and wealth.

"I am opposed," Rand told Mike Wallace in 1959, "to all forms of control. I am for an absolute laissez-faire free unregulated economy. I am for the separation of state and economics."[19]

In Rand's world, those who could do well would be freed from all constraint to express and articulate the full capacity of their talents;

they would achieve joy and fulfillment. Those who weren't up to it—
"parasites," she called them—would fail and get out of the way. It's a
touchingly romantic idea, as long as you assume that you will be one
of the successful ones. It reminds me of adolescents who think all their
troubles would be over if only their parents would stop telling them
how to behave.

Greenspan wasn't in love with Ayn Rand, but he was in love with
her ideas and they framed everything he did. In his autobiography,
The Age of Turbulence, he describes her as a "stabilizing force" in his
life.[20] Describing himself as a convert, Greenspan was clearly in awe of
her, though proud that he had been able to "keep up with her most of
the time." Ayn Rand was right there, standing next to him, when, in
1974, he was sworn in as chairman of President Gerald Ford's Council
of Economic Advisors. And his ideas hadn't changed a bit when he
took over the Federal Reserve in August 1987. The man with a religious belief in the evils of regulating was now in charge of money
supply.

"I do have an ideology," Greenspan told the U.S. Congress. "My
judgment is that free, competitive markets are by far the unrivaled
way to organize economies."[21]

"He wanted to do whatever he could to deregulate the market," says
Partnoy, who has studied Greenspan's career critically for many years.
"But he was very clever about it. Rather than lobby upfront for the
repeal of Glass-Steagal, he pressed for a series of small incremental
changes. I think of it as Swiss cheese: put a few holes in, then a few
more—and eventually there's no cheese left! He honestly believed that
we would all be better off if regulated markets got smaller and smaller,
and the deregulated markets got bigger and bigger. That's how you get
to the promised land."

What's so striking, however, is that all the time Greenspan was
nibbling away at regulation, the market was being rocked by a series of
warning tremors that offered strong evidence that its most deregulated
sectors—the sector Greenspan was so eager to help grow—threatened
to blow everything up.

In 1994, when Greenspan raised interest rates from 3 percent to 3.25
percent, the marketplace was full of derivatives that assumed interest
rates would stay low. When interest rates rose instead, all hell broke
loose. David Askin, one of the most active traders in complex mortgage
derivatives, ran a six-hundred-million-dollar fund that went up in

smoke in a matter of weeks, filing for bankruptcy on April 7. Five days later, Gibson Greetings, Air Products, Dell, Mead Corporation, and Procter & Gamble admitted to billions of dollars in losses from derivatives, many of which even their internal financiers did not understand. Congressional hearings were held, in which George Soros testified that "there are so many of them and some are so esoteric, that the risks involved may not be properly understood even by the most sophisticated investors."[22]

In May 1994, Greenspan's Fed raised the rate another half percent—and there was a bloodbath on Wall Street. Property and casualty insurers lost more than they had paid out on Hurricane Andrew in 2002; hedge funds, banks, securities firms, and the life insurance industry lost billions. According to Frank Partnoy, virtually every kind of institution, from every sector of the economy, suffered massive losses.

In Orange County, California, the seventy-year-old county treasurer—and college dropout—Robert Citron, bet twenty billion dollars of public money on derivatives sold to him by Merrill Lynch; in December 1994, the county filed for bankruptcy. And Orange County wasn't alone. Dozens of smaller municipalities, from California to Georgia to Maine and Montana, along with public utilities, city colleges, and pension funds, had invested in collateralized mortgage obligations and other derivatives, losing millions.

In 1994, Procter & Gamble sued Bankers Trust for the huge losses they'd suffered from derivatives. The prosecution used taped phone calls that demonstrated just how deliberately and knowingly the bankers had misled the firm. For once, a chink of light was shed on the "dark market" of derivatives, and what it showed wasn't pretty—and wasn't regulated. At the same time, Kidder, Peabody, which was part of General Electric at the time, under the legendary Jack Welch, discovered losses of $350 million. It turned out that no one at Kidder, Peabody really understood what traders in the firm were up to. The quarter in which the losses were reported was the first time in fifty-two quarters that earnings were less than they'd been in the previous year. But after all this mayhem, the only legislation that emerged actually made life far harder for would-be plaintiffs when Congress limited securities lawsuits in 1995.

Frank Partnoy has chronicled each of these debacles, from what he calls "Patient Zero" in 1987 through to Enron in 2002 and the banking crisis twenty years later. "It was foolish," he wrote, "to deregulate markets simply because large institutions instead of individuals were involved. It was a well-established economic principle that markets with large sophistication and information gaps did not function well. The more they carved up markets, the harder it was for anyone to keep tabs on risk."[23]

Each of these debacles reinforced the same lesson: derivatives were a "dark market." No one knew what went on in these deals and because there was no statutory requirement to report anything, even the parties to the deals often did not know what they had. Had there been any reporting requirement, at least those with the most at stake might have gained some insight into their own exposure. Instead, the freedom to report nothing meant that not only did the government not really know what was going on; no one did.

That this could continue was possible only because so many people shared Greenspan's ideology. The *Financial Times* journalist Gillian Tett compares such blind faith to the medieval Church.

"If this was a religion, Alan Greenspan was the pope," says Tett. "He blessed derivatives. Then you had the high priests up at the altar, passing out blessings in the financial Latin that the congregation doesn't understand. The pope is saying it's all miraculous and wonderful and the blessings come in the form of cheap mortgages."[24]

A few dissenting voices had the temerity to stand up to Greenspan and argue that derivatives posed a major risk and required oversight. In 1988, stockbroker Muriel Siebert testified before the congressional subcommittee on telecommunications and finance, in the wake of the 1987 market crash. The major problem with the market, she said, was derivatives.

"Program trades and index arbitrage end up bringing the volatility and rampant speculation of the futures pits to the floor of the Big Board. Futures have become the tail wagging the dog."

In 1996, Brooksley Born was appointed to head up the Commodity Futures Trading Commission, the regulator uniquely tasked with regulating the twenty-seven-trillion-dollar derivatives market. And after the string of catastrophes in 1994, she was one of the few eager to impose some oversight. But Greenspan was having none of it. In 1998, Born's CFTC issued a "Concept Release" outlining how regulation might work; Greenspan instantly issued a statement condemning it. Born was trying to devise mechanisms to monitor risks to a major segment of the economy; Greenspan marshaled all his friends, allies, and political capital to blast Born's proposals out of existence.

"It seemed totally inexplicable to me," Born recalled later. "It was as though the other regulators were saying, 'We don't want to know.'"[25]

Six weeks later, the hedge fund Long Term Capital Management, which included Greenspan's former deputy at the Fed, David Mullins, became insolvent. The size of the failure threatened the entire U.S. economy.

"Long Term Capital Management was exactly what I'd been worried about," Born said. "No regulators knew it was on the verge of collapse. Why? Because we didn't have any information about the market."[26]

At last, the LTCM crisis provoked some support in Congress for regulation. But Greenspan once again moved quickly to quash it, saying "I know of no set of supervisory actions we can take that can prevent people from making dumb mistakes. I think it is very important for us not to introduce regulation for regulation's sake."

And Greenspan and his friends won the day: no regulation for over-the-counter derivatives was introduced. They could continue to trade without any capital requirements or rules against manipulation or even fraud. Greenspan's free market was allowed to get bigger and bigger, and Brooksley Born resigned.

Three years later, in 2001, the sixth largest corporation in America, Enron, went bust. Inside an intricate web of malfeasance lay deadly derivatives, tied to the company's stock price, which left its investors with nothing. Those investors weren't all Enron employees; many were small investors, like Mary Pearson, a Latin teacher who testified before Congress after the company failed.

"I am just a pebble in the stream, a little bitty shareholder. I did not lose billions but what I did lose seems like a billion to me. I was going to use my Enron stock as my long-term health care. I was disappointed in the people that I put my trust in years ago. And after a little time passed on, bitterness came into being, and bitterness will eat you alive if you let it. But sometimes at night I do feel real bitter over what I have lost, because it was a big part of my future, and I do not know how I am going to handle the future now. All I can do is hope and pray I do not get sick."[27]

This was not a narrative Greenspan could see. From his perspective, "creative individuals and undeviating purpose and rationality" went on to "achieve joy and fulfillment" and the parasites perished. Until, that is, the banking crisis of 2008.

"This was my worst nightmare coming true," said Brooksley Born. "Nobody really knew what was going on in the market. The toxic assets of our biggest banks were in over-the-counter derivatives and caused the economic downturn that made us lose our savings, lose our jobs, lose our homes."

Just as Rand had wished, the state and economics had been separated; Greenspan had proved true to the big idea of his life, but blind to the realities of it. Even after the biggest financial catastrophe of his lifetime, when Greenpan went to testify to Congress about what had gone wrong, he held fast to his big idea. It wasn't wrong; it was just flawed.

CHAIRMAN WAXMAN: You had an ideology. "My judgment is that free, competitive markets are by far the unrivaled way to organize economies. We have tried regulation, none meaningfully worked." That was your quote. Now our whole economy is paying its price. Do you feel that your ideology pushed you to make decisions that you wish you had not made?

MR. GREENSPAN: Well, remember, though, whether or not ideology is a conceptual framework with the way people deal with reality, everyone has one. You have to. To exist, you need an ideology. The question is whether it exists, is accurate or not. What I am saying to you is yes, I found a flaw, I don't know how significant or permanent it is, but I have been very distressed by that fact. I found a flaw in the model that I perceived is the critical functioning structure of how the world works.

CHAIRMAN WAXMAN: In other words, you found that your view of the world, your ideology, was not right, it was not working?

MR. GREENSPAN: Precisely. That's precisely the reason I was shocked, because I had been going for forty years or more with very considerable evidence that it was working exceptionally well.[28]

Greenspan's performance was mesmerizing drama: a proud, old man wriggling to protect himself from the sharp, hard prongs of fact. His adversaries had prepared long and hard for this inquisition and neither they, nor the nation as a whole, were prepared to offer him room to maneuver. They demanded his recantation but he fought hard to evade the cognitive dissonance implicit in events that would not change shape just to fit into his ideology. Despite failure after failure, he still could not deny his big idea. He could just admit a flaw, not that he was wrong. Just like Mrs. Keech, he acknowledged only that he had gotten a minor detail wrong. He couldn't see and wouldn't see the financial wreckage strewn right across his career, but instead insisted that his big idea had worked just fine for forty years. The free-market economist Friedrich von Hayek once said that "without a theory, the facts are silent." But for Greenspan, with his theory, the facts became invisible.

"Greenspan was blind to two things," says Partnoy. "He missed the fact that in the modern regulated state, you can't have a truly free market. There are always partially regulated markets and therefore there are opportunities for people to exploit information traps. And he didn't understand that even to the extent that the market isn't regulated, there are serious potential downsides to a free-for-all. That's why in the U.S. and UK we have common law. Because if those things are absent, you have problems. Not just unfairness and injustice—but also just this kind of volatility and destabilization."

Of course, Greenspan did not act alone. He had the support of the powerful, he had the support of the crowd—as long as the economy was doing fine. You could say that he was blind, but he operated within a collective myopia that reinforced his ideology. And he hasn't recanted.

"Greenspan isn't atoning," says Partnoy. "It would be very hard for him to do that. He'd be escaping from a long tunnel."

In that, Greenspan is more like Marian Keech than like Richard Doll. In 1997, his reputation secured by his having proved the connection between smoking and lung cancer, Doll did recant, although with the most modest of mea culpas. In a paper titled "Risk of Childhood Cancer from Fetal Irradiation,"[29] he quietly announced the death of threshold theory.

"The association between the low dose of ionizing radiation received by the fetus *in utero* from diagnostic radiography, particularly in the last trimester of pregnancy, and the subsequent risk of cancer in childhood provides direct evidence against the existence of a threshold dose below which no excess risk arises, and has led to changes in medical practice."

But by the time Doll changed his mind, millions of pregnant women had been X-rayed. And Alice Stewart had moved on to confront the nuclear power industry.

4

THE LIMITS OF YOUR MIND

ON MARCH 23, 2005, Warren Briggs got into his car and set off for work. The commute to the British Petroleum refinery in Texas City usually took thirty to forty-five minutes, but that day it felt longer. When he got to the plant, just before six A.M., he could scarcely remember driving there. Warren had been working twelve-hour shifts, seven days a week, for twenty-nine days in a row. He couldn't remember the last time he'd had time off. He had mixed feelings about his shifts. Twelve hours off meant more time with the kids. But he still wasn't getting much sleep.

He spoke briefly to the departing night-shift operator and then read the log book to prepare for the start-up. There was just a one-line log-book entry: "isom brought in some raff to unit, to pack raff with." That told him more or less nothing, he thought, grumpy as he started to work.

In front of him sat the control board for the ISOM/NDU/AU2 complex: twelve monitors divided into twenty-four screens. Some screens had pages and pages of information behind them; others were pretty simple alarms. Visitors said it looked like something from NASA; Warren wished it were that exciting.

Warren's boss was late and, when he got in, he was busy. He was always busy because he had a stack of paperwork and a bunch of contracting crews to look after. A lot of the men hated contractors, said they were unsafe and cut corners. Warren didn't mind. Those guys needed to feed their families same as he did. It wasn't their fault BP brought them in with fewer benefits, lower pay. There weren't that many jobs around Texas City to choose from.

"We're running so thin": that was the phrase everybody used. At first it just meant the pipes were wearing thin but now the whole place was wearing out. The plant and the people. So much cost-cutting, you could do the form-filling but not the repairs. Warren's supervisor was buried in paperwork and he had two new operators to train. He probably wouldn't be around much during the shift.

With no one to relieve him, Warren ate his lunch at his desk in front of the control board. Some weird pressure spikes caught his attention and he wanted to keep an eye on them. It was boring, lonely work, cooped up in a darkened room. The equipment he was supposed to be controlling stood outside in the Texas sunshine, one small part of the vast refinery. When people first saw it, they'd say it looked like something on the moon, a space-age settlement full of towers and spheres that went on for miles. Warren didn't share their romance. It was just a refinery, making 3 percent of America's gasoline. That was a lot of cars.

The isomerization unit Warren looked after boosted octane levels in the gasoline produced at the plant. Flammable hydrocarbons, or raffinate—the "raff" in the log book—went into a 170-foot tower that would distill and separate gas components. Higher octane meant higher performance and higher prices. That was the name of the game. Starting the unit was always a tricky time, when it would have been nice to have an extra pair of eyes. In the old days, there had been two operators, but cost cutting had changed all that. Then they'd added a third unit—the NDU—and said it was so easy to operate that you didn't need an extra person. So instead of two people for two refinery units, now it was just Warren, on his own, looking after all three.

Around 12:40, an alarm went off, but Warren couldn't figure out where the high pressure was coming from. He decided to open a manual chain valve to vent some of the gases to the emergency relief system and to turn off two burners in the furnace. Just after one P.M., Warren's boss called in to see how things were going. When Warren mentioned the weird pressure spikes, his boss suggested opening a bypass valve to the blowdown drum to relieve some of the pressure. What neither of them knew was that the isomerization tower was too full, fifteen times higher than it was meant to be. But Warren's control panel wasn't configured to display flows into and out of the tower on the same screen and nowhere did it calculate total liquid in the tower. Running thin.

An adventure, one of the guys had called working there. An adventure? Sure, he said: Each morning when I walk into this place, I wonder if today's the day I'm gonna die. That wasn't Warren's idea of an adventure.

At 1:14 P.M., three emergency valves opened in the tower, sending nearly 52,000 gallons of hot, flammable liquid to the blowdown drum. When the liquid overflowed into a process sewer, it set off alarms in the control room. But the high-level alarm didn't go off. While Warren sat in front of his twenty-four screens, a geyser of liquid and vapor erupted from the top of the stack, propelling nearly a tanker full of hot gasoline up into the air and then down to the ground like a tall, ungainly fountain. Within ninety seconds the whole unit and all the contractors' trailers were engulfed in a vast flammable vapor cloud.[1] Then a nearby car backfired.

A mile away, Joe Bilancich was negotiating for a new apprentice scheme. He felt one concussion in the room, then another. Everybody moved to the window. Flames and smoke filled their view while pieces of pipe and metal rained down on the ground.

Forty-five minutes from the site, Eva Rowe heard the blast. Both her parents worked at the site; she called them at once. No answer.

Fifteen people died that day at BP's Texas City site, killed by the "blunt-force trauma" of the explosion. Eva Rowe lost both of her parents. It was one of the worst industrial accidents in American history.

When investigators, lawyers, and executives arrived to investigate the cause of the tragedy, everybody talked about blind spots: problems, processes, and warnings that everybody could see but somehow managed not to see. Some of the causes were complex and technical, but some were not. What happened to Warren Briggs was simple and obvious and not unique to oil refineries. As we know from the banking crisis, companies don't have to kill people to be dangerous.

According to the U.S. Chemical Safety Board (CSB), which spent two years investigating the accident, Briggs was one of the most rested members of his team. The night lead operator, who had filled the tower from the control room before Briggs had come on duty, had worked thirty-three consecutive days, while the day lead operator—who was training two new operators, dealing with contractors, and working to get a replacement part to finish the ISOM turnaround work—had been on duty for thirty-seven consecutive days. In other words, they were all dog tired. The CSB estimated that Briggs was getting 5.5 hours of sleep per night, and therefore was suffering from what they call an accumulated "sleep debt" of about a month and a half. That didn't just mean that he felt lousy. "It is common for a person experiencing fatigue to be more rigid in thinking, have greater difficulty responding to changing or abnormal circumstances, and take longer to reason correctly," said the CSB. Focused attention on one thing, to the exclusion of everything else—often referred to as cognitive fixation or cognitive tunnel vision—is a typical performance effect of fatigue.[2]

Briggs and his operators could not see the problem. They were simply too tired. The UK Health and Safety Executive found that subjective levels of fatigue increase with consecutive early shifts (those starting around six A.M.) The third day of working an early-morning shift results, it said, in a 30-percent increase in fatigue, while the fifth consecutive day of working early-morning shifts results in a 60-percent increase in fatigue, and the seventh consecutive day results in a 75-percent increase compared to the first day. The study doesn't even contemplate what happens to peoples' minds when they've been working like this for thirty days nonstop.

Fatigue, overwork, and burnout are not unique to the oil and gas industries. On November 11, 2004, the computer games company Electronic Arts woke up to find itself the target of a blogger called "EASpouse" who complained with shocking eloquence about the hours EA expected its programmers to work. Addressing herself to then-CEO (now chairman) Larry Probst, the spouse asked, "You do realize what you're doing to your people, right? And you do realize that they ARE people, with physical limits, emotional lives, and families, right? Voices and talents and senses of humor and all that? That when you keep our husbands and wives and children in the office for ninety hours a week, sending them home exhausted and numb and frustrated with their lives, it's not just them you're hurting, but everyone around them, everyone who loves them? When you make your profit calculations and your cost analyses, you know that a great measure of that cost is being paid in raw human dignity, right?"

Electronic Arts—whose tagline at the time was "Challenge Everything"—is the world's leading producer of computer games. The year 2004 was a good one for the company. *The Sims, Lord of the Rings, FIFA,* and *Medal of Honor* generated record revenues ($3 billion) and record profits ($776 million).[3] The year was particularly noteworthy because technology breakthroughs—faster processors and improved screen resolution—resulted in a boom for handheld game devices. The introduction of Sony's PSP promised even greater opportunity. But writing in the company's annual report about the challenges the company faced going into 2005, Probst made no mention of a workforce that was fried, or of an engineering team with a turnover rate of nearly 50 percent.

When EASpouse's essay, "EA: The Human Study," was posted online, it tore through the computer game community like wildfire. "I was so angry and in such pain, I thought, either I get a response to this or there's something seriously wrong with the world!" said Erin Hoffman, its author. "It was students and gamers who propelled the thing. Within forty-eight hours, everyone read it. But it was students who were most angry! They dreamed of working in this industry—and were desperately disappointed to learn how awful it was."

Today, Hoffman is in less pain, but she's still angry. The gist of her complaint then was that EA routinely scheduled engineers to work eighty-five-hour weeks. When her fiancé, Lan, had interviewed for a job at EA, neither of them had been naïve. As veterans of the computer games industry, they knew that just before a product shipped, most teams went into crunch mode, which involved a lot of long hours.

"They asked Lan in one of the interviews: 'How do you feel about working long hours?' It's just a part of the game industry—few studios can avoid a crunch as deadlines loom, so we thought nothing of it. When asked for specifics about what 'working long hours' meant, the interviewers coughed and glossed on to the next question; now we know why."

Crunch is only supposed to be the mode of working at the tail end of a project. At EA, the team started by doing eight-hour days, six days a week. But that quickly turned into twelve hours, six days a week and then into eleven hours a day, seven days a week. Crunch wasn't an emergency; it was a standard. Watching what was happening to her fiancé horrified Erin. "After a certain number of hours, the eyes start to lose focus; after a certain number of weeks with only one day off, fatigue starts to accrue and accumulate exponentially. Bad things happen to one's physical, emotional, and mental health. The team is rapidly beginning to introduce as many flaws as they are removing. The bug rate soared in crunch."

As the debate inspired by Erin's essay continued, she and her friends became better informed about the iron laws of human productivity. The forty-hour week is there for a reason; it gets the best work from people. The first four hours of work are the most productive and, as the day wears on, everyone becomes less alert, less focused, and prone to more mistakes. In 1908, the first known study by Ernst Abbe,[5] one of the founders of the Zeiss lens laboratory, concluded that *reducing* the working day from nine to eight hours actually *increased* output. Henry Ford, who studied productivity issues obsessively, reached the same conclusion and infuriated his manufacturing colleagues when, in 1926, he had the audacity to introduce a forty-hour work week. Subsequent studies by Foster Wheeler (1968), Procter & Gamble (1980), members of the construction industry, and many, many more show that, as the days get longer, productivity declines. No study has ever convincingly argued otherwise.[6]

Once you are doing sixty hours a week or more, you don't just get tired, you make mistakes; the time you spend rectifying errors consumes all the extra hours you worked. The classic, and comic, example of this was Frank Gilbreth, the efficiency-obsessed father in *Cheaper by the Dozen*. He found he could shave faster if he used two razors—but then he wasted all his saved time covering the cuts with Band-Aids.

In software companies, a lot of developers like working late; they relish the silence that comes when the sales and marketing folk go home. But that means they need to start later, too. Otherwise, the extra hours produce only errors. Software bugs or accidental file deletions can have knock-on effects that take much longer to repair than did writing original code. EA's working patterns weren't just inhumane; they were counterproductive.

Then there is the sleep factor. Missing just one night's sleep has a noticeable impact on the brain's ability to function, as Dardo Tomasi[7] and his colleagues at the Brookhaven National Laboratory discovered when they took fourteen healthy, nonsmoking right-handed men and made half of them stay awake through the night. In the morning, both rested and groggy subjects were put through a serious of tests that involved tracking ten balls on a screen. As they completed the tests an fMRI scanner took pictures of their brains to see how the rested brain differed from the one that was deprived of sleep. They found, not so surprisingly, that the sleepier the subjects, the lower their accuracy in the tests. But it was the detail that was most interesting.

The scientists found that two key areas of the brain—the parietal lobe and the occipital lobe—were less active in the sleep-deprived participants. The parietal lobe in the brain integrates information from the senses and is also involved in our knowledge of numbers and manipulation of objects. The occipital lobe is involved in visual processing. So both areas are highly involved in processing visual information and numbers. What was Warren Briggs of BP looking at on his twenty-four screens? Visual information and numbers. What do computer-game engineers work with all the time? Visual information and numbers. The higher-order brain activity that was most needed in those jobs was the first thing to go.

While the parietal and occipital lobes were less active, the thalamus, on the other hand, was very busy in the sleepy subjects. Scientists hypothesize that the thalamus attempts to compensate for the reduced activity in the parietal and occipital lobes. The thalamus sits at the center of the brain and is responsible for the regulation of consciousness, sleep, and alertness. It was, in other words, working extra hard to stay alert. All the energy you might want to concentrate on solving a hard problem is devoted to the challenge of staying awake.

In evolutionary terms, this makes sense. If you're driven to find food, you need to stay awake and search, not contemplate recipes. But now that, for most of us, work isn't primarily about physical endurance, mere wakefulness is not enough. These and other studies indicate that, yes, we can stay awake for long periods of time with little sleep—but what we lose, progressively, is the ability to think. "A tired worker tends to perform like an unskilled worker."[8] Or, you could say, a smart worker starts to work like a mindless one.

Moreover, sleep deprivation starts to starve the brain. There is a reason why we start to eat comfort food—doughnuts, candy—when we're tired: our brains crave sugar. After twenty-four hours of sleep deprivation, there is an overall reduction of 6 percent in glucose reaching the brain.[9] But the loss isn't shared equally; the parietal lobe and the prefrontal cortex lose 12 to 14 percent of their glucose. And those are the areas we need most for thinking: for distinguishing between ideas, for social control, and to be able to tell the difference between good and bad.[10]

To Charles Czeisler, professor of sleep medicine at Harvard Medical School, encouraging a culture of sleepless machismo is downright dangerous.[11] He's amazed by today's work cultures that glorify sleep-lessness, the way the age of *Mad Men* once glorified people who could hold their drink.

"We now know," says Czeisler, "that twenty-four hours without sleep or a week of sleeping four or five hours a night induces an im-pairment equivalent to a blood alcohol level of point one percent. We would never say 'This person is a great worker! He's drunk all the time!' yet we continue to celebrate people who sacrifice sleep."[12]

A blood alcohol level of 0.1 percent is higher than all legal limits for alcohol while driving. The U.S. and UK limits are 0.08 percent. At 0.1 percent, you are liable to be prone to mood swings; be emotionally overexpressive; lose peripheral vision, depth perception, and distance acuity; and exhibit poor reasoning.

Czeisler's research team found that hospital interns scheduled to work for twenty-four hours increased their chances of stabbing themselves with a needle or scalpel by 61 percent, their risk of crashing a car by 168 percent, and their risk of a near miss by 460 percent. Twenty per-cent of car crashes are attributed to nothing more complex than lack of sleep. Since companies vigorously prosecute alcohol policies, Czeisler argues they should do the same with corporate sleep policies.

But they do just the opposite.

Erin's fiancé Lan joined a successful class-action suit against EA's working practices and he left the company. The "spouse" turned out to be a little premature: they never married and have since split up. Erin sits on the board of the International Games Developers Associa-tion (IGDA) but says the industry hasn't learned much: Engineers are still too tired to see straight and the executives who manage them are too tired to see the problem.

"EA changed for a while, but only really because one group saw this as an opportunity to get rid of the guys responsible for the crazy hours. So there was a big political bloodbath and a new regime. Every-thing got better for six months and then it started all over again. They're destroying people who should become our top developers! A lot of studios now won't hire former EA employees because they're so burned out; they say there's just too much work involved in rehabbing them."

Even rested and alert, you may not be able to see what's right in front of you. In one of psychology's most famous and stupefying experiments, Dr. Daniel Simons made a video at Harvard that set out to test just how much the mind can see when it's busy.

"It started as a lark," Simons recalled.[13] "There had been earlier experiments into visual cognition but in all of them, the display was so weird that it didn't feel like real life. So I thought: What if we make this whole thing live? This was quite a lot of fun—I'm a big fan of doing fun research. I do the boring stuff, too, but the purpose here was to ask: How extreme can you make this and illustrate the point?"

(Before you read farther, you might want to try the experiment for yourself on YouTube: http://www.youtube.com/watch?v=vJG698 U2Mvo.)

In 1999, together with Chris Chabris, Simons made a short film of Harvard students moving around and passing basketballs. One team wore white shirts, the other wore black. Although Simons had appeared in some of his earlier video experiments, this time he chose to stay behind the camera and film it. When they finished making the film, Chabris and Simons asked volunteers to watch it and count the number of passes made by players wearing white. Less than a minute later, when the video ended, they asked viewers if they'd seen anything else. About half said no, they'd seen nothing.[14]

What they had missed was a female student wearing a full-body gorilla suit who walks into the scene, stops in the middle of the frame, faces the camera, thumps her chest, and walks off. She is on screen for approximately nine seconds.

The experiment has been shown repeatedly, around the world, in front of diverse audiences. I first saw it in Dublin, in an audience full of executives. Like them, I was so focused on counting the passes, that I never saw the gorilla.

Simons was so stunned by the result that he says that for several years afterward, he still kept expecting people to spot the gorilla. But results were always the same. In 1999, Simons and his colleagues published an account of the experiment entitled "Gorillas in Our Midst" and, in 2004 they won an Ig Nobel Prize for "achievements that first make people laugh and then make them think." Simons has since gone on to make an academic career studying how we pay attention.

"We experience far less of our visual world than we think we do. We feel like we are going to take in what's around us. But we don't. We pay attention to what we are told to attend to, or what we're looking for, or what we already know. Top-down factors play a big role. Fashion designers will notice clothes. Engineers will notice mechanics. But what we see is amazingly limited."

We see what we expect to see, what we're looking for. And we can't see all that much. I asked Simons whether some people saw more than others.

"There is really limited evidence for that. People who are experienced basketball players are slightly better at seeing what's happening in the video—but that's probably because they're more accustomed to watching passes; it isn't so hard for them to read what's going on. You can train yourself to focus on more than one spot. You might improve your eye muscles somewhat. But the limits are pretty fixed. There's a physical and an evolutionary barrier. You can't change the limits of your mind."

Simons' video is used for all kinds of safety training. "The airport security people, you know—they can find what they're looking for but they won't find what they're not looking for, no matter how dangerous it is." Trained baggage screeners are better than Simons' respondents at spotting weapons, but not much: a third of the time, they will fail to spot weapons of any kind.[15]

Simons is amazed by the strange, sometimes convoluted interpretations of his film. "The video gets talked about a lot in relation to national security forces and why they didn't see terrorists in their midst. My favorite one is a Baptist preacher who was giving a sermon in which he referred to the gorilla and said that's why the Jews didn't spot Jesus for what he was! But it is most commonly used for safety training, in power plants, for example, where people will focus on procedures and not notice anything that isn't part of the procedure."

After a decade of experiments[16] by himself and others, Simons concludes that we see what we expect to see and are blind to the unexpected. And there are absolute hard limits to how much we can take in at any given time.

"For the human brain," says Simons, "attention is a zero-sum game:

If we pay more attention to one place, object, or event, we *necessarily* pay less attention to others."

Simons now researches and teaches at the University of Illinois at Urbana-Champaign, where he continues to research visual cognition. His work is far from academic: On September 6, 2006, a graduate of the university, Matt Wilhelm, was riding his bicycle when Jennifer Stark hit him from behind with her car and killed him. In the subsequent investigation, it turned out that Stark had been downloading ring tones at the time she hit Matt, a tragic reminder of the realities behind Simons' experiments.

"There was a huge debate, when radios were introduced into cars," says Simons. "I'm still not sure I buy the argument but I suppose we can tune out a radio. But driving a car while talking on a cell phone or texting is different. They can seem really effortless but they both use your mind's limited attention resources. You can't do it. Your brain can't do it."

It isn't about the phone—which is why hands-free sets won't help you. It's about the mental resources that are available to you at any one time. In what sounds like another piece of fun research, Frank Drews, an assistant professor of psychology at the University of Utah, divided forty students into three teams.[17] The first team operated a driving simulator; the second team drove on the simulator while talking on cell phones. The third team got to operate the simulator after drinking enough orange juice and vodka to take their blood alcohol limit to 0.08 percent, the legal limit for driving in the United States and the United Kingdom.

Comparing the three teams yielded surprises. The team using cell phones had more rear-end collisions and their braking time was slower. The intoxicated participants exhibited a more aggressive driving style, following the vehicle in front more closely and braking with greater force, but they had no accidents. You should not take from this that it is better to drive drunk than while using a cell phone! What Drews and his colleagues concluded was that the drivers using cell phones were dangerous because they simply did not have enough attention to devote to their driving.

Shortly after running the experiment, Drews himself experienced the phenomenon firsthand when a driver next to him on the highway drifted into his lane, forcing the psychologist onto the shoulder. Both drivers took the next exit and Drews got out of his car, very upset. "I knocked on his window. He was still on his cell phone!" Drews recalled. But when he finally stopped talking, the chatty driver had "no clue" about the disruption he'd caused. He hadn't seen a thing.

A study from the Harvard Center for Risk Analysis estimates that cell-phone use while driving contributes to 6 percent of crashes—which means 636,000 crashes, 330,000 injuries, 12,000 serious injuries, and 2,600 deaths each year in the United States. Or $43 billion. When the National Safety Council asked its member businesses whether they had safety policies prohibiting on-road cell-phone use, 45 percent said they did—but of those, 85 percent said the policies made no difference.

Meanwhile, technology whiz kids are busy inventing yet more forms of distraction for us as they bring the riches of personal computing to the car. Soon album covers, e-mail, and Wikipedia entries will all be available to us as we drive.[18]

"Cars are going to become probably the most immersive consumer electronics device we have," according to Michael Rayfield, a general manager at Nvidia, the chip company that works with automotive manufacturers on visual displays.[19]

For Audi cars, Nvidia's Vibrante multimedia software will provide passengers with "dual zone" entertainment enabling them "to simultaneously enjoy two different movies on two different screens in the backseat monitors."[20] This traveling picture palace will give drivers access to photos of their destination, reviews of nearby restaurants, and background information, along with navigational advice. USB ports and wi-fi capability will allow them to plug in keyboards, too, although if they want further online access, a notice pops up reading "Please only use the online services when traffic conditions allow you to do so safely." We already know what a great safeguard that is. We know, but we don't want to know. We just do not have enough mental capacity to do all the things that we think we can do. As attentional load increases, attentional capacity gradually diminishes.[21] One frustrated psychologist has argued that the case for multitasking is on a par with "urban legend";[22] that is, it's a story we like the sound of but that is really nonsense.

It's particularly important to remember that the intellectual capacity we appear to lose first may be what we need most: the ability to discriminate, to make good judgments. Remember Warren Briggs sitting in front of his computer screens, so tired that he suffered from tunnel vision. He worried about how to get rid of the pressure spikes because he was too tired to contemplate the harder issue of what was causing these spikes to appear in the first place.

The bottleneck[23] that characterizes our ability to receive information explains why we cannot intelligently absorb all the information presented to us on TV screens like those displayed by CNN, Fox, or CNBC. The scrolling text, sidebars, and stock prices don't make us smarter or better informed; they make us stupid. While we are watching such a busy array, we can't efficiently think, discriminate, or make critical judgments.

When we are tired or preoccupied—conditions psychologists call "resource-depleted"—we start to economize, to conserve those resources. Higher-order thinking is more expensive. So too are doubt, skepticism, and argument. "Resource depletion specifically disables cognitive elaboration," wrote Harvard psychologist Daniel Gilbert.[24] "Not only does doubt seem to be the last to emerge, but it also seems to be the first to disappear." Because it takes less brain power to believe than to doubt, we are, when tired or distracted, gullible.[25] Because we are all biased, and biases are quick and effortless, exhaustion makes us favor the information we know and are comfortable with. We're too tired to do the heavier lifting of examining new or contradictory information, so we fall back on our biases, the opinions and the people we already trust.

This higher-order functioning that we lose when overloaded or exhausted is important—and not just in oil refineries. In the late 1990s, I worked for a company, CMGI, that in the heat of the Internet boom bought large numbers of companies. Regularly on a Monday morning, I would walk into the boardroom where I would find bleary-eyed executives hungover with exhaustion, having pulled an all-nighter or two in order to complete the latest acquisition. They were fried but triumphant; they were heroes: the deal was done! But I lost count of the number of transactions that were, even at the time, strategically mindless and ultimately wasteful. Why had we bought these businesses? Too much tunnel vision, too little sleep: No one thought—quite literally—to ask, why are we doing this in the first place?

Although CMGI was a remarkable environment to work in, it wasn't—and isn't—unusual in pouring vast resources into deals that bring armies of lawyers and bankers into paneled boardrooms to work through the night completing the latest acquisition. The leading law firms, investment banks, and accounting firms require long hours and weekend work from any employee who wishes to be considered for partner, or even to be taken seriously. Many leading investment bankers tell me that, however much they hate it, these are the rules of client service. When I point out that they could solve their problem by having more employees, each doing fewer hours, they look abashed by the simplicity of the arithmetic. The truth is, many of the participants love it: the thrill of the deadline, the mountains of documents, the legal, financial, and regulatory complexity of the task.[26]

Yet most of these deals achieve worse than nothing. A study by KPMG found that 83 percent of the mergers and acquisitions they studied didn't boost shareholder value; 53 percent actually reduced it. Another study by management consultants at A. T. Kearney found that total return to shareholders on 115 global mergers was a *negative* 58 percent![27] And while business-school professors dissect the corpse of each dead deal, it might be wiser to remember the fried executives who signed off on the strategy. Tunnel vision blinds us to the wider consequences of our decisions. It isn't just control-room operators who are dangerous.

Many psychologists have studied these phenomena, in many cases (like Kahneman and Tversky) to understand why we make mistakes. Others work more tactically, to devise guidelines for safer instrument panels, for example. But one of the earliest was the social psychologist Stanley Milgram, who is more famous for his experiments in obedience (see Chapter Six). Although Milgram himself was a native of New York City, he was fascinated by the way urbanites behaved. In "The Experience of Living in Cities" he reflected that the very large number of people who live in the city, together with their heterogeneity, meant that "city life, as we experience it, constitutes a continuous set of encounters with overload, and of resultant adaptations." He wondered what the effects of living with so many people, so many impressions, so much information might be. "Overload characteristically deforms daily life on several levels, impinging on role performance, the evolution of social norms, cognitive functioning, and the use of facilities."[28]

A natural, as well as a professional, observer of human life, Milgram noted that the country shopkeeper might engage his customers in conversations whereas the cashier in a city supermarket barely had time to complete one checkout before starting on the next. "The urbanite disregards the drunk sick on the street as he purposefully navigates through the crowd," Milgram argued, not because he was less friendly or warmhearted, but because city dwellers had learned to manage the demands made on them by a crowded city. They adapted by reducing the amount of information they took in. If a city was a system that yielded more "inputs" than anyone could handle, inhabitants responded by taking in less. It was Milgram's unique insight to see that the city is a system, just as the brain is a system. And Milgram's fellow New Yorkers were managing themselves in just the same way that our brain manages information: letting some impressions in and leaving many behind.

Milgram's argument was provocative because he maintained that what got lost wasn't random but precise: When people felt overloaded, he said, they restricted their social and moral involvement. "Overload is made more manageable by limiting the 'span of sympathy.'" Milgram wasn't out to enrage city-lovers the world over. He was concerned that the load-balancing trade-offs weren't just operational; they were moral. If it is hard to doubt when you're tired, it may be even harder to care.

What is true for cities may equally be true for any large organization in which individuals operate under tremendous "resource depletion." Jack Kaminsky[29] worked at the Countrywide Mortgage Services for four and a half years.

"I loved my job. I'd usually do a fifteen- , sixteen-hour day—I loved it! When business was booming, I'd be getting up at five A.M., logging in to check e-mails and plan my day. It was like a high, the whole day."

Didn't you, I asked, get tired?

"Sure! Our office was a sweatshop. But the longer you worked, the more you made. We built a very successful team—out of fifty-four offices, we were near the top every year I was there. If you couldn't handle it, we'd find someone else. Countrywide was a well-respected lender, everyone wanted to be part of it. It was easy to replace people."

Jack's job was to package up mortgages to sell on to banks.

"Everybody turned a blind eye to fraud. They're still uncovering fraud from four years ago! The frauds were so obvious. You'd have seven files from seven different brokers. In each one, the same buyer was going to be the owner occupier; I'd have the same owner buying *seven* properties from seven different banks! And I'd tell the banks but they'd just turn a blind eye. We knew it was fraud but what can you do? We packaged them up and sold them on."

When the mortgage market collapsed, Jack was laid off—on a conference call.

Propagandists and brainwashers know what managers and corporate leaders choose to forget: the human mind, overloaded and starved of sleep, becomes morally blind. This would appear to be part of the explanation of what took place at Abu Ghraib.

"Not only did this soldier work half around the clock [from four A.M. to four P.M.], he did so seven days a week with not a single day off for a full forty days! I can't imagine any job where such a work schedule would not be seen as inhumane."[30]

The psychologist Philip Zimbardo served as an expert witness for one of the Abu Ghraib reservists, Chip Frederick. Although his sympathies lay more with reservist Joe Darby, who had handed in the shocking photographs taken at the prison, Zimbardo understood better than anyone the impact that the situational influences of a prison environment could have on young men and women. In 1971, he had designed and run the Stanford Prison Experiment, in which twenty-four mentally and physically healthy young men endured a prison simulation for six days. Zimbardo's detailed account of the experiment is hair-raising, but it taught him volumes about the ways in which a situation dramatically transforms behavior.[31] A landmark in the study of power and environment, the experiment eerily presaged many of the abuses committed at Abu Ghraib by Chip Frederick and his colleages.

"There is absolutely nothing in his record that I was able to uncover that would predict that Chip Frederick would engage in any form of abusive, sadistic behavior," Zimbardo wrote. "On the contrary, there is much in his record to suggest that had he not been forced to work and live in such an abnormal situation, he might have been the military's all-American poster soldier on its recruitment ads. He could have been the best of apples in their good barrel."[32]

Many forces—fear; corruption; inadequate resources; absence of supervision, written procedures, formal policies, or guidelines; and an absolute lack of training—conspired to erode those all-American qualities. But, as Zimbardo observes, that was just the beginning. Frederick not only worked a twelve-hour shift, seven days a week. After working for forty days, he got just one day off, followed by two more solid weeks on. Even when his shifts were over, he wasn't able to leave the prison but went to sleep in a dirty and noisy six-by-nine prison cell.

That Frederick was surrounded by colleagues just as ill-trained and just as exhausted meant no one was awake enough to have any moral sensibility left. Of course other factors contributed to the abuse of prisoners, but what is so striking about Zimbardo's analysis is that, at the simplest level, frightened, untrained guards were left with so little cognitive capacity.

Working hours seem such a small issue—but, by the same token, such a small thing to get right. But there's a great deal of bravura attached to overwork. For men especially, complaining of tiredness can look and sound weak. And there's no biofeedback: If you don't eat, you starve and everyone can see there's a problem. But when we don't sleep, or when we work too hard, often even we can't see there's a problem. Sure, we don't feel great; but what we can't see is what we are losing: the capacity to reason, to judge, to make good and humane decisions, to see consequences and complexity.

The allure of exhaustion is baffling. I've lost count of the number of corporations I've worked with that positively boast about the number of all-nighters they pull. Investment banking may not be the absolute worst, but it's up there, full of pride when they describe their requirement to work three weekends out of five. Client service, they say, just demands it. But I wonder how thrilled their clients would be if they knew how brain-dead the service they receive often is.

"You can't change the limits of your mind," says Dan Simons. But we keep trying. Why? Is it the last vestige of a physical model of heroism for which we lack any intellectual corollary? If so, then we'd better find that new model fast, before more reputations and lives are ruined. At the very least, as western democracies struggle to define some kind of regulatory framework that could protect the economy from future disaster, we could do worse than demand that, after forty hours of work, everybody just go home.

5

THE OSTRICH INSTRUCTION

Lie to me just a little bit longer
Lie to me until I'm stronger . . .
I'm not ready yet
To accept
The truth
So lie to me.
—Philip Ridley and Nick Bicat,
"Lie to Me," from the film *Heartless*

QUITE OFTEN WHEN people come in here, they don't really lie—they just, what shall I say, underestimate the truth. Some deny it. They're all embarrassed. No one ever quite tells the truth."

John Hawk isn't a priest, he's a dermatologist at St. Thomas's Hospital in London. When he sees skin that has been damaged by the sun, he asks his patients whether they've been sunbathing.

"You get the most extraordinary vehemence from people who've been using sunbeds constantly. They're prepared to shout at me, insisting they are not harmful. There was one lady, we'd been quite friendly. She said, 'I use sunbeds all the time and I love it and you aren't going to stop me. I don't want to know!'"

Professor Hawk's angry patient isn't alone. Thousands of people don't want to know that tanning is bad for them and that tanning beds can kill them. Hawk has heard all the arguments.

"You get people saying it boosts their vitamin D levels—but you don't need to boost your vitamin D levels; food and homeostasis will take care of that. Or people saying it produces endorphins and relieves pain. It's all nonsense. I've been campaigning against tanning and tanning salons now for decades and the evidence just grows. What's so sad about these patients is that they do know tanning is bad for you—that's why they're embarrassed—but they choose not to know."

That refusal runs very, very deep, even outliving its victim.

"You can go around in circles, asking yourself why this happened," said Penny Birch, talking about the death of her daughter Hayley. A flight attendant for Virgin airline, Hayley loved the sun and used her freedom to travel to maintain a good tan. "She did enjoy sunbathing and would often top up her tan on rest days between flights," her mother recalled. "But she was naturally dark and never overdid it."[1]

But at the age of twenty-five, Hayley died of skin cancer. By anyone's measure, that is overdoing it. It's hard to know now why it was so important to Hayley to stay perfectly tanned—but it clearly did matter, or she wouldn't have devoted so much of her free time to it. Described as a "girly girl who always liked to look her best," Hayley was perhaps no different from any of us who want to feel good about ourselves.

Her story was tragic but it wasn't unique. In Britain, someone dies of skin cancer every four hours.[2] In Canada, every day more than ten people will be diagnosed with melanoma; one out of every 284 Canadian men and every 486 Canadian women will die of it.[3] While most people now recognize that overexposure to the sun is unhealthy, the fact remains that a great many still do not protect their skin from the sun's harmful rays.[4]

"I know I shouldn't—but you feel so great, you look slimmer, and everybody always says I look so fit," a tanned mother of three told me on her return from a beach vacation.

Defenders of suntans argue that sunlight feels so good that it's counterintuitive to see it as dangerous. Or that the risks of melanoma are relatively new—linked to the depletion of the ozone layer—and not everyone's caught up yet. But the research shows that, for the most part, we all know how dangerous overexposure to the sun is. And none of those arguments explains one of the most cognitively dissonant industries of the modern age: the tanning salon.

The "incandescent light bath" was invented by John Harvey Kellogg. A physician and Seventh-Day Adventist, Kellogg ran a sanitarium where he attacked a range of ills using exercise, vegetarianism, and sunshine. (His other claim to fame was the invention of granola and corn flakes.) Kellogg was a passionate believer in the moral and physical benefits of sunlight and throughout the end of the nineteenth century, sun baths and sun lamps were used for a wide range of therapies.

In 1903, Niels Finsen won the Nobel Prize in medicine for using sun lamps in the treatment of lupus. As natural suntans became more popular, sun lamps and sunbeds did too, supplementing tans in the winter or "preparing" the skin prior to summer vacations. The early association of tanning machinery with health has proved very persistent.

"The tanning industry likes to emphasize• beneficial health effects from tanning salons, saying things like 'Come to our tanning salon and protect yourself against cancer!'" says Dr. Mona Saraiya, the Centers for Disease Control's expert on melanoma. Coolly discussing the latest research, she's at pains to be as objective and fastidious as she can, nevertheless manifesting the scientist's utter bewilderment at irrational human behavior.

"Or they say sunbeds are good for vitamin D deficiency or Seasonal Affect Disorder. I do wonder why they're legal."[5]

The focus of Dr. Saraiya's bafflement isn't just the individuals who use tanning salons but the companies that run them, and the disinformation they disseminate. The Indoor Tanning Association's Web site, for example, plays on the association between health and indoor tanning: "The industry's roots are therapeutic and many Americans do in fact visit tanning facilities for that purpose." The association goes on to claim that, in fact, indoor tanning is "more responsible" than outdoor tanning—because it is so much more controllable.

"I disagree," Dr. Saraiya rejoined. "Although tanning beds say they emit only UVA rays, many emit UVB rays—and anyway, UVA rays can also cause skin cancer. And many studies show that teens don't adhere to the regulations concerning exposure."

Because skin damage early in life is more likely to develop into skin cancer, the Canadian Cancer Society (CCS) has been arguing for years in favor of legislation that would ban minors from using tanning salons; both NDP health critic France Gelinas and Liberal MPP Khalil Ramal have attempted to introduce appropriate legislation. But even if they succeed in getting legislation passed, the American or British examples suggest the law would not be rigorously enforced.

Health Canada already has voluntary safety guidelines, related to the protection of under-aged youth and the identification of individuals at greater risk of developing skin cancer. But a CCS study showed that 96 percent of personnel in 79 Toronto tanning salons did not communicate Health Canada's tanning safety guidelines to volunteers who posed as potential clients. The report also found 60 percent of tanning facilities did not ask the age of minors who posed as clients, and another 60 percent of tanning facilities visited did not identify that the potential client had type-one skin that never tans but burns. Only 12 percent of facilities visited were reported to have posted the Health Canada voluntary guidelines in a place where they were likely to seen by potential customers. Meanwhile, tanning sessions are regularly handed out as door prizes at teen dances.

Guidelines certainly didn't stop a 10-year-old Welsh girl, Kelly Thompson, from suffering burns to over 70% of her body after tanning for just 16 minutes. Within hours of leaving the tanning salon in South Wales she was taken to hospital where she was told that had she remained on the sunbed for another two minutes she would have needed skin grafts.[6]

In an argument eerily reminiscent of the 1950s love affair with radiation, many tanning aficionados claim that tanning must be better for you than sunshine, because it is a sophisticated technology. It is this argument that finally dents the veneer of Dr. Saraiya's dispassionate professionalism.

"They just are unsafe. Unsafe at any level. It is very frustrating. They are producing more and more cancers!"

The regular use of sunbeds is now known to double the risk of skin cancer and doctors now agree that there is no such thing as a safe tan. But we keep on tanning.

"I see young girls coming out of tanning salons burned and looking like lobsters," Tina Farrelly exclaims. "I feel like grabbing them and telling them what can happen." Her niece, a British mother of three, died at the age of twenty-nine after repeated sunbed use. For seven years, she had tanning sessions twice a week. When her mother tried to stop her, she just borrowed a friend's.[7]

The U.S. Department of Health and the International Agency for Research on Cancer has defined tanning beds and sun lamps as "known carcinogens" but the use of tanning salons persists because there is widespread social support for a tanned body.[8] On any day in the U.S. you will find more than a million people in tanning salons. In the UK, the number of privately operated sunbeds has increased by 30 percent since 1998; according to the Sunbed Association, over three million people in the UK use one. Rates of malignant melanoma in the UK have more than quadrupled in the last three decades, with 10,410 cases reported in Britain in 2006, an increase of almost 7 percent over the previous year. By 2024, Cancer Research UK expects that figure to rise to 15,500—making this cancer the fourth most common type among both men and women. That's a lot of cognitive dissonance, dependent on a lot of social support.

In their desire to reduce the dissonance they experience, tanning aficionados come up with some peculiar arguments. Surely, consumers argue, tanning salons wouldn't be allowed if they were harmful— would they? The very fact that they are viable, profitable businesses and that they are *regulated* is taken as proof that they must be safe— because otherwise they would be prohibited. That is as powerful a form of social validation as it is possible to find. The very existence of tanning salons—25,000 in the United States alone—provides the confirmation salon customers need to overcome conclusive data. They're blind, of course, but what keeps them confirmed in their blindness is the fact that the salons are flourishing.

"It's incredible, the arguments people come up with to perpetuate something that they know, deep down inside, is bad for them," says Professor Hawk. "They think a tan shows that they have leisure and wealth and people like to look like they're wealthy with lots of free time. The sad reality is they've become creatures of habit. They don't want to change. So they just pretend they don't know."

Pliny the Elder is thought to be the earliest naturalist to have written about the ostrich. In his *Historia Naturalis* he is rather rude about the bird, decrying its stupidity: "They imagine, when they have thrust their head and neck into a bush, that the whole of the body is concealed." Today, natural scientists say that the bird lays its head and neck flat on the ground in an effort to elude its predators. But however you describe ostrich behavior, the one thing everyone agrees on is that they absolutely do not bury their heads in the sand.

It's a shame, really, because we need ostriches as a metaphor for the way we all behave. Judges certainly need the bird. When they apply the legal concept of willful blindness in court cases, they are said to be issuing "the ostrich instruction." Whether the metaphor is scientifically accurate or not, we all recognize the human desire at times to prefer ignorance to knowledge, and to deal with conflict and change by imagining it out of existence.

All of us want to bury our heads in the sand when taxes are due, when we have bad habits we know we should change, or when the car starts to make that strange sound. Ignore it and it will go away—that's what we think and hope. It's more than just wishful thinking. In burying our heads in the sand, we are trying to pretend the threat doesn't exist and that we don't have to change. We are also trying hard to avoid conflict: If the threat's not there, I don't have to fight it. A preference for the status quo, combined with an aversion to conflict, compels us to turn a blind eye to problems and conflicts we just don't want to deal with.

So my children walk straight past the laundry basket on the stairs because they don't want to stop what they're doing and attend to it. And I might not chastise them for it because I can't face another fight. And when I ignore the recycling, I'm hoping my husband will get the message—without a fight—that it needs to be put outside. Of course part of this is just laziness, but a big part of it is refusing to see anything that makes us uncomfortable.

An intriguing study in 1965 showed that our eyes focus on what appeals to us, and avoid what does not.[9] In the experiment, a number of people—men and women, students, housewives, and secretaries—were asked to look at ten different pictures, some of which were sexual in content. A camera photographed their eye movements and later mapped these onto the pictures, to show the path of the viewer's gaze. Later, each participant was asked what he or she recalled of the pictures. Not surprisingly, each gave a very different account of the same picture.

Ten minutes after the experiment, "Mrs. R." could remember six out of the ten pictures. Prompted, she could eventually recall them all but seemed to have difficulty with number seven.

EXPERIMENTER: It is a man reading, near a nude woman. Do you remember that one?

MRS. R.: No, I don't remember that one at all.

EXPERIMENTER: Take a moment. A man reading near a nude woman. You don't remember that one at all?

MRS. R.: I don't remember that one at all.

EXPERIMENTER: A man sat reading a paper.

MRS. R.: I remember the window.

EXPERIMENTER: And you could see her profile. You could see her breast.

MRS. R.: Yes. Now I remember. Just the top. The girl's face turned around, no waistline, that man reading the paper, and that's all I saw.

That was all Mrs. R. recalled because it was practically all she looked at. Photographs of her eye movement show her eyes stuck pretty firmly to the newspaper.

"Miss I," however, had a different experience.

This is a man reading a newspaper. There's a woman by the table with her naked bosom. I thought it was very humorous because he wasn't looking at her at all.

And the photographs of Miss I.'s eye movements confirm that they strayed far more widely across the entire picture.

Many psychologists argue about why we behave like this: How could we know where *not* to look without looking first? But nobody denies that we do do this: We studiously avoid seeing, and remembering, those things that may cause us discomfort. In the same way that we tend to gravitate toward people who are like us, our eyes—and our minds—focus on information, objects, ideas that confirm our sense of self.

This phenomenon isn't quite as extreme as the tunnel vision in the BP Texas City control room, but it is similar. Both are stress responses. For Mrs. R., who is described as timorous and vague, the picture posed a threat of embarrassment and potentially of conflict: Why was she being made to look at this picture? For Miss I., an attractive young woman trained in the arts, the picture posed no threat at all.

Fear of change and fear of conflict have the same effect. It isn't just dermatologists who have to deal with patients embarrassed by their own habits. Doctors' offices witness a parade of patients who knew they should have come in earlier, who missed appointments or scans or check-ups. Debt counseling services too witness the same ostrich-like behavior.

"We have people who come in with whole sacks full of notices, letters, bills and dump them on my desk, saying 'I have been afraid to open them.' Truly!"

Elma Warrick is the executive director of HomeFree-USA in Kansas City. She says she is the "boots on the ground" when it comes to dealing with people who are over their heads in debt. For someone dealing with grim realities on a daily basis, she's remarkably jovial describing the lengths to which her clients will go to avoid seeing just how much trouble they're in.

"They'd dump these bags on my desk and somewhere in them will be a notice saying, 'We are going to sell your house on this date.' They avoid answering the phone, they don't listen to their messages because they're afraid of who'll be on the other end. A lot of these people were just trying to provide better living conditions for their children. They were only guided by love—wanting their kids to have their own bedroom, be respected in the neighborhood. But they got way out of their depth and now they just bury their heads in the sand."

By 2005, for each dollar of disposable income, Americans owed $1.24. By May 2009, that meant that every American household was carrying on average $121,953 of personal debt.[10] That same year, just over 1.4 million Americans filed for bankruptcy, a surge of nearly one third, driven largely by foreclosures and job losses.[11]

"This foreclosure tsunami has not left anyone untouched or unscathed," Warrick says. "You have people who believed they were knowledgeable or so well educated they couldn't be caught buying more than they could afford. But they did buy more than they could afford because very few bothered to make their own determination of what they could afford. They thought the lenders' estimate was the right one—because they wanted it to be! The lender would say 'You can afford four hundred thousand dollars' and they'd say, 'Oh yeah, I thought I was at that level' when really they had no idea. They had never done the numbers."

In many instances, the clients Warrick sees never paid attention to the detail of their mortgages, never kept track of the house payments, never knew if they were ahead or behind. Nor did they pay any attention to what was happening around them.

"We had a woman in here who just never looks at her bank account and didn't realize her payments weren't going through. So now she's so far behind, they're foreclosing on her house. Then you have people who say 'I knew it was a thirty-year obligation but I didn't know I'd wind up paying more.' Now the HUD1 is a document provided to every buyer and it says, this is the interest rate for this period of time. But people see what they want to see—they don't see what they don't want to see."

Warrick says this isn't a matter of intelligence or education; sometimes it's the most educated who have been most blind because they believed they knew what they were doing.

"People say, 'Those people should have known better.' But those same critical people are coming in now and they're unemployed and they suddenly are in trouble too. It crosses racial lines, socioeconomic lines. And it's not like their situation is completely hopeless—sometimes there are things we can do so they won't lose their home.

But they left it so late! They come to us after months and months . . ."

Warrick laughs wryly. She runs financial education classes, she'll comb through clients' expenses to see where they can cut back, she'll do whatever she can think of to get them back on the straight and narrow. When she talks about her clients, it's with warmth and respect, tinged with disappointment. The hard thing, she says, isn't just that they don't want to know. They don't want to change.

"Do people learn? People don't. We had a man in here, he canceled his appointment because he had a date at a club he belonged to. He was continuing his club membership, which he couldn't afford because he also couldn't afford his house payments—and he couldn't afford the time to come in here to figure it out! They think they can't live without so many things. I'll say, 'Cable TV—how about cutting that?' 'Oh no, you can't get the programming I like.' 'So what about your cars? Maybe you should trade one in.' 'Oh no, I can't sell my cars!'"

In business circles, this is known as the "status quo trap":[12] the preference for everything to stay the same. The gravitational pull of the status quo is strong—it feels easier and less risky, and it requires less mental and emotional energy, to "leave well enough alone." Nobody likes change because the status quo feels safer, it's familiar, we're used to it. Change feels like redirecting the riverbed: effortful and risky. It's so much easier to imagine that what we don't know won't hurt us.

One reason business executives worry so much about the status quo trap is that inertia exerts inordinate pull within organizations. Every change carries with it the possibility of conflict, uncertainty, danger. The business environment is dynamic and difficult enough without going to look for trouble.

Nowhere was this more true than in the financial services industry in the years leading up to the global banking crisis of 2008. Well before that, anyone breathing knew property prices and mortgage lending were out of control. By August 2006, the economist Nouriel Roubini described the market as being in "free fall."[13] At the end of that year, the collapse had such momentum that a far more humble observer, Aaron Krowne, who had no expertise in economics or finance, started his Web site, Implode-o-Meter, to track the daily demise of sub-prime lenders.[14] That a huge and fundamental part of the American economy was going bust was not hard to see. Nor was it a state secret that all of those loans and mortgages came from—and went back to—banks. So how could banks not have known about their own risk?

To be fair, of course, some did. Goldman Sachs did, J.P. Morgan did. Cantor Fitzgerald, at the beginning of 2007, quietly shrank its mortgage book. But most of the major banks did not. One reason—and there are many—is that they did not see the risk because they did not want to. As long as everyone was making money, many CEOs either didn't see a reason to change, or lacked the courage to do so.

Pat Lewis discovered this firsthand. An engineer by training, Lewis is a straight-shooting Midwesterner, well liked and highly regarded. His friends and colleagues are never effusive about him, they just say he's a "stand-up guy." He joined Bear Stearns in 1998, working in their treasury department, where he eventually became deputy treasurer. Along the way, he tried to devise a means of capturing the risk carried by each business unit, relative to its returns. He hoped, and assumed, that if the risk and return were wildly out of proportion, this would identify risk that had been underestimated. Lewis was looking for a way to shine a light into areas where risks in the firm were greatest. You'd think that would be helpful—but Lewis couldn't get much help.

"So my discussions with the business units would go like this: 'We want to understand the risks in your business.' And they'd say, 'Why?' And if you said, 'Well, it will drive a portion of your compensation and it's another way—besides just net revenue—to evaluate your business' then they'd say, 'Any number you have is too high.' Because, of course, they knew that a high risk number would impact their compensation. And if, instead, you said, 'Well, we're just curious and want to gain another insight into your business' they'd think you weren't worth the time of day. So what do you do?"

Lewis is a long-distance runner; he didn't give up easily. For three full years, he plugged away at the project, building a mathematical model that could give ongoing visibility to the risk in each business unit relative to the capital it employed. Finally, when it was sufficiently well honed, Lewis and his boss, Sam Molinaro, presented a simplified version of their model to their CEO, Jimmy Cayne. He dismissed it as just too complicated.

"The CEO didn't understand it so he didn't want it used internally. It was too political. I was too old to do something useless, so I quit doing it. Nobody else wanted to take it on."

Lewis surmised that Cayne had rejected his risk-based capital allocation project not just because it was complicated. He understood it well enough to know that, if it worked, the project threatened huge amounts of change and conflict within a highly political organization: People might lose money, they might lose bonuses, they might lose status.

Cayne's decision left his bank structurally blind, without the capacity to see what it was doing. Bankers at Bear Stearns (who loved risking other people's money) were as averse to examining their own risk as dear old "Mrs. R." was to looking at the naked breast.

At the time that Bear Stearns collapsed, Pat Lewis was already interviewing; he is now managing director at Cantor Fitzgerald, with no nostalgia for the frustrating inertia of his old employer.

"At Bear," Pat Lewis recalls, "you'd have threats of anarchy and people quitting if anyone interfered in a business unit. No one wanted to be the instigator of that. The surest way to get fired was to be a troublemaker."[15]

The only "trouble" Pat made, of course, was to try to get a clear view of the business. And he was prepared to put up with quite a lot of resistance to do so. But most of us don't persevere as Pat did; most of us stay silent, and silence is the language of inertia. In a groundbreaking study, two professors at New York University's Stern School of Business studied what they call "employee silence": the unwillingness of employees to identify or discuss problems they see around them. Elizabeth Morrison and Frances Milliken are quite the antithesis of the academic cliché: They're neither stuffy, nor pedantic, but bring to their work and to their working lives tremendous humor and engagement. So of course they found their subject not in a textbook but right inside their own academic institutions.

"There was a new initiative coming up and a big meeting to discuss it," Morrison recalled. "And everyone was talking about it and how awful it was."

"It inspired a lot of bad feeling and talk and a lot of anxiety," Milliken added.

"And then we got to the meeting and the subject came up—and nobody said a word! Silence. Nothing. Nada. No one raised a word of complaint. Just sailed on through. And that's when we thought, that was interesting. I wonder if that happens everywhere."

They designed a study to try to understand silence in organizations and what they found was pretty shocking. Interviewing a cross-section of executives, fully 85 percent said that they had, at some point, felt unable to raise an issue or concern with their boss. Only 51 percent said that they felt truly comfortable raising issues or spotlighting problems and a mere 15 percent said that they had *never* felt unable to express themselves openly.[16]

The areas that most provoked silence weren't surprising: Anything to do with a supervisor's competence or behavior, with organizational processes, or with pay were areas to avoid. But Morrison and Milliken's respondents also felt that they couldn't easily talk about ideas for improvement or concerns about the company's financial health.

"When there are holes in the research process, we generally don't say anything to the directors of the projects," said one respondent working for a not-for-profit organization.

"I raised a concern about some policies," replied another, "and was told to shut up and that I was becoming a troublemaker. This made me go into detached mode, making me a 'yes man.' "

One particularly compelling interviewee tells of a co-worker in financial services who was being phased out, he felt unfairly. "I felt it was a moral imperative to act," he recalled. "But in the end, I did nothing."

The recurrent theme in Milliken and Morrison's research is that people stay silent at work—bury their heads in the sand—because they don't want to provoke conflict by being, or being labeled, troublemakers. They may not like the status quo but, in their silence, they maintain it, believing (but also ensuring) the status quo can't be shifted.

"Everybody knew there was a problem," said one young woman, working for an Internet consulting firm. "But people didn't speak up. A lot of people quit. They didn't think speaking up would make a difference."

Reading the testimony of these interviewees is a tremendously sad experience: dozens of smart, engaged, moral individuals who have, on some level, given up. They don't believe that they can change the status quo, and so they've surrendered to it. What's so awful about this is that their decision to turn a blind eye in turn renders their bosses blind. How can the boss see what the employees won't show them? The only consequence of their silence is that the blind lead the blind.

What's also so sad about this research is that it rings so true. Even as I'm writing this, I sit on the board of an organization that has stopped in its tracks because it cannot face a single, mission-critical problem. Each board member will talk about it in private; it never comes up in meetings. Nobody can face the fight. And so the entire organization drifts on, consuming time and resources but making no progress. For this business, the recession has come as a boon, helping everyone studiously to ignore the old, festering sore that no one wants to touch. Many board members say they don't want to raise the issue because they don't know how to solve it. But as long as it remains invisible, it is guaranteed to remain unsolved.

That is the hidden cost of ostrich behavior: Whether your head is in the sand or just lying prone along the ground, you're in no position to defend yourself. You cannot fix a problem that you refuse to acknowledge. And if the problem isn't there—how can you be held responsible for it?

Although most business leaders will admit privately that one of the hardest aspects of running a company is knowing what is going on inside it, many adopt leadership styles that ensure no one will ever tell them the truth. At General Motors, Roger Smith was notorious for getting rid of any executive or board member who brought forth difficult or dissonant information or views. At the BBC, I once had a boss whose response to adverse news was to throw telephones against the wall, a reasonable incentive to keep one's mouth shut.

Yet even in companies that are strikingly more open and that espouse a desire for honesty and transparency, silence can maintain the status quo long after the need for change has become obvious to everyone. About ten years ago, I sat on the board of a private company whose founder had recently died. Everyone in the business was in mourning, with the result that no one was prepared to assume a leadership role; it would have felt indecent, intrusive. That was fine for a week or two, but it went on for months. Routine work continued to be done as it always had been, but economic conditions changed; another bubble burst, another recession. The company had no strategy for dealing with it. Meanwhile cash reserves were falling to a dangerously low level.

"What are you doing to reduce expenses?" I asked at a board meeting. It wasn't exactly a brilliant question but the answer stunned me.

"Nothing."

"Nothing? Why?"

"Well, we don't want to alarm the employees," answered one of the senior executives.

Now, the employees of this firm were smart; they could see what was happening to the economy, and they could certainly tell that the company's order book wasn't as full as it had been. When, after the meeting,

I spoke with a few of them, they were seriously worried—but the economy was the least of their concerns.

"I just think the management hasn't noticed what's going on," one confided in me. "They are so out of touch."

Nobody was cutting costs because everyone was afraid to talk about the perilous state of the business. Managers didn't want to alarm employees and employees felt it was a waste of time talking to managers who were clueless. Nobody wanted to make agonizing choices and they were averse to the conflict those choices must necessarily provoke. It was a mutually assured stalemate; both sides had their heads in the sand.

We know—intellectually—that confronting an issue is the only way to resolve it. But any resolution will disrupt the status quo. Given the choice between conflict and change on the one hand, and inertia on the other, the ostrich position can seem very attractive.

Libby, Montana, is a long way from everywhere: Sixty-five miles south of Canada, a seven-hour drive from the state capital, Helena. The nearest big city is Spokane, Washington—and that's a good three-and-a-half-hour drive away. But as you cross the border from Idaho, entering into Montana, the countryside becomes breathtakingly beautiful. Rising out of icy lakes, the Cabinet Mountains scream into the sky, clad in dense pine forest. This is the America of legend: big skies, bold landscapes, and raw.

It says everything about the people of Libby that, when you reach the town, it doesn't feel remote. Only two and a half thousand people live in the town, but they've made it a place where you want to be. The Libby welcome is warm and proud. They aren't glad to see you because they lack for company; they're glad to see you're lucky enough to share their town. The hotel guide says that Libby's assets "include clean water, clean air, beautiful scenery, and close access to nature's playground" but I'd say its assets are its people.

Stoical is the word most people use when talking about Libby. Because while it's beautiful, it's also a tough place to live. Until the 1920s, most of the men worked in logging. Dangerous work, and seasonal, logging was a hard way to support a family. So when vermiculite was discovered in the mountains, things picked up. Year-round employment, some of it indoors. Gayla Benefield still remembers the day her father, Perley, got a job there, because it was her birthday.

"My father had been out of work prior to 1954," Gayla recalled.

"He had had a rough year and things were tough and suddenly he came home—it was September 17, 1954—and said he had a birthday present for me: he had a job!"

With the blondest hair and palest complexion, Gayla's Norwegian heritage is obvious. She belongs here and knows it. Her parents moved to Libby when she was two and after a string of disappointing jobs, the mine was a godsend. Perley loved his work, loved the men and the sense of doing something important. But most important of all was the chance to earn a regular wage, Social Security, and a pension. Starting off as a sweeper in the dry mill, he hoped he'd move on up to driving one of the big trucks. But what mattered most was that Perley had found a secure future for himself and his family.

The Universal Zonolite Company produced raw materials for housing insulation, concrete, wallboard, roofing, even soil conditioner. There seemed no end to the usefulness of the material. Ninety percent of the country's supply came from Libby and it was shipped all over America. Even though it only employed about a hundred men, it felt like an important business, helping America to grow. And working there had its privileges: In 1959, Perley boasted that the company was such a great employer, it was giving everyone free X-ray checkups.

"Dad was just so thrilled at work," Gayla remembered. "All the guys loved working at the mine; it was like a fraternity up there. Dad loved operating equipment and he worked his way to the top of the mountain, grading the roads. In winter, we hoped for snow because that would mean he'd get paid double time."

What he didn't know, because no one told him, was that concerns about the safety of the mine had started three years earlier, when an engineer from the state health department, Benjamin Wake, had conducted a hygiene study measuring air quality in the mine. It was dusty: so thick with dust that the filters in his vacuum pumps kept getting clogged. And it wasn't, as the men had been told, just "nuisance dust."

"The asbestos in the air is of considerable toxicity," Wake wrote. "Inhalation of asbestos dust must be expected sooner or later to produce pulmonary fibrosis."[17]

Although the toxicity of asbestos wasn't definitively established until 1964, Wake already knew that pulmonary asbestosis was a "progressive disease with a bad prognosis." He returned to the mine in 1958, 1960, and 1962, each time making recommendations for repairs to the ventilation systems and for working conditions that might protect the workers. But levels of asbestos continued to rise, and the workforce increased to 150 men. Nobody told any of them what they were breathing or how dangerous it was; even though state authorities were monitoring the mine, they weren't sharing their findings with anyone but the company's senior management. But the company X-rays—that great free gift Perley boasted of—bore out Wake's prognosis: Of the 130 workers X-rayed, 82 already showed signs of lung disease. But neither the men, nor their doctors, were told anything.

In 1961, Gayla married Gary Svenson. He was serving in the military but when he came home, he went to work at the mine, too. But unlike Perley, he hated it.

"Gayla's dad got me a job there when I came out of the service. I didn't like it, I didn't like the dust. You'd put the ore in sacks, thump them on the ground—the stuff went up your nose. We were given respirators, but nobody used them because they got all clogged up in fifteen minutes."

Gary lasted only four months at the mine, before leaving to go into a car dealership.

But that same year, W. R. Grace bought the mine and production really took off. By now, the medical establishment and Grace knew that asbestos was toxic. Libby's vermiculite went all over the country. Monokote, the company's fireproofing spray, was used everywhere, even in landmark sites like the World Trade Center, where it was applied to steel support beams. The world's leading authority on asbestos estimated at the time (1969) that not one man spraying Monokote would be alive in twenty years.[18] But no one in Libby knew that. A 1969 test showed that 24,000 pounds of dust came out of the large stack at the dry mill daily, with asbestos levels as high as 20 to 40 percent. The Libby mine had several stacks and production continued to increase.

But Perley's joy in his work did not. In 1964, he went to the doctor and was told he had a heart condition, and should find some lighter work at the mine. He was only fifty-two but the management found him some easier jobs and, on the days his chest pains were worse, all his friends at the mine pitched in to help him out.

"He said, 'I'm so lucky they let me work with this heart condition.' He really felt so grateful. Guys would help Dad up the steps and carry his kit; they helped him all the way because he couldn't walk and step up two steps. What he wanted most of all was to be able to stay for twenty years so he could get his pension. But from 1968 onward, he just got chest pains so bad, he got more and more ill, then he got pneumonia and started missing work."

In 1969, the mine manager, Earl Lovick, conducted a study of his employees. With statistical precision, he noted that "although 17 percent of our 1 to 5 years' service group have or are suspect of lung disease, there is a marked rise (45 percent) beginning with the 11th year of service, climbing to 92 percent in the 21 to 25 years' service group."

By now, Perley had been working at the mine for fifteen years. In 1971, Earl Lovick stopped smoking and had an operation to have pleural plaque removed from his lungs. But the men under him continued working at the mine, with no idea of what they were handling or how dangerous it was. At the age of fifty-nine, just five days before he was due to receive his pension, Perley died. And Gayla began to think something was wrong.

"What tipped me off was the tragic way the man died and the way the company never sent a card. I started investigating and started talking to my friends' fathers and there was another man who was forty-nine when he died. I thought perhaps Grace didn't know what was going on. And I didn't really know what it was—I didn't know it was asbestos."

By this time, Gayla had a job reading meters for the power company. She'd spend the daytime going from house to house, talking to people, meeting everyone. And what struck her was how many men were at home, sitting on the back porch using oxygen tanks. The more she talked to people the more she learned, how Grace was paying them off, making private settlements that no one could disclose. All the men had worked at the mine.

"Then my mom, Margaret, got sick. She'd gone to talk to an attorney about Dad's case and he heard Mom cough and asked to see her medical records. He called her back and said she had classic asbestosis. She had been going to the hospital for years here and the doctors that had been treating her for pneumonia knew what it was, but not one of them ever told her."

"And then I remembered once, when Dad was still alive, Mom broke her leg and was in the hospital for two weeks and I think the doctor took two X-rays for her leg and *nine* for her chest! Grace had an underground study going on, examining chest X-rays to understand the progression of the disease. But here's the thing: she never worked at the mine!"

Margaret had never worked at the mine, but it didn't matter. Each day, when Perley had come home from work and hugged his wife, he'd been covered in dust. He tracked dust all the way through the family home. There was dust in the family car. You didn't have to work with vermiculite to be contaminated by it. The dust was all over town. Everyone was at risk.

In 1990 Grace closed the mine. A fall in demand for its product, coupled with increasing and ongoing liabilities, meant the business was no longer viable. But it didn't mean that Grace's involvement in the town was over. They knew—had known for many years—that the legacy of their ownership would be decades of responsibility for their former employees and their families.

Gayla's mother had received an out-of-court settlement from W. R. Grace for $100,000, of which she ultimately received just $67,000. Adding up the medicine receipts alone, Gayla found it cost her mother over a million dollars to die.

"She'd be fine in the mornings but by noon her lungs would be full. It was horrific because she would curse Dad, curse the company," Gayla recalls. "At this time her own mother was ninety-nine and getting a hip replacement—and here was my mom scarcely able to breathe. Her own brother is still alive *today* doing ballroom dancing. This is the way our family is. We just don't quit."

Gayla certainly didn't quit. She talked to everyone she knew—which was pretty much everyone in town. Asbestosis and mesothelioma riddled Libby, and W. R. Grace had known about it ever since they had bought the mine.

Just before her mother died in 1996, she gave Gayla permission to sue W. R. Grace for her mother's death. "Of course they tried so hard to stop me. Made offers of three, four, five hundred thousand dollars. But it always had to be secret and that isn't what I wanted. I wanted it to be public. I wanted everyone to know what was going on in this town. And I wanted to be able to talk about it."

"The last offer they made me was $605,000 and a letter of apology. I asked if I could publish the settlement on the Internet and they said no, so I said no. I had to have a guilty verdict. The jury came back with an award of $250,000—but I got that guilty verdict. But you know, the local press was never there. No press at all. Just a tiny blurb in the paper. We were suing a Fortune 500 company and it was the only time there'd been a guilty verdict for secondary exposure leading to wrongful death. And it didn't make the news."

Full of rage at what Grace had done to her family and to her community, Gayla would talk to anyone who would listen. But mostly they wouldn't listen. Local media, she's convinced, were intimidated by Grace. So too were most local politicians. Everywhere she looked, Gayla saw people dying slow, agonizing, and expensive deaths—and nobody wanted to know.

But in 1999, she struck lucky. Andrew Schneider, an investigative journalist from Seattle, came to Libby researching a feature about the 1872 General Mining Act. He ran into Gayla and, with some knowledge of W. R. Grace's malfeasance in the past, he paid attention to her story. When the *Seattle Post-Intelligencer* published his front-page story, all hell broke loose.

> First it killed some miners. Then it killed wives and children, slipping into their homes on the dusty clothing of hard-working men. Now the mine is closed but in Libby, the killing goes on. W. R. Grace knew, from the time it bought the mine in 1963, why the people in Libby were dying. But for the 30 years it owned the mine, the company did not stop it. Neither did the governments. Not the town of Libby, not Lincoln County. Not the state of Montana, not federal mining, health and environmental agencies, not anyone else charged with protecting the public health.[19]

The Environmental Protection Agency was called in for what would ultimately become the largest Superfund cleanup site in American history.

As Gayla had uncovered W. R. Grace's knowledge of the town's contamination, she'd discovered shocking information: not just secret X-rays but secret autopsies, doctors keeping quiet, and state authorities burying information. But nothing was more shocking than Gayla's discovery that so many of her friends and neighbors did not want to know anything she had uncovered.

"People would cross the street when they saw me coming," she recalled.

"They shunned me as though I had something contagious. People said I was crazy or that the lawyers were giving me kickbacks—and these would be people whose own family members were dragging around oxygen tanks!

"One line of defense was, people would say: If the doctors thought there was something wrong, they'd tell us. But they took the secret X-rays and didn't tell anyone! The mayor said, I know it's really bad but what can we do? I had visions of the town jumping on the bandwagon and fixing it but instead people said nothing. They just buried their heads in the sand."

Gayla was angry and frustrated when townspeople fought against Superfund status and fought against getting the asbestosis clinic established. She was trying to bring help, know-how, and money to the town—but the town didn't want to know.

"The businessmen and townspeople were all making money from the miners! I don't understand why one didn't stand up and say enough is enough. But they didn't. That this community would allow this group to let people die—it was just incredible to me."

Though they were now divorced, Gayla and Gary Svenson were still friends and he listened to her. "It divided the town. People didn't want to believe it. There was real hatred between those who liked the company and those who were sick. To this day there are workers who still believe that W. R. Grace did nothing wrong. They were paid a wage to do a job and made a living for them and they are satisfied with that."

Even in her own family, Gayla encountered opposition. "My brother-in-law used to brag about how much money he was making—said he could buy himself a new pair of lungs. And this was after my mom and my dad had died of the disease. He died a horrible death in six months." His sons and wife were subsequently diagnosed with asbestosis.

"We had old loggers who would say, 'I could go out in the woods and die tomorrow.' But I'd say to them: that tree wouldn't come back and kill your children and wife! We even had people who made bumper stickers saying, 'And no I don't have asbestosis!' No one had the courage to confront me face-to-face, they just muttered and didn't help. They just wanted to deny the whole thing."

"I went along with that whole 'it's not that bad' attitude for quite a while," admits Leroy Thom. He's now one of Gayla's strongest allies. "I had a friend who was on oxygen but, you know, he seemed to get along just fine—we used to go bowling together. And then, just suddenly, he just died. It really made me think: Maybe I haven't appraised this as I should."

Leroy worked at the mine for sixteen years. Today, though he's been diagnosed with asbestosis, he runs a machine shop and devotes a lot of his energies to the town's Center for Asbestos Related Diseases. He's affable and laid-back but he says himself that he's been on a steep and emotional learning curve.

"There was a lot of opposition to the clinic, and some people used to come in the back door. They didn't want to be seen coming in! But the good thing is that people trust it—especially people who have the disease. On the other side though is the fact that people are like ostriches—they don't want to acknowledge that the clinic even exists, because it proves that the disease is here. It divided our community. Still today even among some of the workers, they will say things like, you're not missing an arm!"

Gayla isn't the kind of person to be daunted by opposition, even by the silent intransigence she has encountered for years in Libby. Staunch support from old friends and neighbors helped her persevere in getting all the bad news out in the open. Finally, in 2000, the EPA and the Agency for Toxic Substances Disease Registry agreed to screen all former Grace workers, their family members, and anyone who had lived in Libby for at least six months up to 1990. They were expecting about two thousand people; more than six thousand turned up. Then they extended the screening to anyone who had lived or worked in Libby. One of Gayla's oldest friends and staunchest allies, Les Skramstad, had already been diagnosed with asbestosis; so had his wife, Norita, and his son, Brent. He knew firsthand how everyone in the town felt.

"It was like waiting for your draft notice during the war," said Les Skramstad. "It was like going out to the mailbox—that long walk—hoping that the long white envelope from the government wasn't there."

In December 2000, when the ATSDR released "Mortality from Asbestosis in Libby, Montana," it showed that the death rate in Libby from asbestosis was forty times higher than in the rest of the state and eighty times greater than anywhere else in America.

By now, Gayla was getting hate mail; it just made her more relentless. What kept her going was the belief that the wives and children of the miners could be, must be, helped—by decent compensation and good health care. Inspired by the hope that the next generation wouldn't have to suffer as her own parents had, she hoped fervently that the more the town knew, the more it could do for its children. That dedication received a stunning blow when she discovered that Libby's school was contaminated.

"Grace had tested the running track at Plummer School in 1983 and found that the runners were stirring up dangerous levels of asbestos. Underneath the bleachers was completely contaminated—and that is where the kids play during the game. The skating rink—where kids played in the summer when it wasn't frozen—had vermiculite trailings at its base. That is the angriest I have ever been! Angry at the town, angry at the town fathers who knew the material had been dumped there. The principal of that school loved kids—he had retired—but you'd think he'd have stepped forward to say: Perhaps you should just look at the school. But he hadn't said a word! The story had broken wide open in 1999 and here we were, it was 2002 and nobody had said a thing! And for three solid years, those kids were exposed. My grandkids' first day of latency was their first day of kindergarten."

That same summer, Gayla and her second husband were both diagnosed with lung abnormalities. Neither of them had ever worked in the mine.

As the years have gone by, the EPA has continued to find vermiculite all over Libby and to try to clean it up. In June 2009, the federal government finally declared Libby the site of a public health emergency. An earlier attempt in 2002 had been thwarted by the previous administration's Office of Management and Budget.

Today, if you go to the center of Libby and stop for coffee, you can sit and watch as EPA trucks drive up and down the roads, removing contaminated topsoil or bringing in fresh topsoil for Libby gardens. But to this day, not everyone has participated in the cleanup; some still don't want to know. So what does it mean if your garden is cleaned up—but your neighbors refuse to have theirs done? The EPA can't stop the wind blowing.

"There are still plenty of people who blame me for bringing this up," says Gayla. She's at home now, mostly retired from her activism that brought help and the EPA and the clinic to the town. "People would just have got sick and died but business would have gone on as usual. Kids would still be at risk of contamination when they played at school! But I wanted people to have everything that my parents didn't have. I didn't want them to just go home and die—die broke. I thought it was better to look this thing in the face than just pretend it wasn't there."

How does she explain the ostrich-like behavior of so many people in the town? With the mine closed, no jobs were at risk; what could they hope to gain by ignoring the health crisis all around them?

"I think," she starts, accustomed to having answers. She stops. "I think," she starts again, and stops. "Maybe they thought that if you didn't talk about it, if you didn't look at, it would go away. They didn't want a fight. It's the emperor's new clothes: If we say it's fine, maybe it is fine."

People who've lived in Libby a long time all comment on the stoicism of its people. They don't whine and they don't want to think of themselves as victims. Gayla understood that they were victims of W. R. Grace when it came to lung disease but they'd be victims of their own blindness if they did nothing about it.

The story of Libby is an epic tragedy and it's important to remember that at its heart is W. R. Grace, a corporation that knowingly put its employees in danger and then concealed that danger from them. It tracked the rates and risk of asbestosis, mesothelioma, and other lung abnormalities without any of its victims knowing their condition. And in 2001, Grace declared bankruptcy as a way out of mounting, apparently endless litigation. On one level, the people of Libby refused to see what was happening around them because it simply beggared belief that a publicly traded American business could be so cavalier with the lives of its employees and their families and get away with it. But what makes the story doubly tragic is that, once the facts were known, still so many of its victims refused to see what had happened to them.

When Gayla Benefield's mother gave her permission to sue W. R. Grace, she hoped the case would make her daughter rich. Gayla insists that it did, but not financially. The wealth that Gayla gained was in learning how powerful she was, in discovering how smart and well informed she could make herself, and in articulating her powerful passion for making Libby a stronger, healthier community. She was hungry for change and she was not afraid of conflict. It was only her determination, over a period of twenty-five years, that finally allowed everyone to see what had happened and how it could be different.

Pliny would have been proud of her. For although we can blame him for first creating the inaccurate image of the ostrich with its head in the sand, we can't blame him for being one. In A.D. 79, Mount Vesuvius erupted, covering and then preserving the city of Pompeii. While most people ran away from Vesuvius, Pliny went straight into the danger zone to look, learn, and rescue survivors. He died in the attempt. But in his honor, the most violent volcanic eruptions (such as that of Krakatoa) are called ultraplinian, in testimony to the man who preferred knowledge over ignorance.

6

JUST FOLLOWING ORDERS

IN SEPTEMBER 2004, the wreck of HMS *Victoria* was discovered off the coast of Tripoli. With its prow buried in the sand, it stood perfectly vertical, like a skyscraper, the ten-thousand-ton iron-plated leviathan serving as the burial ground for 358 British sailors who had died in one of the most bizarre blunders in naval history.

At the time of the disaster, Sir George Tryon, vice admiral in the British navy, was sixty-one and at the height of his powers. Standing six feet tall, with long sideburns, beard, and mustache, he looked every inch the Victorian gentleman and man of authority in his position as commander-in-chief of the Mediterranean fleet. From the time he'd joined the navy as a cadet at age sixteen, Tryon had enjoyed a brilliant and unimpeded career. He had served all over the world and was highly regarded, well connected, and, by all accounts, affable, energetic, deeply knowledgeable; he was praised for his humanity, insight, and love of a prank. Contemporary portraits suggest someone rather intimidating, though it is hard now to know whether that was a feature of personality or of rank.

What is clear is that Tryon was far from the Victorian archetype his picture suggests. He thought long and deeply about the traditions of the British navy and sought to restore the verve and initiative for which it had once been famous. Under Admiral Horatio Nelson, Tryon believed, men had been inspired with a mission and entrusted to make their own decisions in the heat of battle; only that way could commanders react with the flexibility and spontaneity that intense naval warfare demanded. Just obeying orders was dangerous because too much about war at sea was unpredictable. The very fact that Nelson's own death in 1805 at the Battle of Trafalgar had not compromised Britain's victory was testament to the independent initiative Nelson had inculcated into his navy. It was that spirit Tryon longed to recapture.

Although he may not have labeled them as such, Tryon knew that his officers were capable of being ostriches—conflict-averse and eager for a friction-free career. He took the unusual step of encouraging greater openness by specifically asking all of them to tell him about any risk or threat to the British fleet that might not come to his attention in the normal course of business. He insisted that the safety of the ship and its men should always come first: mere obedience was not enough. In an age of deference and intimidation, he worked hard to inspire in his men a sense of autonomy and independence sufficient for the most threatening and unforeseeable of naval encounters. In today's terms, you might say that he preferred open-door management to micromanagement. His was a controversial, even radical, position; many of his contemporaries clung to the practice of sending highly detailed instructions, signaled through flags, which could be long-winded, slow, and hard to see in the smoke and clutter of war. For Tryon this issue wasn't theoretical, but a matter of life and death. On occasion he could be deliberately uncommunicative, believing this was the best way for his men to learn how to think for themselves in unpredictable circumstances.

June 1893 found Tryon on maneuvers, commanding HMS *Victoria*, heading a column of six ships; his deputy, Rear Admiral Markham, headed a second, parallel column of five ships. Tryon's orders stated that each column was to turn 180 degrees to change direction. But each ship needed at least 730 meters to turn and there wasn't space enough between them for both to complete their turn without colliding. With orders so ambiguous and dangerous, Markham hesitated; surely the intention was not to turn the ships into each other's paths. When no action ensued, Tryon sent a signal saying, in effect:

What are you waiting for? This rather public rebuke stung Markham into action; it is said that, right up to the last minute, he hoped his orders would be changed. But he did as he was told.

The orders were not rescinded or changed. Inevitably, the two vast battleships collided, causing the largest peacetime loss of life in the history of the Royal Navy. HMS *Victoria* capsized in just thirteen minutes, taking Sir George with it. His last words, apparently, were, "It's all my fault." How could two battleships and two experienced seamen be so blind? A court-martial was never able fully to explain the incident to everyone's satisfaction. Tryon, of course, was not there to explain or defend himself; Markham did survive and was both blamed and exonerated for following orders: "Admiral Markham might have refused to perform the revolution ordered, and the *Victoria* might have been saved," wrote two admirals at the time. "Admiral Markham, however, would have been tried by court-martial, and no one would have sympathized with him as it would not have been realized that he had averted a catastrophe. Unconditional obedience is, in brief, the only principle on which those in service must act."

Parodied in the Ealing comedy, *Kind Hearts and Coronets* (1949), in which Alec Guinness plays a Tryon-like figure gleefully crashing his ships, what today might strike us as absurd was tragedy to the Victorians; certainly Tryon would have regarded it as such. For it was precisely Markham's failure to seize the initiative and *not* blindly obey that could be seen as the heart of the problem. Everything Tryon had believed in was proved by the accident—but, at the same time, his foolish death discredited everything he stood for. Whether for comedy or tragedy, the event is chiefly remembered for revealing the tension and difficulties inherent in following orders.

Such blind obedience is not, of course, the exclusive province of military men. Hierarchies, and the system of behaviors that they require, proliferate in nature and in man-made organizations. For humans, there is a clear evolutionary advantage in hierarchies: a disciplined group can achieve far more than a tumultuous and chaotic crowd. Within the group, acceptance of the differing roles and status of each member ensures internal harmony, while disobedience engenders conflict and friction. The disciplined, peaceful organization is better able to defend itself and advance its interests than is a confused, contentious group that agrees on nothing. The traditional argument in favor of hierarchies and obedience has been that of the social contract: It is worth sacrificing some degree of individuality in order to ensure the safety and privileges achieved only by a group.

More recently, psychologists have come to understand that this social contract may be more than utilitarian. A significant component of human happiness, they say, lies in being able to contribute to a purpose larger than oneself. Because, in the developed world, most of us can satisfy our immediate, or hedonic, needs pretty easily, doing so soon ceases to feel very rewarding. Once we're warm enough and safe enough and have sufficient food, getting more heat or housing or hot dogs—the hedonic treadmill—becomes progressively less gratifying.[1] So we yearn to contribute to something beyond our own immediate self-satisfaction and, as we find our greater purpose, we become happier and healthier and may even live longer. For very few people can that greater purpose be achieved alone. We need other people and organizations to build great art galleries or ballparks, scout teams or governments, companies or charities. We can do more with each other, we can do more good with each other, and therefore we surrender some of our autonomy in exchange for happiness, impact, and evolutionary survival. We surrender to the authority of the larger purpose and, in doing so, we become responsible *to* it. This may not feel like a radical shift—indeed we may not be conscious of making it. But how we act and what we see is profoundly altered when we obey.

The great psychologist of obedience was Stanley Milgram, the social scientist who was so thoughtful about the overload of city life. Influenced by the then-recent experience of the Holocaust, he conducted some of the world's most famous psychology experiments in the 1960s. Milgram sought to understand whether and why individuals obey authorities even when the task is morally repugnant, there is no reward for doing it, and, just as important, there is no punishment for disobedience. Using today's jargon, he would have asked: Is obedience hardwired?

He did so by running a series of eighteen experiments, each of which was a permutation of the first. A volunteer was invited into Milgram's basement lab at Yale University and told that he (or she) was involved in an experiment to gauge whether or not punishment was effective in learning. The volunteer—or "teacher"—was to read word pairs to the "Learner," who was in reality an actor. The learner had to indicate which word pairs went together. If the learner made an error, the teacher had to administer an electric shock. Each shock would be progressively stronger, starting with 15 volts and progressing to 450 volts: a lethal dose. The learner (the actor) would simulate pain so that the teacher (the volunteer) would believe the electric shocks to be real. Milgram wanted to know: How far would the volunteer teachers comply with a series of instructions that came increasingly into conflict with their conscience? Would the teachers continue to deliver the shocks, even though they were clearly causing pain and even, perhaps, death? Since there was no punishment for quitting—and no reward for continuing—how far would the volunteers go before refusing to obey?

Because the experiment has become so famous, it's important to reiterate a number of critical points about it that have become widely forgotten or misunderstood. The experiment was not about violence or aggression; what Milgram sought to test was obedience to authority. Participants were not being explicitly violent—though the distance between the teacher and learner would become germane. Nor was there any great incentive for the teacher to continue with the experiment. Each volunteer was paid four dollars plus carfare for his or her participation. It was central to the experiment that it be colored "by a cooperative mood,"[2] conducted without fear or threat of any kind. Any volunteer could stop, or leave, at any moment. The authority present was a well-mannered scientist in a white coat: not a boss, not a troop commander, merely an ostensibly objective observer trying to do research, which the volunteer was assisting.

Before setting out to conduct his experiments, Milgram asked three groups—psychiatrists, college students, and middle-class adults—how they expected the volunteers to behave. "They predict that virtually all subjects will refuse to obey the experimenter; only a pathological fringe, not exceeding one or two percent, was expected to proceed to the end of the shockboard."[3]

Although it was an academic exercise taking place in a college setting, the experiment was "vivid, intense and real" for all of the participants, and what Milgram discovered shocked and troubled him so much that it was ten years before he published a complete account of his work.[4] Sixty-five percent of the volunteers obeyed fully. "Of the forty subjects, twenty-six obeyed the orders of the experimenter to the end, proceeding to punish the victim until they reached the most potent shock available on the generator. After the 450-volt shock was administered three times, the experimenter called a halt to the session." What Milgram found wasn't aggression, for he observed "there is no anger, vindictiveness, or hatred in those who shocked the victim. Men do become angry; they do act hatefully and explode in rage against others. But not here. Something far more dangerous is revealed: the capacity for man to abandon his humanity, indeed the inevitability that he does so, as he merges his unique personality into larger institutional structures."[5]

Many permutations of the experiment followed.[6] Some of Milgram's colleagues found his results so surprising that they attempted versions of their own. One of these addressed the criticism that Milgram's situation depended too much on the performance skills of an actor. Perhaps its outcome could be explained by the fact that the actor had not really been very convincing and therefore the volunteers had suspected all along that they were doing no real harm; it just wasn't real enough. To test that critique, Charles Sheridan and Richard King enlisted thirteen male and thirteen female students to participate in a similar experiment in which, instead of an actor simulating pain, a cute fluffy puppy was used. In this version, the level of shock was exaggerated on the display cabinet but real (albeit lower) shocks were administered to the dog. "The first of the three actual voltage levels produced foot flexion and occasional barks, the second level produced running and vocalization, and the final level resulted in continuous barking and howling."[7] There was no danger of bad acting spoiling the reality of this experiment.

Other conditions remained the same: There was no sanction or punishment for disobedience and the team adopted Milgram's script to ensure a like-for-like comparison. Like Milgram, too, this team had asked a classroom of male and female students (not participants) what they expected the outcome to be. Everyone anticipated high levels of disobedience. Sheridan and King were also interested to find out whether there was a significant difference in responses from men or women, hypothesizing that "women would be less willing than men to inflict harm on a cute puppy."

Once again, they were wrong. Levels of obedience obtained from the male volunteers were close to those obtained by Milgram in the original experiment. But without exception, 100 percent of the female volunteers "complied with instructions to shock the puppy all the way to the end of the scale."

Milgram's experiment has been repeated often, and in many countries. (Milgram himself had hoped to repeat it in Germany but his early death prevented him from doing so.) The highest rates of full obedience were found in South Africa and Austria; the lowest in Australia and Spain.[8] A more recent replication of the study was conducted in 2006 and results closely mirrored Milgram's; if anything, rates of obedience had increased. In particular, in one version of the experiment (Experiment 5), which featured scheduled and scripted protests from the learner, the obedience rate went from 70 percent to 82.5 percent; howls of protest did not cause participants to doubt their actions.[9] In March 2010, French television producers seemed to think that recreating Milgram's experiments would make a fine game show;[10] their motives may have been different (and Milgram would have hated the use to which his work was put) but their results were the same: most participants went all the way.

Milgram struggled long and hard to understand his own highly disturbing findings. He concluded that when we are part of a group, or an organization, we change our focus. "Although," he wrote, "a person acting under authority performs actions that seem to violate standards of conscience, it would not be true to say that he loses his moral sense. Instead, it acquires a radically different focus. His moral concern now shifts to a consideration of how well he is living up to the expectations that the authority has of him. In wartime, a soldier does not ask whether it is good or bad to bomb a hamlet; he does not experience shame or guilt in the destruction of a village: rather he feels pride or shame depending on how well he has performed the mission assigned to him."[11]

That shift of focus is fundamental. It blinds us both to the alternatives we have to obedience (every one of Milgram's participants was free to stop) and to our moral responsibility for our actions. We focus so intently on the order that we are blind to everything else. When we obey orders, our concern to be a good soldier means that we no longer see that we have a choice or that we are morally responsible for our actions. Rear Admiral Markham felt that he had to obey Tryon's orders and, when he did, it was the order and not Markham that was deemed responsible for the deaths that ensued.

Another way of thinking about this is that when we agree to submit to authority in order to pursue a larger good, we exchange an individual self (with responsibility for our conscience) for a social self that is responsible to the whole. The most traditional way of portraying this is that the individual self lives at home and the social self goes to work. But if you think of yourself on your own and then in a party, you recognize the same person but in different roles with different manners, styles, and connections. The individual self is an actor, responsible and autonomous; the social self is an agent, working with and on behalf of others. Same people, different roles, different focus.

Milgram concluded that this shift of focus wasn't a personal failing and the problem of obedience wasn't wholly psychological. It was an inescapable aspect of belonging to a group. When the individual is working alone, conscience is brought into play. But when working within a hierarchy, authority replaces individual conscience. This is inevitable, because otherwise the hierarchy just doesn't work: too many consciences and the advantage of being in a group disappears. Conscience, it seems, doesn't scale.

It may even be that the more committed we are conscientiously to the moral purpose of an organization, the more obedient we become. Taking this out of the laboratory into the real world, a group of Ohio psychiatrists decided to find out whether nurses would obey doctors, even when the doctors' orders clearly endangered the lives of their patients. What is so interesting about this study is that it involves a highly conscientious group of individuals, working in a hierarchical organization. When asked, nurses are quite clear about their primary concern for patients; that is typically what has brought them into their profession in the first place. So they bring a high degree of commitment and enthusiasm not just to the tasks of their work but to the purpose of their work. But this, it turns out, doesn't protect them from the dilemma of obedience.

In the study, twenty-two nurses—twelve from a municipal hospital and ten from a private hospital—were instructed to administer an obviously excessive dose of medicine. The drug itself was unauthorized, which is to say it wasn't on the ward stock list and hadn't been cleared for use. The doctor ordering the drug would do so on the telephone and would be a physician whom the nurse did not know. (The drug itself, of course, was a placebo so that the patients were never in any danger.) Rather like Milgram, the Ohio team also canvassed thirty-three graduate and student nurses, asking them what they would do in these circumstances. Thirty-one said that the subjects would not give the medication.

But in the experiment, it turned out that twenty-one of the twenty-two participating nurses were prepared to administer the drug. Moreover, they expressed no real resistance to the order and did not appear to experience any internal conflict or even any conscious awareness that there might be a problem. Only one refusenik felt any hostility to the doctor ordering the wrong drug. The rest merely felt somewhat tetchy or confused. "Insofar as the nurse is concerned," wrote the Ohio team, "the psychological problems involved in a situation such as the one under discussion are operating to a considerable extent *below the threshold of consciousness*"[12] (my italics). What most surprised the team that conducted the experiment was not that the nurses obeyed but that their obedience had rendered them so entirely blind to their primary duty of care for the patient that they could see no conflict at all.

The Ohio nurses had just one test, one chance to disobey. In Milgram's original experiment, the volunteers had multiple points at which they could have refused. But the fact that they were operating a sliding scale—from 15 volts to 450 volts—may, in fact, have helped them to obey. There was never a single moment at which the delivery of the shock suddenly seemed absolutely wrong. Instead, applying lethal shocks was something the volunteers learned to do only by making baby steps along the way.

"There was never a moment when it seemed so bad that you had to stop." That comment comes not from one of Milgram's volunteers but from Walt Pavlo, a mid-level executive at MCI Telecommunications. Unlike a hospital, the long-distance phone company didn't have a high moral purpose that instilled commitment and obedience. What it did have was a highly competitive culture and big rewards for employees who played the game. But most of all, says Pavlo, it had people who wanted to be good employees.

"When I started out, I was thirty, eager and ambitious. Everything was going right. I had a new job, a great family, and MCI was a big go-ahead company, full of smart young people just like me. I was psyched."

Now fifty, Pavlo is a likeable, soft-spoken but intense conversationalist. If you didn't know his background, his seriousness might worry you; it is as though he's still puzzling over a problem that just won't go away. His mind is restless and even if he's talking about old times, he's still looking for new insights. As we sat together in a hotel in Washington, D.C., we must have looked like just another couple of executives having a business meeting. But this conversation was different because Pavlo is a convicted white-collar criminal.

"My boss, Ralph McCumber, had been a navy commander, had served in Vietnam. He had a kind of military bearing: very neat, very methodical. And you just knew he was tough. I don't know how you knew, you just knew."

Pavlo's job was to make sure that the outstanding amounts owed by the long-distance carriers to MCI got paid. He was really a debt collector but excitement around the new, entrepreneurial company and around the newly deregulated industry made him feel bigger and more important than that. And highly dedicated.

"I'd get up at four thirty every morning, get to work about five thirty. I'd have a meeting with McCumber around seven thirty to go through problem accounts. It took me about three months to become McCumber's first lieutenant."

There was much about MCI's operations that Pavlo didn't understand: how they let their customers run up such huge debts, why they took on customers delivering trashy products like sex chat and psychics, and why they paid commission on sales to customers who didn't pay up. But Pavlo was the new boy and he trusted the business would eventually make sense. In the meantime, he was most concerned to make a good impression. So when McCumber came and told him about a forthcoming RIF, Pavlo felt anxious.

"What's a RIF?" he asked.

"Reduction in Force," McComber explained. "We fire people in the fall to save a few months' salary, then re-hire in January. It's an annual ritual around here so MCI can make its year-end earnings numbers and clear out the dead wood."[13]

Pavlo's assignment, three months into his job, was to fire one of the bookkeeping clerks, Eslene. She was fiftyish and suffered from vertigo but, he was told, she had to go. From Pavlo's perspective, he had to be the bad guy to a nice old lady who needed her job for the health benefits, if nothing else. And he did as he'd been ordered.

"Cheer up," Eslene told him as she left. "You're going to be a great manager."

Pavlo says he felt like an executioner. But he didn't leave. He was being a good employee and a good provider to his family. A few months

later, Pavlo and McCumber came up with the idea of getting delinquent customers to sign promissory notes—legally binding promises
by clients to pay back what they owed. Since they represented obligations to MCI, they could be counted as assets and the company's bad
debt disappeared. Pavlo knew it was a fudge but it seemed to work, so
he kept doing what he was told.

"Of course there was never a direct order to cook the books," Pavlo
explained to me. "Instead it was just a kind of willful neglect. No one
would ever ask how the debt disappeared. So since nobody told you to
stop, you kept going. The only order we had was just: make the debt
vanish. Don't bring me problems, bring me solutions. Nobody wanted
to look into the detail.

"The other thing about it was: nobody seemed to get hurt. The
company did fine. The shareholders were doing great. The customers
were still running their sleazy businesses. Where was the harm? You
couldn't see any. What you could see was the reward: promotions,
swanky hotels, nice resorts. So you just look away. You do what you're
told and you don't look too close."

After two years, Pavlo started smoking, something he had despised
in the past. Turning a blind eye to the mess that he couldn't clear up—a
mess that, in fact, he was exacerbating—was a horrific, cognitively
dissonant experience. The good guy and the bad deeds just couldn't
coexist. The only way he could deal with it was to anesthetize himself:
drinking, smoking, and working such crazy hours that he couldn't feel
a thing.

"I hated myself. And I hated my customers. And I hated the company. Because, in my mind at the time, I thought: they're making me
do this. MCI is making me smoke and drink and write these notes. It's
not me, it's them. And how do you go back? I went into that company
with such high ideals and after a while, I couldn't figure out how to
get out."

Twenty years later, and after serving a two-year jail sentence, Pavlo
is still in pain, trying to reconcile in his own mind how he could have
done things that he knows were wrong. He's devoted years of his life
to teaching college and business-school students how he went wrong,
hoping he can help them recognize the traps he fell into. The problem, he says, is not that you are asked to do one big, bad deed; it is
that there are so many tiny steps along the way that there is never a
moment when it's simple to say no.

"I don't consider myself a bad person. I know right from wrong. But I could rationalize some very irrational behavior that now appalls me. Why did I think that this was right? I was doing my job. I did what I'd been told to do."

Pavlo moved, by baby steps, from doing things that felt bad to committing acts that were illegal. His is a rare experience, though the phenomenal cost of white-collar crime—2 percent of all business revenues, according to Madoff whistle blower Harry Markopolos—suggests that it may be less rare than we would like to imagine. But obedience in most cases is not about knowingly doing something illegal. It may be as simple as following orders that—like Pavlo's promissory notes—just don't make a lot of sense.

Obedience poses a troublesome problem for large corporations. In 1998, when BP bought Amoco, the new combined company instantly ordered a 25-percent cut in fixed cash costs across all refineries. The order was made regardless of the condition of each site. And so, over the next three years, the management responsible for the Texas City site reviewed everything: maintenance, service agreements, personnel, equipment testing, and tools. Everything was cut—down, it was said, to the number of pencils.

The 25-percent cut was not a target; it was a "directive," and the cadre of managers responsible for Texas City implemented it. They did so despite their knowledge that, under Amoco's ownership, the plant had been run down and despite repeated warnings about the site's safety. An internal BP presentation made in 2002 says, "If we do not achieve a significant improvement [in] safety performance at the Texas City refinery, one of our co-workers or a contract employee will be killed."[14] A graph illustrating fatalities in the past twenty years powerfully illustrates the point. A further report showed the poor state of the infrastructure, citing high rates of absenteeism and a large backlog of overdue inspections. A safety report written the following year says that "the 'checkbook mentality' blame and status culture still exists throughout most of the Texas City site and this limits health, safety, environmental, and general performance. Budget and HSE priorities are not aligned."

Cost-cutting, personnel reductions, and cutbacks on training put everyone at Texas City under increasing pressure. Between 1994 and 2004, the site experienced *eight* blowdown drum incidents, of which only three were investigated. In 2004 alone, three major incidents caused three fatalities.[15] Yet that same year, prior to a meeting to discuss cuts, one manager sent the following e-mail:

> Which bit of 25% don't you understand? We are going to be wasting our time on Monday discussing this topic unless you come prepared to commit to a 25% cut. I have much more interesting things to do with my time than getting up at 3am to travel to Chicago for a non-productive meeting![16]

The order that came from London to cut costs was followed clearly and effectively—even in the face of repeated warnings that the infrastructure was not safe and that, as one report put it, "we have cut routine budgets to the point where we are not doing the routine maintenance essential to keeping units up. We cut 10%, cut 10%, cut 10% . . . without regard for risk."[17] When consultants working at Texas City asked executives whether they felt there were any safety problems not being addressed, those in high management positions answered "I am not aware of any." They had been instructed to cut costs and that's what they focused on.

Just as no one told Pavlo to cook the books at MCI, no one at BP headquarters in London said, "Make the cuts, we don't care if people die." Of course they didn't. But the effect of the cost-cutting directives was to block out other considerations. When employees were surveyed on corporate priorities, they cited number one as making money and number two as costs and budgets. And even though managers on site knew there were safety problems, were grief-stricken by accidents, and were honestly anxious about how to make the refinery safer, they turned a blind eye to the problems and obeyed.

That, of course, is the problem with targets, and with managing by objectives. Implicitly they communicate the same message as Pavlo's management did: We don't care *how* the target is achieved, as long as it is achieved. Such is the power of obedience that other considerations (ethics, legality, safety) simply become invisible to social beings who want to make a contribution. When the inexperienced jailers at Abu Ghraib were told to "soften up" prisoners, they were not given detailed instructions, and they were not informed as to the usefulness of their work. They simply tried to do as they were told. That their cruelty elicited not a single valuable piece of military intelligence was

not relevant: They followed orders, which eliminated other concerns.[18]

Hierarchies and obedience persist even in the face of extraordinary
danger. A National Transportation Safety Board review of thirty-seven
airplane accidents in the United States concluded that up to a quarter of
all plane crashes are caused by "destructive obedience" inside the cockpit.[19] In a study eerily reminiscent of Sir George Tryon and the HMS
Victoria disaster, many flight crew errors were attributed to accepting
the authority of the captain even when he was getting things wrong.
Commercial airplane pilots typically enjoy tremendous authority: They
have three to four times more experience than their first officers, and
many have come from the military and are not accustomed to being
questioned. Only the pilot in command has explicit authority to devi-
ate from rules in an emergency. As a consequence, it feels very difficult
to challenge them. The NTSB study, which analyzed cockpit communications captured on flight recorders prior to crashes, found that 25
percent of all accidents could have been prevented if the pilot had been
challenged when making an error.

Obedience is even strong enough to blind us to our own self-interest.
The classic example of that extreme is the kamikaze pilot or the suicide
bomber, for whom obedience to a cause (and, in some cases, the promise of intangible future glory) is powerful enough to destroy the instinct
for survival. Those cases are always cited as being culturally determined—by the Japanese love of the emperor or by religious extremism. But in far tamer, academic experiments, in which volunteers have
been ordered to harm not an anonymous "learner" but themselves, the
same results have been found.[20] Volunteers will more readily harm
themselves than disobey.

This is a problem the military has had generations to ponder. From
a legal perspective, military law states that a soldier must obey orders
unless that order is manifestly illegal. If the law is illegal, then the
superior who issued it is held responsible. But any doubts that a soldier
may have about the legality of the order should be resolved in favor of
obedience. (Intriguingly, the same rules of conduct apply to lawyers,
too.)[21] We may tend to think of the military as having a culture of
blind obedience, but that is far from the case. One of the few of Milgram's volunteers who did *not* obey was, he said, inspired by his military training in which he was taught that he had a right to refuse illegal
orders.

The Nuremberg trials that followed the Second World War did not allow obedience as an excuse because the prisoners being tried there were the superior officers and also were high-ranking political officials. And even in more recent times, the charters establishing international tribunals relating to war crimes in the former Yugoslavia and in Rwanda have not allowed obedience as an excuse. Only in the Communist bloc and some parts of the Third World does following orders provide any kind of legal protection.[22]

Lieutenant Colonel Fred Krawchuk, of the U.S. Army Special Forces, knows the military law, knows the theory behind it, but also has to put it into daily practice. When I spoke to him, he was in Kabul, Afghanistan, in the midst of Operation Mushtarak. As you might expect in a highly volatile context, he thinks about obedience very, very carefully.

"Obedience is too simple. And in a highly complex situation, like this one, anything too simple doesn't work. There is a tension between obedience, the duty to do the right thing, and the notion of blind obedience when you're struggling to suppress your own conscience despite evidence that things are wrong. I think one of the things that is clear for us is that we are taught to speak up when we witness something negligent, abuse, criminal conduct. That piece is pretty clear."

Krawchuk says that what the military wants is "prepared minds" and that preparation consists not of abstract theory but of exercises and scenarios.

"A lot of our units train in Louisiana. When we know they have the skills they need—how to use instruments of force individually and collectively—we put them through exercises where they will be put in a lot of different situations and under all kinds of different stress. And we're working with them to develop negotiating skills, to see how they develop relationships with people, how they deal with danger. They'll be going through a town and you throw situations at them to see how they react. As soon as the exercise is done, we call an After Action Review when the unit goes through what they did and asks: What went well, what didn't go well? How could we do better? And we try to put time into the schedule so they go right back into retraining to internalize what they've just learned."

The Army is not just trying to teach soldiers how to use their weapons but how to use their minds, making difficult decisions under stressful conditions of great complexity. But this isn't the only training the soldiers get. Krawchuk says all of them are taught a great deal of history. The massacre at My Lai during the Vietnam War is a standard topic: what to do when you are served with an illegal order.

"My Lai is a story I've heard over and over again. Everyone does. But I think one of the experiences that has inspired me the most was when I was in an orientation briefing and the commander came to speak to us and what he said was: 'I've already written up my letter of resignation and it is in my desk.' And we're all sitting there thinking: What's going on? 'Because if it comes to the day I'm asked to do something not proper or ethical, I am ready to stand my moral ground and make a difficult decision.' That was really something! It has stayed with me. Someone is taking a stand. My own interpretation was that this person's integrity was so high, it wasn't about career or promotion, it is about the right thing."

Krawchuk doesn't feel he's ever been in a situation where he has had to choose between doing as he's been told and doing what he thinks is right. He feels exhaustively trained for that, but he hasn't been there yet. And while he readily accepts that there is, necessarily, a culture of obedience in the Army, he believes that in practice this turns out to be a lot more complicated than it sounds.

"I had this conversation once at business school. I was the only one there who was a military officer on active duty. We were discussing leadership and someone said: 'For you, Fred, leadership is easy. You give orders and people follow.' It is not that easy. If people don't respect you, don't trust you, there are lots of ways to get blown off without 'disregarding orders.' It isn't black and white. But what I think about is: we are very results oriented. Take care of the mission, that's what we're trained to do. And there's a lot that's healthy about that. But when dealing with conflict situations, how much room is there for independent thinking?"

Before going to Afghanistan, Krawchuk served as a U.S. Army Special Forces officer assigned to the U.S. Pacific Command in Hawaii, where he was responsible for communications, security, and development strategies in Asia. This has meant working with host nations, local populations, nongovernmental organizations, and local governments to build infrastructure—water, medical care, education—in highly volatile conditions. The job doesn't, he says, lend itself to quick or simple solutions.

"It is a misservice to sit back and wait to be told what to do. Of course you do as you're told but there is something else about moral courage, about standing up for what is right. It might mean you assume some risk and write a position paper or schedule a briefing to help solve some of these difficult problems we're facing right now. You don't just wait to be told what to do. When do you pick the fight? How far do you take your ideas? As someone who believes we need comprehensive answers to complex situations, I think we need more than just people doing what they're told or waiting to be told. My experience is there is a lot more struggle with that than with illegal orders."

Krawchuk is struggling not with obedience itself, but with its side effect, which is blindness. When all we do is obey, we become blind: We do not see consequences or alternatives or better solutions. I'm haunted by that e-mail from the harried BP executive: "Which bit of 25% don't you understand?" It sounds so desperate, frightened of the consequences that will rain down if the order to make cuts isn't obeyed. Under these conditions, the independent thought Krawchuk values simply isn't possible.

Milgram's experiments demonstrate that, however much we think we won't obey, for the most part we do. It is a default behavior, at least in part because its opposite—reflection, independent thinking—is so much more effortful. Obedience is another kind of shortcut, in which we trust someone else's thinking above our own. It's easy and simple, especially when we're tired, distracted, and don't want a fight. And so obedience both amplifies and articulates all those other forces that make us blind.

The military has no choice but to grapple with the full spectrum of obedience from Nelsonian initiative to the unquestioning following of orders. More than a few tragedies—from the sinking of HMS *Victoria* to My Lai and Abu Ghraib—demand thoughtful consideration of the challenges that obedience presents. This has made the military very wary of the power obedience confers. Dealing daily in life and death, military leaders recognize that the costs of their mistakes are high and irretrievable. But Fred Krawchuk's story about being at business school is telling: His business colleagues seemed to envy what they imagined to be the military model of obedience—just do as you're told—and were unaware that the model is dangerous and out of date. That the military itself doesn't regard blind obedience as an admirable goal should give any executive pause. Some of the gravest mistakes in both the business and the political world have been caused by eager executives, keen to please, hungry for reward, and convinced that blind obedience was their path to success. Who is more willfully blind: the executives who believe this, or their leaders who allow them to? Military law would blame the boss.

7

THE CULT OF CULTURES

Madness is the exception in individuals but the rule in groups.
—Nietzsche

WALT PAVLO DIDN'T stop at writing promissory notes. As bad debts at MCI ballooned, he found himself spending more and more time with crooks and charlatans. Some went into liquidation; when Pavlo met with TelRoute, he caught their executives stealing crystal glasses and bottles of liquor from the office bar. This was not, he reflected, liquidation the way he'd studied it at business school. One of his more bizarre clients made its money from porn lines and from selling prepaid calling cards, exploiting new immigrants eager to phone home but too poor to own a phone. When Pavlo called on their New York office, he felt, he said, "like a lost kitten in a jungle full of predators." The tables were piled high with cash but still the company's $25 million debt remained unpaid.

"Everywhere you looked," Pavlo recalled, "everybody was on the make and on the take. At MCI, sales sneaked deadbeats onto the network. Finance wrote worthless promissory notes. Accounting hid MCI's past-due balances. The customers on MCI's network were ripping off MCI and I was covering them up on behalf of the company."[1]

Everybody Pavlo spent time with seemed to be ripping people off. One of the most colorful, and the most dangerous, was Harold Mann, who dreamed one day of running a vast, vertically integrated porn empire. Along the way, he ran sex chat lines for his own and numerous other phone companies. He owed MCI money, of course—that's how he and Pavlo met—but he also owed about six hundred thousand dollars to a smaller company called TNI. And TNI owed MCI two million dollars. Everybody was collecting from consumers, but no one was paying their bills.

One day, bubbling with enthusiasm, Mann approached Pavlo with an idea. Mann would take over collecting TNI's debt. But the money he collected wouldn't go to MCI; Pavlo and Mann would keep it for themselves—and Pavlo could cover the traces with another promissory note. After all, Mann reasoned, it's not like MCI was ever going to get the money anyway.

"Holy shit. That's what I thought. I realized that Mann knew exactly what was going on at MCI. Deadbeat balances were being shoved into every hidden corner and crevice they could find. Who'd miss a lousy two million dollars?"

As Mann pointed out, Pavlo was surrounded by cheats; he was the only one who hadn't yet figured out how to make money at it. Until now. If he couldn't beat them, why not join them?

"I also thought: I've been on the road for years, chasing these deadbeats, and what do I have to show for it? No time with my family. Everybody else is getting rich—and I'm taking home a lousy salary. When I could be . . ."

Four years after he'd joined MCI, Pavlo was sitting with his wife on a Cayman Islands beach, smoking Cohiba cigars, and thinking that life had never been sweeter. He'd finally made it.

At MCI, Pavlo had learned to obey orders, even when they were repugnant—such as firing the clerk—or stupid, such as issuing promissory notes. But spending most of his time with fraudsters and cheats, he learned to conform—to them. They ripped the company off; so would he. They operated without concern for anyone but themselves, and so could he. Despite a moral upbringing and a nagging sense that he was doing the wrong thing, Pavlo conformed to the crooks around him. At the time, he said, it was as if he'd lost sight of everything he was and everything he stood for.

Stanley Milgram distinguished clearly between obedience and conformity. Whereas obedience involves complying with the orders of a formal authority, conformity is the action of someone who "adopts the habits, routines and language of his peers, who have no special right to direct his behavior."[2] Milgram knew what he was talking about; he had been a student of Solomon Asch, the great American psychologist of conformity who, in the 1950s, had conducted a series of experiments that demonstrated just how readily individuals will conform to a group.[3]

In his experiments, Asch assembled college students for a simple test: Shown a single vertical black line of a certain length, they needed to identify which of three separate lines matched it in length. All but one of the students had been told beforehand to choose an obviously "wrong" line. The isolated student gave his opinion last. In nearly 40 percent of the cases, the isolated student chose the obviously wrong answer. Repeated trials of the experiment showed that only a small minority—8 percent—could be counted on always to conform and only about a third could be counted on never to conform but the vast majority of us—58 percent—will, under certain conditions, conform. Under social pressure, most of us would simply rather be wrong than alone.

The distinguishing feature of conformity is that it is implicit and it feels voluntary; after all, no one is telling us to choose the wrong line and there is no legitimate or formal reason to do so. Just as we prefer to spend time with people like ourselves, so we like to fit in. When we find that we don't fit in, we can change whom we associate with or change ourselves. Conforming is the choice—sometimes conscious, sometimes not—to change ourselves.

Since Asch, a great deal of work has been done trying to discover whether some people are more likely than others to conform—whether there is a "conforming personality." Not surprisingly, it's been found that people in general are more likely to conform to those of higher status than to mere peers: we'd rather conform to models of success.[4] Members of minority groups are likely to conform when they are the sole member of their minority. Unlike in Asch's study, when the experiment was repeated at the University of Oregon in 1979 men were found to be more likely to conform than women. Perhaps most interestingly, those who conformed were more likely to believe in external factors, such as luck, chance, or fate; those who believed that they alone had control over their lives were less likely to choose the wrong line. But, just as when Asch conducted his original experiment, when those conforming were shown their error, they all responded with astonishment: "Oh, god, I must be blind! What's the matter with me . . ."[5]

Competitive environments seem to exacerbate conformity. Pavlo had always felt keenly that he wasn't quite as smart, quite as sophisticated, as some of his peers, but he was determined to match them.

"So I have an MBA from Mercer, which is a small private college. And some of the others are from Northwestern, Wharton. So they think they're better than me—and maybe I think they're better than me. So what can I do to make myself better? We judged our effectiveness by how many hours we worked—so I'd come in at four A.M. and leave at eight P.M. If I see there are already cars in the parking lot, I wonder, should I get in at three A.M.? You get so competitive that the hours or the numbers aren't enough, so you start talking about how many e-mails you get a day, how many frequent-flyer miles you have. I'm platinum on Delta—are you?"

Companies foster this kind of competitiveness because they believe it will bring out the best in people. And they put employees into teams because a diverse group of individuals is thought to be more likely to make a better decision than one person alone.[6] But the problem is that the superiority of group collaboration starts to wane when individuals influence each other, which, in teams and corporate cultures, they inevitably do.

"When I was at Lehman, if you didn't fit in, you just weren't there," recalled Brad Ruderman, a veteran of the defunct firm. "I mean, the mentality of the business culture there—it was their way or no way."

Ruderman sits in a Los Angeles synagogue wearing flip-flops, shorts, and a T-shirt. He's forty-six and his hair is only just beginning to gray. He has beautiful manners but also, like Pavlo, an air of sadness that is strangely touching. Far from boastful, he describes his years in investment banking with a mixture of nostalgia and bafflement.

"I was a blank slate when I got in there," he recalls. "I had a job in investment management and one day I met a friend who worked two floors down in sales and trading. When I walked onto his floor I saw a situation I couldn't believe: energetic people just knocking the cover off the ball; energy, activity, just the most amazing scene to behold, and I said, 'What's going on here?' He hooked me up with the managing director downstairs and I was able to start and work my way up. And I was one of them."

Ruderman had grown up on the west coast, where his father enjoyed a successful career in the securities industry. But Ruderman never thought he was quite top tier; he hadn't gone to Harvard or Wharton, he'd graduated from UCLA. So when he joined Lehman Brothers, he felt he had to prove himself.

"The people I'd work with were from Harvard, Yale, Princeton; all Ivy League people. Only two or three of us were non–Ivy League and I was gonna get them! The rewards of belonging—well, it was everything! The self-satisfaction of knowing what you had accomplished monetarily but also intellectually and that you had joined a club, a group of people seen as the best and the brightest—that was something money can't buy. When you're twenty-nine and you have a direct phone extension to the vice chairman of the firm; it doesn't get much better. It is every cliché rolled into one. For someone with low self-esteem, this was the way to show I belonged."

As a child, Ruderman had been a good boy, looking up to his father, working hard to get good grades and stay out of trouble. He was, he says, always looking for a pat on the back and validation, always feeling a cut below his expectation of himself.

"And then I get into Lehman and it is so competitive as to boggle the mind! We're all on commission and every day of the week, our prior day's commission would be posted on the window of the managing director's office. So every day you walk into work your net income is posted for everyone to see. If that doesn't foster competition for someone already competitive, what would? Of course, that's what it's for. For someone like me, if you're not up there somewhere near the top, it's a disaster. You have to do something because otherwise, well, you're nothing."

The minimum Ruderman felt he had to earn was $100,000 a month—anything less and he was a loser. But if he'd made $140,000 in July, then anything below $120,000 in August would be a flop, too. Every month, he needed a bigger and bigger hit to stay in the gang.

"I was so motivated to gain acceptance. It wasn't greed. I didn't need anything. I had a car. A house. Once I had that, I had what I needed. It wasn't about stuff. It was about my personal scoreboard with everyone else. Sometimes there'd be three days left in the month and I hadn't hit last month's target, so I'd push the envelope to do some things not always in the best interest of my client. I lost all morals, all ethics, in the interest of staying in the gang."

He got to the point, he says, where he really didn't care about his clients, only about the commissions he earned. Of course, the firm always said that client interests came first, but in the competitive environment in which Ruderman worked, what came first was fitting into the Lehman culture. To an outsider, one of the more bizarre features of the gang in this investment bank was the preponderance of gambling.

"You would walk into the restroom and see racing forms on the floor—because that's what everyone did in their downtime! There was nothing hidden about it. Then there were huge poker games going on after work, twice a week maybe. It would cost fifty thousand dollars to buy in. We would bet on anything that moved, like which window washer would finish first. Any time you take a chance, that is gambling."

Getting sucked into the poker game meant that now Ruderman was working hard to hold his own in two highly competitive environments. When he returned to the west coast to start his own firm, he became a big fish in a small pond, taking investments from Larry Ellison, CEO of Oracle, and from Michael Milken's brother, Lowell. CNNMoney even quoted him as an authority on financial bubbles.

> "Everybody is in a bubble," said Brad Ruderman, managing partner at the Beverly Hills, Calif.-based hedge fund Ruderman Capital Partners. "Everybody that missed the stock market bubble is intent on identifying the next one. There are people almost daily talking about a housing bubble—but every home that's getting built, people are moving into right away. Is that a bubble?"[7]

Desperate to stay and look successful in a town where he was surrounded by the rich and famous, Ruderman used his family connections to get new clients and new money to start his own fund. Most of them, he says, were just like him: professionals who'd done well, upper class, well educated.

"There's such cachet involved in being part of an exclusive group of investors. I managed a fund with limited entry and my investors walked around their country club saying "The economy is in disarray but I have Brad Ruderman managing my money!" And I'd walk around talking about the people whose money I managed. And we all—there was a kind of reflected glow!"

The glow began to dim when the market went down and Ruderman couldn't maintain high rates of return. But to stay in the club, he couldn't admit that to anyone. So he misrepresented his results and hoped that something—gambling, lottery tickets—would provide enough cash to keep his place secure. But he was in over his head and in April 2009, the SEC obtained a court order halting his hedge-fund fraud.

"It wasn't that I didn't know what was going on. I have intellect. But I couldn't see any other life. I had to keep it going because—I mean, if I wasn't part of this, what was I? What else was there?"

In 2010, Ruderman was sentenced to 121 months in jail. Having felt that he would lose everything if he did not fit in, he discovered too late that conformity itself had cost him everything.

It's easy, and perhaps comforting, to look at people like Pavlo or Ruderman, condemn them for their white-collar crimes, and imagine that they're utterly different from us. But the powerful urge to belong, to which they succumbed, isn't a criminal urge but a human one. It runs very deep because our self-esteem is delicately dependent on what society thinks of us. Every morning, Brad Ruderman confronted a brutal announcement of his worth on his boss's door; that was enough, he said, to torment him. But in a 2007 study, psychologists at Tufts and Princeton experimented with something far more subtle. They invited forty-six female college students to take an Implicit Association Test which measured self-esteem. Some of the students were overweight and of these, some were supervised by an experimenter wearing a T-shirt that read "everyBODY is beautiful," while the others were supervised by an experimenter wearing a plain T-shirt. Would the self-esteem of the overweight students be influenced by the mere sight of a supportive T-shirt?[8]

Of course it was. The one-time expression of an egalitarian attitude about weight on the T-shirt of an experimenter was enough to improve the self-esteem of the overweight women. While Pavlo and Ruderman were receiving hundreds of thousands of dollars as signals that told them they were part of the in-crowd, even as indirect an expression of support as a T-shirt slogan might have made them feel better about themselves.

There is a physical reality to the pain that we feel when we are excluded. Uncomfortable feelings of social exclusion and physical pain arise, in part, from the same regions of the brain, and the same neurochemicals that regulate physical pain also control the psychological pain of social loss. When we form and validate our social relationships, this stimulates the production of opioids that make us feel great. (When relationships dissolve, likewise, opioids aren't produced and we feel awful.) As the pioneering psychopharmacologist Jaak Panksepp put it, "social affect and social bonding are in some fundamental neurochemical sense opioid addictions."[9] In other words, our desire to seek social connections with others comes from chemical rewards as well as social ones.[10]

We can all remember how this feels from school days: the fun of being part of a clique, or the misery of being left out. The silent treatment, being shunned or "sent to Coventry" (or, within the penal system, being sent to solitary confinement)—these are all forms of punishment because they make us feel cut off from sources of power and self-esteem. However independent we may be (or want to be), we know that we can achieve little alone; to be excluded is to be both lonely and impotent. But when we gang together in like-minded groups, we become more effective, learn shortcuts, and feel ourselves validated.

Conformity is compelling because much of our sense of life's meaning depends on other people. Walt Pavlo felt like an idiot because he didn't have any of the measures of success valued by the people he spent most of his time with; Brad Ruderman had no coherent sense of his own life without the approbation of his peers. Both conformed because, by doing so, they could join a group that appeared to give their lives meaning and respect. Even though both were aware that what they were doing was wrong, their need to belong blinded them to alternatives and consequences. And just as our sense of well-being may be sufficiently fragile to be influenced by T-shirt slogans, so our sense of leading a meaningful life hinges crucially on being included.

Cyberball is mostly known as a 1980s arcade game, first released by Atari and maintained, to this day, for lovers of retro video games. Multiple players, each on a separate computer console, can throw a ball back and forth. But there's another version, one that was refined by psychologists with the aim of studying social exclusion. Using this software, you can pit volunteers against each other or against preprogrammed players who will behave as you need them to. So you can play this cyberball with lots of players or, as in one experiment, with just one real participant who, after a brief period of inclusion, is slowly but surely ostracized. This experiment wasn't designed to prepare students for college life or investment banking; it was designed to measure how 121 individuals respond when they're not part of the game.[11]

In the experiment, after the experience of ostracism, the volunteers took a test, the Kunzendorf No Meaning Scale, which assesses the extent to which life is viewed as meaningless (e.g. "Life is a cruel joke" or "I don't care if I live or die"). As you might expect, the excluded players were more likely to feel their lives to be meaningless. A similar experiment, but with real people delivering positive or negative feedback, showed similar results: Those who were rejected not only found less value in life; they also felt no desire even to search for new meaning. The experience of exclusion left them feeling hopeless and demotivated.

The Florida State University team that conducted these studies devised several more, but they all led to the same conclusion: Ostracism makes individuals feel they lack purpose, have less control over their lives, are less good moral beings, and lack self-worth. Those high school cliques aren't uniquely adolescent experiences: Human beings hate being left out. We conform because to do so seems to give our life meaning.

This is so fundamental a part of our evolutionary makeup that it is strong enough to make us give the wrong answers to questions, as in Asch's line experiments, and strong enough to make us disregard the moral lessons we've absorbed since childhood. The carrot of belonging and the stick of exclusion are powerful enough to blind us to the consequences of our actions.

Once we conform, there are many rewards. Not just Cayman Islands bank accounts and media coverage, but tiny, daily reinforcements that come from being with the in-crowd. Of these, perhaps the most profound is jargon, the secret language that identifies those in the know, reinforcing the bonds of conformity. All groups use acronyms, nicknames, and abbreviated technical language to communicate quickly but also, subliminally, to reinforce belonging: We know what we're talking about but no one else does.

In the thousands of hours of recorded phone conversations by Enron power traders, what's most striking (after the criminality of the deals they're discussing) is their language: not just the code names of illegal power contracts (Get Shorty, Death Star, and Fat Boy) nor the saturation of language in expletives, but the pervasive derogation of anyone or anything that is *not* Enron, from "little old grandmothers" to "dumb consultants" to the whole state of California: "Best thing that can happen, fucking earthquake, let that thing float out to the Pacific . . . they're so fucked." There's even tacit recognition of the company operating as a quasi-cult, in repeated references to "drinking the Kool-Aid." The sense of belonging to a superior team was so strong that no one seems to have remembered that the real people who conformed by drinking the Kool-Aid (in the Jonestown massacre) all died.

Nicknames operate in the same way as jargon: denominating the in-crowd from the outsiders. If you don't have a nickname, you clearly aren't an important member of the group. If you do have one, then that provides some status; and, of course, if you are the person doling out nicknames then you're the most powerful of all. Many contemporary accounts of George W. Bush's White House illustrated this dynamic in action, where a nickname bestowed by the president was a sign of favor even if some of the names ("Turd Blossom" for Senior Advisor Karl Rove, "Big Time" for Vice President Dick Cheney, and "Fredo" for Attorney General Alberto Gonzales) didn't seem especially complimentary.

Aggressive, cultish language is characteristic of highly competitive, deeply conformist organizations, as Frank Partnoy recalled when writing about his time as a derivatives trader at Morgan Stanley.[12] Partnoy arrived shortly after an internal coup had placed John Mack—"Mack the Knife"—at the top of the firm. Mack had displaced Robert Greenhill, whose supporters had been known as the "Branch Dividians" [sic], named after the Branch Davidian religious cult best known for the siege at Waco, Texas. "This kind of aggressive fervor was new to me. I had never belonged to a militia before. The salesmen at First Boston might have played practical jokes on their clients, but they certainly hadn't discussed firing shotguns at them or blowing them up or ripping their faces off. In contrast, Morgan Stanley was a savage cult."

Partnoy found the pull of the cult irresistible. Before long, he was as eager to rip someone's face off or blow someone up as any of his peers. He honed his killer instincts at the Fixed Income Annual Sporting Clays Outing (FIASCO for short) but he was dimly aware that he had started to become just like his boss, nicknamed "Scarecrow."

"I wondered how much I had changed in the past months. Scarecrow's influence was pervasive and I suspected we were becoming more and more like him. Why were two intelligent young men awake before dawn on a dreary April day, excited about sloshing through the mud in the pouring rain so that we could, if we were lucky, pump a few pounds of birdshot into little pieces of clay? What was happening to us?"[13]

What was happening to Partnoy turns out to be physiologically interesting. Asch's conformity experiments have puzzled psychologists and neuroscientists for years, but now the development of fMRI technology allows them to study the brain at the point at which it conforms.

In 2005, neuroscientist Gregory Berns and a team of researchers at Emory University placed thirty-two "normal, right-handed volunteers" into an fMRI brain scanner and asked them to compare not lines, but three-dimensional objects.[14] In one version of the experiment, they had to decide by themselves which two objects were the same. In another, they decided after knowing what their fellow participants had decided. And in a third version, they cast their vote after knowing what a computer had decided. What the scientists sought to discover wasn't whether the volunteers would conform; they knew by now how likely it was that they would. Instead, they wanted to know what kind of brain activity was involved. If, in the act of conforming, activity in the prefrontal cortex was dominant, this would indicate that conformity was the result of conscious decision making. But if activity centered in the occipital and parietal regions of the brain, then that would suggest that conformity was an act of perception—that social influence had altered what the volunteer *saw*.

The three-dimensional test was harder than Asch's and so the participants made more mistakes, even without any external input. But they conformed at the same rates. And when they did so, there was *no* activity in the prefrontal cortex—that is, a conscious decision was not being made. The brain's activity centered on those areas of the brain responsible for perception. In other words, knowing what the group saw *changed* what the participants saw; they became blind to the differences.

The scientists concluded that the areas of the brain responsible for perception are altered by social influences. What we see depends on what others see. That was a remarkable enough finding. But several other insights emerged from this experiment. Knowledge of the group's decision seemed to reduce the mental load on the volunteers; less thinking took place when they knew what the others thought. A good match could stop thinking because it felt right. So instead of the group benefiting from the collective wisdom of many, in fact what it got was reduced thoughtfulness from each one.

When asked in a debriefing questionnaire how they explained their conforming errors, the participants had no sense of having conformed; they believed that they had all reached the same decision purely seren-dipitously. They may have thought that they'd made a free choice where in fact, they had not. Just as Asch and Milgram had surmised, the conforming decision was not experienced, not felt at all, but was entirely implicit.

Furthermore, in the rarer examples of a participant taking an inde-pendent stand against the crowd, something else happened: the amyg-dala, the area of the brain that governs emotions, became highly active. Something tantamount to distress seemed to take place. Inde-pendence, it seems, comes at a high cost.[15]

Berns's findings have all kinds of interesting applications, from the profound to the trivial. Studying teenage taste in popular music, the same researchers found that a big determinant is anxiety about not matching the taste of the in-crowd. The same may be applied to all kinds of fads and tastes: Do you read the new Dan Brown novel be-cause you want to—or because you worry about being left out of the discussion? Does the little black dress make you feel good because it suits you, or because it reduces your anxiety in a crowd? To what ex-tent did clients who invested with Brad Ruderman or Bernard Madoff do so because they carefully considered their options or because they wanted to belong to the same club? How far are we capable of even scrutinizing our choices, never mind summoning the emotional en-ergy to make them? How often in life are we really just going along for the ride?

Of course, we all assimilate to a degree; society would cease to func-tion if we did not. But one of the biggest risks of conformity, according to the psychologist Irving Janis, is that our sense of belonging (which makes us feel safe) blinds us to dangers and encourages greater risk-taking. He cited the example of Picher, Oklahoma, a mining town that was, at one time, the largest producer of lead and zinc in the world. Residents were proud of the fact that bullets for two world wars had

been made from lead in their mines. But the mines were so extensive
that some of them ran underneath the town. In February 1950, some
two hundred residents were told to evacuate because of the imminent
danger of a cave-in. The city fathers just laughed; one attended a Lion's
Club meeting wearing a parachute, just to show how silly the rumors
were. Unfortunately the other inhabitants in Picher followed their lead,
costing some of the men and their families their lives when the town
center collapsed days later.

Irving Janis was working in the 1970s, well before the advent of
fMRI scanners, but he hypothesized that lack of vigilance and excessive
risk-taking are a form of "group derangement." He argued that this
kind of behavior could be found in any kind of group. Most famously,
he outlined his hypothesis in detailed studies of military disasters: the
Bay of Pigs, the Korean War, Pearl Harbor, and the escalation of the
Vietnam War. Well before the neuroscience was available to support
his theory, Janis believed that, in a group, the pressure to maintain a
consensus results in less thinking. Members don't look for information
to confirm or disconfirm. "Selective bias is shown in the way the
group reacts to factual information, mass media, experts, and outside
critics. They spend little time deliberating the obstacles to the plan and
therefore fail to work out contingency plans." And he concluded by
summarizing a groupthink "law" that is the central irony lying at the
heart of all corporate cultures: "The more amiability and esprit de corps
among the members of a policy-making in-group, the greater is the
danger that independent critical thinking will be replaced by groupthink, which is likely to result in irrational and dehumanizing actions
directed against out-groups."[16] The downside of the cozy feeling of
togetherness is that everyone's less vigilant and more vulnerable to bad
and dangerous decisions.

Groups subject to groupthink typically imagine themselves invulnerable, as did the city fathers of Picher, Oklahoma. They rationalize
warnings out of existence and believe passionately in the moral superiority of their group. Enemies and outsiders tend to be demonized
and dissenters are subjected to immense pressure to conform. Dissent
is rare and difficult because self-censorship mostly expunges it and
because consensus and unity are deemed the ultimate good. In most
organizations, the good team player is implicitly defined as the person
who goes along with the team, not the one who asks hard questions.
I've even heard boards discuss how, and why, they are invulnerable to

groupthink, oblivious to the irony inherent in their confidence. In fact, of course, being a truly good team player involves having the confidence to dissent—but this is rarely what's implied in this trite accolade.

Serving on the Bear Stearns board of directors, Henry Bienen, the president of Northwestern University, learned just how prized board unanimity can be. Completing an annual questionnaire about the board's effectiveness, he opined that some meetings seemed somewhat perfunctory, short on discussion and debate. He was subsequently subjected to what he called a "woodshed" discussion when he was roundly chastised by Jimmy Cayne, the same CEO who had rejected Pat Lewis's risk-assessment model. Bienen quickly saw that criticism was not welcome and he was not invited to stand for re-election when his term expired.[17]

Just before the UK bank HBOS was taken over, I chaired a panel in the City of London about board governance. Taking part was Dennis Stevenson, then chairman of HBOS. Those of us on the panel were pretty amazed when he turned up at all; everyone knew the bank teetered on the edge of collapse. But he did more than turn up: He eulogized the outstanding board he chaired, citing as evidence the fact that, even in this crisis, "we are as one." He seemed oblivious to the notion that the "unity" of his board may have been a contributing factor in the bank's mess in the first place.

Since Irving Janis first published his hypothesis in 1972, it has been applied to a wide range of decisions, from the launch of New Coke to the Iraq War. The emphasis within the Bush White House on loyalty and consensus meant that dissent, dissonant data, or disconfirming information could not be entered into discussions. The desire to be part of the in-crowd, at the center of power, played heavily against discursive, exploratory debate.[18] As Scott McClellan, a Bush spokesperson and fan, wrote, "[Bush] failed to spend enough time seeking independent input from a broad range of outside experts, those beyond the White House bubble who had firsthand experience on the ground in Iraq, and—perhaps most important—those with different points of view, including those who disagreed with his policies. The failure to open up the Bush White House to fresh perspectives in the second term was already beginning to exact a price."[19] Otherwise intelligent human beings, with the nation's best interests at heart, steadily blinded themselves to alternatives and to the consequences of their choices.

Thinking themselves masters of the universe, they became slaves to their group.

But the concentric circles of conformity and groupthink may ripple wider still. Individuals influence each other, reducing thought. Groups influence other groups, pushing each other into positions of greater extremism. But in a competitive marketplace, the moral dislocation that Ruderman and Pavlo and Partnoy experienced may spread to entire institutions and industrial sectors. That's certainly what it looks like when you examine the chain reaction that led to the implosion of the mortgage industry in the United States in 2008.

In California, Florida, and most of the northeastern states, house prices appreciated at an average rate of 10 percent in the years 2001 to 2006. Because, during that same time, Alan Greenspan at the Federal Reserve was bringing interest rates down to record lows (reaching 1 percent by 2003), you didn't need to be a great mathematician to understand that you would get a higher rate of return on your house than on your savings account. So home ownership ballooned, reaching an all-time high of 69.2 percent in 2006. But many of these new purchases weren't really homes; they were investments.

"I started buying houses because, well, that's what everyone was doing!" Looking somewhat abashed, Deborah Laird still struggles in her effort to capture how she felt just a few years earlier. A high school science teacher with a pension, she'd never been a very active investor. Left a small sum of money by her mother, she had put it into mutual funds that, after the tech bust of 2000, had delivered disappointing returns. Laird wasn't greedy; she had always lived modestly and remains rather proud of her thrifty lifestyle. But in 2003, that started to change.

"All you ever heard was how much money people were making, selling houses, buying houses. I'd lived in the same house for fifteen years; I started to feel stupid! I reasoned with myself that it wasn't like I was actively helping anybody by staying out of the market. So I decided to trade up."

Laird sold her Boston apartment and bought herself a house. She was surprised by how much money she'd made. And it had been so easy.

"The mortgage was simple. Finding properties wasn't hard. And after teaching physics all day, it was fun to have something else to talk about in the staff room. I realized that everyone was doing it and it was, well, it was kinda fun!"

By 2006, Laird wasn't just a science teacher any more; now she was a landlord, with three apartments and two houses. But whereas being a schoolteacher and a property investor might have made Laird peculiar years ago, now it made her part of the club.

"And then I had a cancer scare. It wasn't a big deal—I mean, now I can see it wasn't a big deal. But at the time, my god, I was scared. And I just stopped everything. I mean—it's not like I needed another house! And between appointments and scans and teaching and looking after all the properties, I was just burned out. And the money seemed so stupid—if I was going to die next year, what would it bring me? So I just stopped."

Her home today is comfortable but not ostentatious. It's decorated mostly with pictures of nephews and nieces; the sofas are dotted with cushions she embroidered herself. It's not the headquarters of a property tycoon. But Laird feels she had a lucky escape.

"Looking back, I feel like I went kind of mad. It was like: property was the hot thing and I was doing the hot thing and everyone was doing the hot thing and we were all in it together. And I have *never* been someone who ever cared about that stuff before! Now I think my cancer was a kind of warning, or a blessing. Because if it hadn't come along—I might never have stopped. And where would I be now?"

Halfway across the country, in Plano, Texas, Catherine Clark (not her real name) had just been hired as a senior executive at Countrywide, the company that had supplied mortgages for Deborah Laird's tiny property empire. With deep experience at a senior level in large corporations, Clark had an exemplary résumé and had been attracted to Countrywide by its entrepreneurial energy and ostensible appetite for change.

"They told me they wanted my experience of different corporate cultures in other places I'd worked. But once I got there—they just wanted me to conform. Working at Countrywide, there wasn't a lot of change and no desire for change. There was no real liking for new people. Everyone talked about the 'Countrywide way' and that's what you were supposed to stick to. It meant that newcomers were all frustrated—they wanted to change, and had often been recruited for change—but we were just shut down."

The company needed her to bring in more senior executives, to deepen the talent pool and diversity of the team. But once again, she was frustrated.

"I found an African American from Bank of America—perfect for the position. And my boss says, "Why would we consider him? He would be hard to understand.' In other words: he's not like us. There was another potential candidate from WAMU [Washington Mutual]. He was very well qualified but he was gay."

What shocked Clark most was the lack of dissent within the organization. "Where I'd worked before, my most trusted advisors would argue with me. No one was afraid of conflict. People would scream at each other—and then the next day, they'd be playing golf together. It wasn't that it was a culture of screamers, either; it's just that dissenting voices were okay.

"At Countrywide, in meetings, there was no dissent. There were lots of whispers afterwards, but no argument in the meetings. In the Consumer Markets Division, Joe was known for his tirades. You would be called to his office, he'd scream and yell at you with his door open so everyone could see. So everyone got the message: toe the line or else."

Clark started as an outsider and left because she felt she couldn't accomplish anything. The overwhelming conformity of the aggressive sales culture, however, was part of the appeal to many who stayed.

"I love this business!" says Pamela Vincent, who stayed with Countrywide until it merged with Bank of America. "Housing is an important American value. There is something worthwhile in what we do, helping someone buy their first home. And I love the sales culture; there's a lot of celebration, a lot of deadlines, a lot of ups and downs and it's exciting because this is where the money is made. Each month you start from zero and you can see the money made producing loans."

Vincent isn't persuaded that anyone did anything wrong. She defends NINA loans (available to those with no income and no assets) as "great for the self-employed." All she will concede is that the company shouldn't have let sub-prime lending extend quite so far or expected appreciation to continue indefinitely.

"At Countrywide, we weren't the first to do sub-prime mortgages but we did start applying sub-prime practices because we continued to see housing appreciation. The bedroom ATM! The house goes up—why not take a new mortgage? These kinds of loans can be very valuable in the hands of a very astute homeowner who is economically savvy. My former brother-in-law put four girls through college, just refinancing his house. Lots of people did that. Appreciation was thought to cover all ills."

But didn't she think that, some day, market appreciation of properties would have to stop—or at least slow down?

"Well, no one else thought they would. And it's like Chuck Prince at Citigroup said: You had to keep dancing. Why wouldn't you? It was fine as long as everyone else kept doing it too!"

That infamous quote from the CEO of Citigroup perfectly describes how conformity works in the marketplace: Everything's fine as long as no one dissents, bucks the trend, or fails.

Vincent worked in retail mortgages. In Florida, Jim Kennedy saw what was happening at the wholesale end of the market.

"With wholesale mortgages, you are the middle man," says Kennedy. "The retailers originate the deals and we fund them. That meant we saw what happened when you put a lot of loans together. And what we saw was a lot of fraud—like seven homes all being bought by one guy as an owner-occupier. I'd report it back to the broker and he'd just say, 'Jim, we are just focused on getting the sale.' So I'd report it to headquarters and all they ever did was turn a blind eye. We took it to upper management because it left a sour taste in the mouth. We knew what was going on. And what did management say? If we didn't do it, someone else would. All they cared about was market share. It was just like a game of chicken, waiting to see who'd bail out first. No one was gonna go first."

"There was endless willful blindness," says Michael Sarnoff, chief credit officer at a large Midwest bank. "The entire food chain from borrower to lender to securitizer to auditor to rating agency to end investor. They all went along for years, they all got sucked in and conformed to perpetuate the madness."

Sarnoff worked in the mortgage industry for twenty years. His vantage point allowed him to see how, at every step of the way, all the participants conformed to the same errors.

"In 2003, I think we hit an all-time high in terms of volume. The sub-prime lenders were multiplying and everyone knew the loans were just stupid: [lending] to people with terrible credit, no income, occupancy fraud, income fraud—but nobody cared because appreciation was taking place. Then they all started throwing wood on the fire in the form of additional lending so you could lend to anybody, to a dead person! The amount of crime in the mortgage industry was just incredible but even if you segment that out, you still, today, have incredible greed and stupidity among consumers who are buying property they can't afford."

Theoretically, the market was hugely diversified: a plethora of borrowers, lenders, securitizers, auditors, and rating agencies competing with each other was supposed to spread risk and generate a wide diversity of products and business models. But competition among the participants was so fierce that instead they all copied each other. The drive to compete just created more and more uniformity. It wasn't just that everyone was working from the same assumptions; they all used the same software.

"Desktop Underwriter is software that has about a hundred fields and you put the data in and it produces either an approval or a caution," says Sarnoff. "You can't close a loan with a caution. So it's really the industry standard—everybody uses it—so everybody was judging the same people the same way. The software was written by employees at Freddie Mac and Fannie Mae; they were right there at the table and because they're such a force in creating standards in the marketplace, they just perpetuated it."

That so much of the market was fraudulent perturbed Sarnoff and he'd complain to anyone who would listen. But even so, and despite his seniority and proven competence, he couldn't change the game. In order to compete, he needed to be able to attract and retain a sales force. And no salesperson would stay working for Sarnoff if he or she didn't have the same chance to earn the huge commissions as their peers were making. So even at his own bank, Sarnoff sometimes had to turn a blind eye to the absurdity of NINA loans and the proliferation of fraud.

Nevertheless, he remains especially critical of the ratings agencies who were asked to grade the debt that was packaged up into mortgage-backed securities. "Moody's, Standard and Poor's were manipulating the data to keep securities going through, making them appear larger or more secure than they were. I knew people who'd rate a security and by the time the paperwork got through, all the data had been changed and falsified. The real problem was that since the seller paid for the rating, they didn't mind incompetent audit teams or falsified results, as long as they got their AAA ratings. I have friends on audit teams who'd see their final results changed. I wouldn't do it, but many did. Everyone was in on it. But it really was, if you can't beat 'em, join 'em."

And of course by the time the packaged securities reached Wall Street, there were plenty of traders to sell them and rip someone's face off.

Sarnoff says the last few years have been like watching a plague sweep through a town as, slowly but surely, each part of the industry succumbed to the same disease. This was conformity on an epic scale, as institution after institution caved in to the same thinking: if you can't beat 'em, join 'em; if we don't do it, someone else will; toe the line or else; you have to keep dancing.

What he was seeing was willful blindness amplified: individuals conforming to institutions that conform to the market. We may not have seen collaborative, collusive conformity on such a scale since the totalitarian regimes of the 1930s. This time, however, there were no dictators; there was only the market. And the central challenge of the episode is the revelation that the more competitive the market became, the more it also became uniform. What Pavlo and Ruderman and Partnoy saw on a personal level turned out to be true on a global scale: the more competitive a society becomes, the greater is the compulsion to conform.

With so many involved, did Michael Sarnoff think that any one person could be said to have been responsible? Who was blind?

"Insane consumers, greedy lenders, loan officers who'd do anything to get information through the system, poor underwriters who were no more than box checkers, a cheap labor force, Fannie Mae and Freddie Mac and a president who pressured them to increase home ownership, biased rating agencies, securitizers, and all the stupid investors who bought CDOs and CDOs squared," he says. "All equally blind. All greedy. There was just a horrible deterioration in the moral fabric of people. And a lot of wishful thinking. But the structure of the industry means no one feels responsible."

In their mutually reinforcing conformity, each of these businesses perpetuated and exacerbated each other's errors and flaws until they comprised a system that could not change without collapse. Though many claimed merely to be "obeying the market," no one had told them what to do; they merely had copied one another. What none of the experiments or the neuroscience or the biochemistry can tell us about conformity is how bad it feels when it goes wrong. Because in choosing to stick with the crowd, we steadily blind ourselves—to alternatives, to bad news, to doubt, to the individual values that we think are steady but turn out to also be susceptible—until we find ourselves dazed and confused in the dark.

8

BYSTANDERS

*"As I was leaving the tier that night, I was told that I didn't see shit.
And me being the person that I am—I try to be friends with
everybody—I said, 'See what? I didn't see nothing.' "*
—U.S. Army Specialist Jeremy Sivits on Abu Ghraib[1]

IN JANUARY 2001, Walt Pavlo pleaded guilty to wire fraud and
money laundering and was sentenced to two years in prison. It might
as well have been twenty, for he had lost everything: his job, his wife,
his family, most of all his sense of himself. The little boy who'd been
brought up to know the difference between right and wrong now had
to wrestle with the incontrovertible fact that good Walt had done bad
things. Who was he now? A bad-guy fraudster who'd burned through
shareholder cash partying like a rock star on the Cayman Islands? Or a
fundamentally good guy who had, somehow, lost himself?

Pavlo doesn't think many people with a conscience get away with
white-collar crime because, he says, you can't bear the reality of what
you've done. To this day, you can read the anguish on his face as he
struggles to reclaim the good man he always thought he was. He's
working again, for a small recycling firm that's glad to have someone
more qualified than they might be able to afford. But the battle still goes
on inside Pavlo's head. He's neat, well dressed, attentive, punctual—and
these things matter to him, disproportionately: every detail signals
whether he's still on track. He has to convince a tough jury: himself.
But he still isn't sure of the verdict.

When he got out of prison, Pavlo contacted Frank Abagnale, the famous fraudster whose life story was the subject of Spielberg's film *Catch Me If You Can*. Abagnale advised him to start talking to people about his experience. If you stay at it, Abagnale advised, you can be successful, but you have to have the right message. You have to bear the consequences of what you've done, and you have to go it alone. Pavlo took this advice and started teaching business-school students how easy it is to go wrong. He would give up to eight talks a day for a single fee. Punctilious about not making too much money, he didn't want to profit from his crime.

One day, he was giving a talk in South Dakota.

"It was very cold outside. I was talking to a bunch of sophomores and I smelled smoke. But I kept on with my talk. Ten minutes later, smoke started rolling in through the air vents. We evacuated the building. About ten minutes later, it turned out it was no big deal—just someone burning pizza boxes. But when we all came back in, I asked, 'How many of you smelled smoke and said nothing?' Everyone giggled and raised their hand. 'How come no one said anything?' Some said they didn't want to look stupid; others said they weren't sure it was smoke. But that is how it is in business. You smell the smoke. You know there's something wrong and you think: maybe it's just me, maybe I'm wrong—and you don't do anything. By the time there's a fire in the building, it's too late."

Although he didn't know it, Pavlo had witnessed an accidental reenactment of a famous experiment conducted in 1968 by two young psychologists, Bibb Latané and John Darley, in which they placed one, two, or three volunteers in a room and asked them to fill in a questionnaire. As they did so, the room slowly began to fill with smoke. The two psychologists wanted to know under which conditions the volunteers would be most likely to do something about the smoke: Were you more likely to respond to an emergency when alone or with confederates?

Their results were shocking. One person alone would, within two minutes, do something about the smoke: look for its source, check its temperature, go and get help. But when there were two people in the room, only one out of ten reported the smoke. The rest stayed there, doggedly filling out their questionnaires while coughing and rubbing their eyes. And when there were three people in the room—which the psychologists theorized should produce three times the response rate of one person—only one in twenty-four people reported the smoke within the first four minutes, even though, by then, they could scarcely see.[2]

Darley and Latané coined the phrase "bystander effect" to describe what they'd discovered. Their interest in the phenomenon had been sparked by the murder of a young New Yorker, Kitty Genovese, who was stabbed to death in the middle of a street in New York City in 1964. At the time, it was thought that up to as many as thirty-eight people had witnessed the attack, which had lasted more than thirty minutes, yet not one had so much as phoned the police. Preachers, news commentators, and politicians instantly pontificated about callous New Yorkers and inner-city anomie, but Darley and Latané were skeptical—and they were living in New York themselves at the time. Was it just New Yorkers who were especially venal—or would anyone respond passively to an emergency? Which, if any, of us was so superior?

The very first experiment isolated volunteers in booths and led them to think they were overhearing someone having an epileptic seizure. In cases in which the volunteers thought they alone knew what was happening, 85 percent reported the incident. But in cases in which the volunteers believed that others elsewhere would also know about the seizure, only a third did anything about it. The experiment indicated that the larger the number of people who witness an emergency, the fewer who will intervene.[3] Collectively, we become blind to events that, alone, we see readily.

In that first experiment, the witnesses knew others shared their knowledge, but they were isolated from one another because Latané and Darley wanted to rule out conformity as one of the explanations for the behavior, to focus on individual decisions. By the time they did their version of the experiment in the smoke-filled room, they knew that bystander behavior might be exacerbated by conformity but was not determined by it.

Their results provoked repetition in a flurry of variations, in which men and women, black and white, young and old were witness to all kinds of emergencies: robberies, faints, asthma attacks, screams, falls, crashes, and electric shocks.[4] They all confirmed the original thesis: the more people who witness an event, the less likely it is that any will respond to it. Even just thinking about other people reduces levels of altruism.

News headlines keep confirming their findings. The advent of cell phones should have made reporting incidents faster and easier, but they haven't changed behavior. In October 2009, a fifteen-year-old girl in Richmond, California, was raped by ten high school students, an event witnessed by at least twenty people.

There is no reason to conclude that the witnesses were exceptionally bad people. That's what Latané and Darley's work had proved. We are all likely to behave this way. When we are in groups, we see bad things happening but act as though we are blind to them. Just as we all think we won't obey Milgram's instructor, so we do not believe that we would be passive bystanders. But the evidence is against us.

Internet chat rooms have shown just how far bystander behavior can scale. In 1998, Larry Froistad, a twenty-nine-year-old computer programmer, confessed to two hundred people in a chat room for recovering alcoholics that he had set his house on fire to murder his five-year-old daughter.

"When she was asleep, I got wickedly drunk, set the house on fire, went to bed, listened to her scream twice, climbed out the window and set about putting on a show of shock and surprise."[5]

Only three of the two hundred members of the chat room reported him. Froistad was subsequently tried, convicted, and sentenced to forty years in prison. Subsequent studies of the behavior of more than four hundred chat groups just reinforced the bystander thesis: more people, less response. But one salient detail did emerge: you were more likely to get help if you could ask for your helper by name.

The bystander effect demonstrates the tremendous tension between our social selves and our individual selves. Left on our own, we mostly do the right thing. But in a group, our moral selves and our social selves come into conflict, which is painful. The nonintervening subjects of Darley and Latané's experiments had not, they said, *decided* not to intervene. Rather they were frozen in a state of indecision and conflict about whether and how to intervene. Looking for a way out of that discomfort, they choose the easier path, a kind of moral shortcut.

One of the initial explanations for bystander behavior was ambiguity: It can be hard to know quite what's happening or what response is most appropriate. But perhaps we are also ambiguous about our own role within the event. We hope that the situation isn't so dire that it needs our intervention. Perhaps it will pass or we've just misinterpreted it. Responding could provoke conflict and we don't like conflict. Conformity comes into this, too: I sure would look like an idiot if I rushed to help and it turned out to be nothing. Our fear of embarrassment is the tip of the iceberg that is the ancient fear of exclusion, and it turns out to be astonishingly potent. We are more likely to intervene when we are the sole witness; once there are other witnesses, we become anxious about doing the right thing (whatever that is), about being seen and being judged by the group.

A great deal of bystander behavior is trivial, or at least feels that way. You see a young employee being mocked by her peers for her dress sense. It doesn't matter to you, but being trivialized is professionally damaging—yet it's the rare boss or colleague that doles out clothing advice. Our most frequent exposure to bystander apathy occurs at work, where we see (or think we see) colleagues indulging in abusive, unsafe, or illegal activity. We don't want to be the ones to complain and, anyway, we might be wrong. Where this concerns clothing, it may not matter. But where it involves vulnerable, less powerful people, it can be highly dangerous. This emerges powerfully in a study of nurses who regularly observed a colleague, Annie, cruelly abusing patients.

"She had a really negative effect on patients, especially the elderly ones or those who were long-stay," one of the nurses, Sean, recalled. "Making a big deal about getting them a bed pan or helping them to the bathroom during the night meant a lot of them would stop taking anything to drink from late afternoon to ensure they didn't need the bathroom during the night . . . and yet dehydration is a big problem with elderly patients. And we had a number of patients who suffered a long, painful night because she had been really abrupt with them when they'd first asked for something for the pain, and they were too scared to ask again."[6]

Annie was the talk of the hospital; everyone—even those on other wards—knew she was a terrible nurse. But no one did anything. Some said she was intimidating: "When drunks were admitted to the ward, she never had any trouble from them. If even a big, drunk aggressive guy gets the vibe that he should behave himself or else, you can imagine how easily the rest of us were intimidated by her." They were afraid that if they did say anything, and nothing happened, working with her would only get worse. Others blamed themselves, hoping they could learn how better to work with Annie.

"At first, I thought of this as my problem," Sean admitted. "I was pretty new and I'm not the most assertive of people."

Some nurses made excuses for her, explaining what a hard life she had had, while others tried to focus on her redeeming qualities: she was good in a crisis (when caring takes a back seat). All the nurses tried to avoid working with her and they all talked about her. As in all workplace gossip, the fact that everyone knew what was going on was part of the problem.

"Knowing that colleagues were concerned and keeping an eye on her made me feel a bit better about it for quite a while," recalled another nurse, Mandy. "It was only gradually that it dawned on me that nothing had actually changed: She was no better, in fact she was probably getting worse." Responsibility for Annie was being diffused: Since everyone knew about it, in theory everyone was responsible for it—which means that they all wanted someone else to act. But by remaining passive, the nurses actually *reduced* the likelihood that anybody would bring about a positive solution.

Diffusion of responsibility—the rule of nobody—is a common feature of many large organizations, where almost nothing is done alone. Even one of the most famous whistleblowers of all time—Daniel Ellsberg—succumbed to it for a while.

Ellsberg started working in 1964 for U.S. Assistant Secretary of Defense for International Security Affairs John T. McNaughton "on secret plans to escalate the war in Vietnam, although both of us personally regarded these as wrongheaded and dangerous. Unfortunately, by decisions of President Johnson and Secretary [of Defense] McNamara, these plans were carried out in the spring of 1965."[7]

Despite his belief that the war was wrong, Ellsberg continued to work for the government. In 1967, he was assigned to work on the top-secret McNamara study of U.S. decision making in Vietnam—what came to be known as the Pentagon Papers, a seven-thousand-page analysis of twenty-three years of American policy in the region. Ellsberg kept hoping—quite reasonably—that those with access to the papers would read them; he personally urged Henry Kissinger to do so. He also kept hoping that someone else—any of the "scores of officials, perhaps a hundred" that had access to the papers—would give them to the Senate. Still no one did. It was not until 1971 that Ellsberg finally took action himself, risking life imprisonment by leaking them to the press.

That Ellsberg waited in no way undermines his courage; rather it illustrates how even a tremendously brave man could think, and hope, that someone else—with more authority, more power, more protection—would act. In Ellsberg's case, as in the more mundane case of the nurses, there were so many people who could act—or could be expected to act—that no one felt uniquely responsible for doing so.

Sometimes diffusion of responsibility can be no more than a fancy phrase for passing the buck. We take our cues from those above us—especially in hierarchical organizations—and if they do nothing, what are we supposed to do? We can always use our salary, our career, to justify turning a blind eye to what we know is wrong.

When she worked at Enron as a contract specialist, Lynn Brewer completed a legal brief concerning a large gas contract that she knew to be "a quarter-billion-dollar scam." Enron simply did not own the gas it had used as collateral; the company was in default of the agreement the day it entered into the deal. But no one else seemed worried by it. Brewer had the nerve to track down the detail—something no one expected her to do—but she had absorbed enough of the company's competitive ethos to know not to include details of the fraud in her brief. She agonized at length, knowing that ignoring the scam and helping to cover it up was wrong, but she was loathe to jeopardize her salary, her career, and the excitement of a new job. So she drafted the brief as though there were nothing wrong with it, and then, in a wonderful piece of displacement activity, deemed others to be the bystanders.

"Bound by attorney-client privilege and a legal code of ethics, going outside the company and blowing the whistle was not an option. It would cost us not only our jobs but our careers . . . Why hadn't the banks caught the minor missing detail? Or had they too been wooed by the promises of Enron's Yellow Brick Road the same way I had?"[8]

The "Yellow Brick Road" reference is germane. In 1997, Enron's mining and metals team had staged a holiday skit of *The Wizard of Oz.* Sherron Watkins played the Wicked Witch and the Wizard was played by Jere Overdyke in a scarlet satin pimp suit pretending to be the CFO, Andy Fastow.[9] Everyone could read the subtext: Just as the wizard is a fraud, so the company's financial wizardry was nothing more than smoke and mirrors. In the audience, everyone laughed knowingly—every one of them a bystander. They may have felt themselves merely passive witnesses to a crime too big for them to stop—but the reality was that, with every crooked contract, the Enron employees were validating their crooked corporation. The crucial point about by-standers is that they have potential influence, and their choice not to use it means that they aren't neutral but run the risk of morphing gently into perpetrators. A neutral stance isn't possible. After all, you can't bring down the sixth largest corporation in America without a great deal of help.

That everyone was well paid, that they all liked each other and had so much in common, that many were exhausted by long hours and global travel, all helped to secure their collusion. But what moral clarity they might have had was also severely confused by the intense ambiguity of their environment. Orientation videos and TV ads for Enron specifically celebrated the "defiant and the visionary." CEO Jeff Skilling and chairman Ken Lay deliberately set out to build a vast company that operated with the freedom and latitude of entrepreneurial start-ups. They actively scorned rules and regulations and encouraged competitive risk-taking. At the same time, they were spending a fortune lobbying Washington to get any inconvenient regulation abolished. It could be very hard, at any given time, to know whether a law was to be taken seriously, or merely an obstacle to be circumvented. The cliché "don't ask for permission, ask for forgiveness" was understood as license to do anything that generated revenue.

Such shifting sands make it intensely difficult to keep hold of any clear sense of moral norms. If everyone is doing crooked deals, and being rewarded for it, then what is normal? If everyone is taking moral shortcuts, where can you see signs for the main road? How can you maintain a sense of yourself as a good person if the definition of *good* keeps changing?

"As a child," says Walt Pavlo, "when you did things wrong, your parents said so. I know right from wrong. But as an adult when I was hiding money, I knew I was doing wrong but I was being rewarded and promoted! It's extremely confusing. You rationalize: it can't be that wrong if nobody's stopping me. So I'm going to call it okay because it fits my life model that good things happen to good people. Good things are happening and therefore I must be good."

Of course, Pavlo had a boss. Didn't the boss start to wonder how such huge debts managed to disappear? No. In a classic example of "don't ask, don't tell" his boss—who was, anyway, under a lot of pressure and exhausted—never asked: What are you doing and how are you doing it?

"If he had asked, that would have relieved me of so much pressure. It would have been a *relief* if he'd said anything!"

But instead the boss chose to be a bystander, too.

Bystander behavior need not always involve a crime. In companies, it is more often implicated in the failure to respond to strategic business threats. Classically, this is taught as the blindness of buggy-whip manufacturers to the all-too-obvious rise of the automobile, or as the myopia of U.S. television manufacturers to the emerging excellence of Japanese electronics. The cases are legion, but teaching the stories of these industrial train crashes never seems to prevent them.

In 1999, the advent of the Internet and the rise of digital music had all of the record labels in conniptions. Why were kids stealing their music? How could they be stopped? The music business, with its own history of corruption, nonetheless was determined to stop kids from ripping off its profits. Years before the iPod had even launched, kids were ripping CDs and sharing them—via e-mail, Napster, Kazaa, or any number of file-sharing sites. Nobody wanted to pay for music anymore; anything you wanted could be found for free somewhere online. The record companies dabbled in a few Internet initiatives but were too corrupt to make good partners for anyone. And they invested heavily in lobbying, hoping that their trade association, the Recording Industry Association of America, would buy enough friends in Washington to stop the future from happening. As profits melted before their eyes, torn between denial and aggression, they presented a disunited, incoherent front to a consumer base years ahead of them. Whatever they tried to do, it was always too late.

If you weren't in the music business, this was easy to see. And it didn't take a gigantic leap of the imagination to see that what was happening in music was just a glimpse of the future for the movie industry. But it hadn't happened to them yet. Broadband penetration in the late 1990s was still under 50 percent in the United States. Even though, theoretically, you could download a movie, in practice nobody had the patience to do it down phone lines. But the music business presaged the looming disaster lying in wait for the film business.

At any rate, that's what it looked like to me when I approached the studios with a proposal that was, in essence, a precursor of iTunes. Wouldn't it make sense to seize the initiative and learn about online distribution and consumption now, rather than wait to have it owned by someone else? At the time, I ran an online media business called iCAST. Well connected and extravagantly well funded, we had a lot of meetings in Hollywood; even if people didn't like or understand all of our ideas, they wanted our money.

I remember in particular one meeting with an army of executives from Disney, many of whom are still in place today. We laid out the threat, as we saw it, and proposed a number of ways we could work together to seize the initiative. I didn't recognize it at the time, but in this meeting, we witnessed the full panoply of bystander behavior. They all saw what was happening in the music business. They understood that the same crisis awaited their business. But no one was willing to take the risk of intervening. The market, they said, was ambiguous; no one knew for certain how digital entertainment would develop. And whose responsibility was it to take the first step?

Corporate politics meant that doing nothing would always be safer than recommending a bold course of action. Besides, the executives asked, if the strategic risk were real, wouldn't some of the other studios be doing something about it? If they weren't, why should Disney? Nobody in the room—though they were all proudly very senior—felt quite senior enough to make a decision. I remember sitting there thinking, in the 1980s, the TV networks were dubbed the "three blind mice" because of their failure to take the advent of cable seriously. Now the film studios were producing the remake.

You only have to mention the words *willful blindness* to hear the same story about a different industry: how beverage companies ignored the advent of vitamin drinks; packaged goods businesses don't think it matters whether products are environmentally sound; pharmaceutical companies don't pay attention to off-label prescribing; and gun manufacturers still pretend a secondary market (selling to kids and criminals) has nothing to do with them. The knowledge is there, spoken or unspoken, but the executives do nothing. In these cases, it is their livelihoods, not their lives, that are threatened—but their pattern of behavior is just the same as that of Kitty Genovese's neighbors.

These are classic business stories, because it is so human and so common for innovation to fail not through lack of ideas but through lack of courage. Business leaders always claim that innovation is what they want but they're often paralyzed into inaction by hoping and assuming that someone else, somewhere, will take the risk. They may see a looming crisis but, like the participants in Latané and Darley's experiments, they would rather continue earnestly to complete their questionnaires than get up and acknowledge that the room is full of smoke and they can no longer see. Just like the witnesses to a crime, once someone does seize the initiative, bystanders are left feeling anxious and uncomfortable, dimly aware that they missed their moment.

Nobody really knows if bystander behaviors are innate or learned, but they certainly start very young. Most children witness bullying at school, by teachers or peers or both, and feel uncomfortably grateful not to be the victim. They may even learn, as my son did, the invaluable life lesson of how to stay off of a bully's radar screen. But a salient characteristic of all bullying is that it craves an audience, which most kids, acting as bystanders, provide.

In recent years, the U.S. Department of Justice and the police have become very interested in bullying, calling it the most underreported safety problem on American school campuses.[10] Two thirds of school shooters who were still alive to report after the incident had previously been bullied; that on-campus shootings occur at all may, in some part, be attributed to the rage and frustration felt by the victim, for whom all bystanders are colluders.

Bystanders play a big part in bullying. Despite many campaigns, and the requirement that all British schools have an anti-bullying policy, a national survey into bullying in 2006 showed that 69 percent of schoolchildren said that they had been bullied, 87 percent of parents said that their children had been bullied, but 83 percent of teachers said that they had not seen bullying at their school.[11]

Bullying is, by its nature, hard to measure but it is ubiquitous, with Canadian rates at least as high as the UK's. Although Canada has laws against bullying, they don't seem to prevent stunts like "Kick a Ginger Day" which inspired over 4,700 Canadians to support the idea of tormenting red-headed people.

In many instances, bystanders act as "reinforcers," by either providing an encouraging audience or protecting the bully by their failure to intervene. Both types of bystander validate the bully by their very presence. Only 10 to 20 percent of witnesses ever provide any real help. Perhaps most disappointing of all is the police observation that bullying is seldom reported because children follow adult examples.

"It is at school that children learn to be bystanders," says Ervin Staub, professor of psychology at the University of Massachusetts, Amherst. Staub has devoted his life to the study of good and evil. He is himself a Holocaust survivor and his work on genocide and mass violence has led him to work in Rwanda, Burundi, and the Congo, as well as in New Orleans and Los Angeles. His interest in bullying derives from his observation that all mass violence requires, and is also inflamed by, bystanders. It's for that reason that he conducted a lengthy study of bullying in schools, which is where, he believes, the behavior starts.

"Sadly, teachers don't intervene often," says Staub. "It turns out that some teachers think kids should take care of their own business. So they don't do anything. But this is problematic because as adults, we should provide kids with guidance. When we are passive, that sends a message that there's no need to act. I very much believe that bystanders give perpetrators and bullies a message that what they are doing is accepted. It tends to make them believe that they are supported."

In western Massachusetts, Staub has begun to develop a curriculum to teach kids how better to respond when they see bullying. Its goal, he says, is to create a sympathetic but unaccepting attitude to bullies.

"We try to help the students understand the impact on kids who are bullied; kids don't process that necessarily. And we train them to engage. They don't have to do it alone, just turn to a friend and say, 'Hey, we need to do something here, we have to stop this.' We also try to get them to turn towards and support the victim because the passivity of bystanders makes victims feel there is no sympathy for them. You know, it often takes very, very little to stop a bully; people just don't realize the power that they have."

So far, Staub has run his program only once, but early indications are that students emerge more confident in ways in which they can and will intervene. He'll be running it again because he wants those kids to understand the power they have. Staub is dedicated to understanding the processes of mass violence in order to understand how to prevent it.

"I have done work in Rwanda for many years now and one of the things we do there is try to help people understand the influences that lead to violence, what are the social conditions and psychological changes that people undergo. By providing this kind of information, I believe it is less likely that people close their eyes. They know what to look for. Things that normally go under your radar, when you know what you are looking for, those things are likely to connect, to click in. You think: I have to pay attention to this, this matters.

"One of my strong positions is that in case of mass violence, we must act early. It is easier to act earlier—before ideologies and positions have developed and intensified. It's just the same in individual situations, even if you're not thinking about ideology, just thinking of a bully. Once they're a little way down the road, they're in a position where if they stop in response to someone, they lose face. So it's easier to intervene before they have too much to lose.

"The same is true in other group situations. We tend to think: this is a small thing, it's not big enough to worry about it. But by the time it is big enough to worry about, it is too late. Mass violence evolves progressively, always with small steps like excluding people, creating offices that serve discrimination. When no one does anything about those changes that sends a sign, too—a sign that they can go farther. I'll give you an example: Goebbels. After the Évian Conference in 1938, when the community of nations gathered in Switzerland to talk about taking in Jewish refugees from Germany and no one wanted to take them in, Goebbels wrote in his diary, 'They would like to do what we are doing but they don't have the courage.' He took the message that if, at the first step, no one would stop him, then he could keep going."

Today, over forty years since he collaborated on the bystander experiments, John Darley works within the leafy enclave of Princeton University. He's since moved on to do important work that explores how large organizations, and the people in them, become corrupt. In many ways, he has not strayed so very far from his original, groundbreaking work. The greatest evil, he argues, always requires large numbers of participants who contribute by their failure to intervene.

Darley was born into psychology; as a teenager, he remembers his father helping Leon Festinger with logistics when he infiltrated the cognitive dissonance of Marian Keech and her flying-saucer devotees. For someone who has spent his life delving into such dark aspects of human behavior, Darley is a delightfully affable and mellow character, open, accessible, and still eager to explore human behavior and the social and corporate structures that reinforce it. He's particularly intrigued by the way morality impinges on thinking only intermittently.

"The moral mind is not a default mind," he says. "In very competitive environments, where you're under a lot of stress, a lot of cognitive load, you won't necessarily even see that there is a moral consideration at all. Most corruption, I think, starts with an intuitive act, not a deliberate one. Is this a System One/System Two error, I wonder."

Darley is referring to a body of work by the psychologist and Nobel laureate Daniel Kahneman, who argues that we operate two modes of thinking: System One, which is intuitive, associative, very fast, and born of habit. It is, in essence, shortcut thinking—and much of the time, it is good enough. System Two is more deliberative, analytical, and slow and requires much more effort; it's what we use if we want to solve a math problem correctly but one of its other purposes is to monitor System One for errors.[12]

"Many decisions made intuitively are reasonable," Darley continued. "But the problem is that sometimes they are not. And the reasoning system monitoring—System Two—is intermittent and lax. That's the problem: no alarm goes off. So you sell mortgages to people who can't afford them but you're in a competitive environment, under a lot of pressure to perform, so you don't monitor the morality of your actions. And of course, as soon as that mortgage is securitized, you're not responsible for it, so you don't care if the owner defaults. Responsibility has been diffused. From your perspective, System One has worked just fine. And of course the most bonused are the most blind because for them to look carefully is, quite literally, too costly. I think when you look at how all of that plays out, you see that in conditions of high stress—from competitive environments, compensation structures, or just company politics—the high stress tends to distance moral reflection."

Darley has written extensively about the degree to which corruption on a wide scale, and evil on a wide scale, require large numbers of participants and bystanders. Corporate meltdowns like those at Enron, MCI, or the banks require the work of thousands of people, all failing to see the moral implications of their work. And you can't have historic catastrophes, like the Holocaust, unless millions of individuals have taken, in effect, the same moral shortcut.

"Under conditions of high stress," Darley continues to gnaw on the problem, "you may still have inklings, suspicions. But you may inhabit an environment that valorizes blindness, so you don't look. Who or

what is it you are blind to? In the end, I think it's you. You become
blind . . . to yourself . . . to your better self."

In 1938, the residents of Mauthausen, Austria, were feeling optimistic.
Their stone quarry was once again being worked, as massive rebuild-
ing in Germany and Austria brought new business to the town. In
nearby Linz, Austria, Hitler had great plans for his hometown: a new
bridge, town hall, art museum, party headquarters, and two monuments, one commemorating the *Anschluss* and one commemorating
the composer Anton Bruckner. The town's economy was looking up,
too, because the building of a new concentration camp created jobs
and new business for suppliers and craftsmen.

When prisoners began to arrive in August of that year, the SS tried
to keep the population at a distance. But the camp was in full view,
and ordinary life had to continue. Inevitably that meant that the
brutal treatment of prisoners was witnessed by many bystanders. One
was a farmer, Eleanore Gusenbauer, who didn't like what she saw. So
she wrote to complain:

> In the Concentration Camp Mauthausen at the work site in Vienna
> Ditch inmates are being shot repeatedly; those badly struck live for
> yet some time, and so remain lying next to the dead for hours and
> even half a day long.
>
> My property lies upon an elevation next to the Vienna Ditch and
> one is often an unwilling witness to such outrages.
>
> I am anyway sickly and such a sight makes such a demand on my
> nerves that in the long run I cannot bear this.
>
> I request that it be arranged that such inhuman deeds be discontin-
> ued, or else be done where one does not have to see it."[13]

9

OUT OF SIGHT,
OUT OF MIND

ST. JAMES'S SQUARE IS one of London's most elegant addresses. A short stroll from Buckingham Palace, it is lined with fine, tall Georgian buildings embracing a quiet, shady park. Prohibitive parking charges prevent it from being too crammed with cars, while the refined inconvenience of its layout stops taxis using it as a rat run. Just off of Pall Mall, it's in the heart of gentleman's clubland. The fine sweeping staircases and high marble halls of the Naval and Military Club suppress the acoustic, while deep armchairs envelope hushed conversations. The dukes of Norfolk and of Cleveland have kept family houses in the square since the eighteenth century, just two of the seven dukes and seven earls in residence.

A few doors down is Chatham House, home of the Royal Institute of International Affairs and scene of many a high-level confidential briefing on world politics. "Chatham House rules" is a byword for frank but confidential conversations that don't leave the building. At one time, the elegant terraced house was home to the Earl of Lovelace and his wife, Ada, daughter of Lord Byron and an early computing pioneer. For the young couple, the square was the perfect London residence: exclusive, close to the heart of power. Next door is the London Library, the world's largest private lending library, founded by Thomas Carlyle.

Thackeray was its first auditor, and Dickens, George Eliot, Kipling, Shaw, Henry James, and T. S. Eliot were among its members. Its Piranesi staircases bind together a maze of buildings packed with more than a million volumes. St. James's Square is picture-book London and typically British: intimidating as an oyster on the outside, seething and expensive within.

It's a long way from the sulfur-scented streets of Texas City, Texas. But St. James's Square is also the headquarters of British Petroleum. It's here that Lord Browne of Madingley issued his order for cost-cutting and here too that the group chief executive of refining and marketing, John Manzoni, ensured that it was implemented. If you look at an organization chart for BP in early 2005, you'll see Browne at the top and Manzoni immediately underneath. From there, it's about seven layers of management down to the guys operating the Texas City refinery. Seven layers, 4,800 miles, a six-hour time difference, and a cultural chasm between the two locations.

As with many multinational corporations, it's impossible to put the whole org chart on a page because nothing is simple. The Business Unit Leader (BUL) is responsible for the refinery but alongside him works an HSSE manager (health, safety, security, environment) and a process safety manager; they're responsible for numerous sites, so on any given day, they could be in Texas City—or somewhere else. Toward the bottom of the pyramid, it gets particularly hairy, with Tier 1, Tier 2, Tier 3, and Tier 4 managers, each with accountability of some kind. It got complicated, not just because there were so many titles, acronyms, and responsibilities, but because the people kept changing: five plant managers alone between the years 2001 and 2003.[1]

Additional organizational change occurred in 2003 and 2004 when BP issued its "Management Framework." The BP South Houston complex was dissolved, the director became the refinery Business Unit Leader, and the process safety department became part of the new HSSE department with a new manager.

The impact of these ineffectively managed organizational changes on process safety was summed up by consultants studying the refinery just weeks before the explosion. "We have never seen an organization with such a history of leadership changes over such a short period of time. Even if the rapid turnover of senior leadership were the norm elsewhere in the BP system, it seems to have a particularly strong effect at Texas City. Between the BP/Amoco mergers, then the BP turnover coupled with the difficulties of governance of an integrated site . . . there has been little organizational stability."[2]

Instability, of course, is just a word that means a lot of people moving up—and out. No aspiring manager wanted to stay in Texas City. Why, the site wasn't even in Houston, America's oil capital, but a thirty-minute congested drive southeast on the Galveston freeway. Highfliers might do a stint but they'd soon be on their way—wasn't that the fun of working for a global business? The managers could move, and did—frequently. Everyone else, the guys they said were "closest to the valve," stayed put; where else were they going to go?

The men running the isomerization unit reported to bosses on site who reported to a regional vice president, Pat Gower, in Illinois, who reported to a group vice president, Mike Hoffman, who reported back to Manzoni in leafy St. James's Square. And Manzoni's job wasn't simple, either.

"I have ultimate accountability for several of the businesses inside BP," Manzoni explained in his deposition taken after the explosion at Texas City. "It's the refining business. There is a retail business. There is a lubricants business. There is a business marketing business. There is chemicals business. If I were to give you a sense of that, these are very diverse businesses. In language and in companies that you may be more familiar with, it's a bit like putting Coors, Whirlpool, GAP, General Motors all together and running those businesses all together."

With so much on his plate, detail was never going to be at the heart of his working day. Asked about the Texas City "assets," Manzoni was unapologetic. "It would be very unusual," he said, "for me to look at individual assets." The year that Manzoni became group CEO, Texas City had been described as "in complete decline." In 2003, an audit claimed that the "condition of the infrastructure and assets is poor at the Texas City refinery." In July 2004, Manzoni finally paid a visit to this, the largest refinery in his portfolio. But, according to his deposition, he still had no inkling that anything was wrong.

Q: And you are telling me no one told you about the problems that existed at the plant during that visit?

A: Actually, I left the plant with a sense that programs were being put in place and that—and there was something called the 1,000 day program.

Q: Have you ever talked to any superintendents?

A: I have done it in the past. I can't remember whether I did on that visit in Texas City.

Q: Did you ever talk to a guy named Ray Hawkins?

A: No.

Q: If he—if you had spoken to him and he told you, "Do you know what? My day-to-day activity is nothing more than crisis management, eventually something is going to fall off the plate," what would that tell you?

A: There is a problem.

But of course, no one told Manzoni; they knew about him, but they rarely saw him. No one at the refinery had the kind of relationship that would make them seek him out to tell him the truth. Just that year, the site had already seen thirty million dollars of damage due to a ruptured furnace pipe, and two months after Manzoni's visit, two workers died opening a pipe flange. But apparently Manzoni didn't notice this, either.

"I am not sure I was made aware of compliance issues or gaps in operations. You know, we obviously focus on continuous improvement in all aspects of our business but I am not sure that I was specifically made aware of any gap. I believe nobody knew the level of risk at Texas City because if they had known, I have absolutely no doubt we would have taken different and substantively different actions."

Manzoni's argument is intriguing because he's using a logical shortcut: assuming that there could not have been a problem because, if there had been, someone somewhere would have taken action. Since no one took action, the problem could not have existed. The deposition, though, reveals all the details Manzoni never saw: the impact of budget cuts, the absence of updated fire equipment, the consequences of deferred maintenance, and cuts in safety training. It rehearses the sequence of reports, audits, consultants reports, surveys, and warnings that all drew attention to safety issues at the plant. But all of it, it seems, passed Manzoni by.

Q: Tell me why the plant wasn't shut down to fix these problems before this explosion occurred.

A: I can't tell you actually because I wasn't aware of the problems before the explosion occurred.[3]

Throughout the deposition, what is so surprising is the frankness with which Manzoni demonstrates his own blindness. Not only did he not know what was going on, he doesn't appear to think that there was anything to know. He is so vague in his deposition that critics might accuse him of lying, but I don't think he is: The very fact that he is so brazenly unconcerned by his own ignorance makes him weirdly credible. Although he acknowledges the gravity of fifteen deaths, he seems at a loss to understand why he should be involved. He has no real understanding of Texas City, is unprepared but also strangely unworried, annoyed only that everyone insists on digging up history when what he really wants is to fix the problem now that he can finally see it.

What comes out loud and clear in his testimony is the unbridgeable gulf between Manzoni—the elite, educated British executive—and the men close to the valve whose issues can neither be heard nor seen. Watching Manzoni, it's tempting to ask the question: Where was he? And the answer would be: a very, very long way away. Separated by miles, by background, by culture, by status. Even the deposition was conducted in Chicago, a long way from everything, and everyone, that mattered in the case.

In 2007, Lord Browne resigned from BP, for a host of reasons not least of which was the damage done to BP's reputation and stock price by the Texas City accident. Between 2005 and 2008, as other oil companies saw their stock prices rise by 30 to 40 percent, BP went through prolonged losses and only modest gains. This provoked a great deal of soul-searching within BP as it struggled, under new CEO Tony Hayward, to reorganize the business. The company chastised itself for "poor listening" and for its celebration of complexity as a virtue rather than recognizing it had become a cumbersome problem. Attempts were made to reduce the organizational chaos of the company, by keeping executives in their jobs longer, by rewarding crisis prevention over heroic crisis management, and by ostensibly simplifying corporate structures. By the end of 2009, the company leadership was feeling confident again, its share price was rising, and management was nearly ready to start talking publicly about how profoundly it had changed. But executives were cautious. After all, it wasn't as though Texas City were over. At the end of the many lawsuits that had followed that explosion, BP had reached a plea bargain with the U.S.

Justice Department, in which the corporation paid a fifty-million-dollar fine to avoid criminal charges for violations of the Clean Air Act related to the fatal explosions. But that deal was contingent on BP fulfilling its settlement agreement with the Occupational Safety and Health Administration, something it hadn't done. Instead, in every year that followed the refinery explosion, another worker died on the job at Texas City; and by October 2009, the corporation still faced 439 outstanding safety violations at Texas City alone. Less than six months later, the Deepwater Horizon oil rig exploded and then sank, leaving the largest offshore oil spill in the United States. When, after weeks of trying and failing to contain the disaster, CEO Hayward complained that he wanted his life back, the distance between St. James's Square and the Gulf of Mexico yawned wider than ever.

One of the arguments put forward to support globalization is that, because we have the technology to connect everyone, business can and must expand across the globe. We don't need to be in the same room together anymore. Between the Internet, video conferencing, e-mail, cell phones, and social networks, distance doesn't matter. But it is painfully obvious in Manzoni's case that none of this technology bridges the gulf. The distance does matter. Manzoni couldn't see the people who worked for him; he had no relationship with most of them. Much more likely is that he truly did not know most of the eighty thousand people working for him, he didn't ever see their working conditions, and, perhaps worst of all, he didn't see that not seeing might pose a problem. When Tony Hayward said he wanted his life back, he seemed utterly impervious to the oil rig workers who would never get their lives back or the fisheries workers who had lost their livelihoods forever.

Technology can maintain relationships but it won't build them. Conference calls, with teams of executives huddled around speaker-phones, fail to convey personality, mood, and nuance. You may start to develop rapport with the person who speaks most—or take an instant dislike to him or her. But you'll never know why. Nor will you perceive the silent critic scowling a thousand miles away. Videoconferencing distracts all its participants who spend too much time worrying about their hair and whether they're looking fat, uncomfortable at seeing themselves on screen. The nervous small talk about weather—it's snowing there? It's hot and sunny here—betrays anxiety about the vast differences that the technology attempts to mask.

Physical distance isn't easily bridged, no matter how refined the technology. Instead, we delude ourselves that because so many words are exchanged—e-mail, notes, and reports—somehow a great deal of communication must have taken place. But that requires, in the first instance, that the words be read, that they be understood, and that the recipient know enough to read with discernment and empathy. It's tragically obvious in Manzoni's deposition that he has no idea who is working for him or what his employees are worried about. It's extremely hard to communicate well with people you don't really know, whose concerns you cannot see.

Communication technologies have developed exponentially since Milgram did his obedience experiments, but there's one version of those experiments that has become more relevant than ever. In the original experiment, the victim could not be seen or heard and 65 percent of obedient subjects delivered shocks to the maximum limit. In that version, one of the subjects commented, "It's funny how you really begin to forget that there's a guy out there. For a long time, I just concentrated on pressing the switches and reading the words."[4] But in a second version, the victim was in the same room as the subject, sitting just a few feet away. That proximity reduced the number of fully compliant subjects to 40 percent. And when the subjects were made to touch their victims' hands, placing them on a shock plate, human contact meant that only 30 percent finished the course. With the victim sitting in the same room, establishing eye contact and eventually physical contact, everything changes. It is so much easier to be blind to the consequences of your actions when you do not have to see them play out.

Similarly, John Darley conducted a variation on his bystander-effect experiments, when he placed some pairs of participants in a room face-to-face, and others sitting back-to-back. They were left to draw. After a few minutes, they heard the sounds of an accident taking place: a workman apparently fell to the floor, groaned, and exclaimed, "Oh my leg!" Eighty percent of those working face-to-face responded to the accident; only 20 percent of those sitting back-to-back did so. Relationships—real, face-to-face relationships—change our behavior.[5]

This is, of course, why some leaders prefer distance; they feel that they could not do their jobs if they were immersed in the messy, human detail of the mission. Britain's General Douglas Haig, who presided over the slaughter of a whole generation of young men in the First World War, could not bear to visit a military hospital. One of his subordinates, on first visiting the battle front, is reported to have burst into tears, crying "Good God, did we really send men to fight in that?"[6] Albert Speer, as I have said, was always very careful to shield himself from the reality of the labor camps he oversaw. Even Adolf Eichmann and Heinrich Himmler became physically ill when confronted with the consequences of their decisions.[7] The argument for distance is that eliminating proximity clarifies the mind and facilitates more objective decision making. But it can also blind one to the details that one would prefer not to see.

Structural blindness was built into the way BP did business, not because its leaders wanted to be blind but because, to be competitive, Browne believed the business had to be big. Built through aggressive mergers and acquisitions around the world, it was inevitably spread across continents, time zones, and cultures. The company was well aware of the problem; it's why so many surveys and processes were put in place to attempt to hold everything together. But structure alone, when presented with such a challenge, won't fix the problem. Manzoni and Browne were both blind to the routine risks being run at Texas City in part because they weren't familiar enough with the site or the people to care about them. They were abstractions, numbers, profit-generators, and cost centers. But it wasn't geography alone that left them so dangerously out of the loop. It was also power.

Power imposes distance between those that have it and those that do not. The powerful are quite often unaware of this; the best struggle against it, but the distance is always there. Power circumscribes whether you're spending most of your time in elegant London clubs or at the Grand Prize Barbeque on Texas City's Palmer Highway. Power determines whether you are talking to chief executives or superintendents. Power decides whether you fly in the splendid isolation of a private jet or in first class instead of in economy, next to the young mother who needs help with her restless child. Limousines and catered lunches, personal assistants and flattering friends teach new habits of privilege and entitlement. But while these may seem attractive luxuries, they come at a cost: isolation. The bubble of power seals off bad news, inconvenient details, hostile opinions, and messy realities, leaving you free to inhale the rarefied air of pure abstraction. Like the cave dwellers of Plato's parable, the powerful watch shadows of outside reality flickering on their walls, grateful to be so comfortably protected from the reality themselves. The rough gives way to the smooth in a frictionless ascent.

Moreover, recent research into power shows that the powerful appraise information differently. A team of American and French academics got together to try to figure out whether power alters judgment. In one experiment, they recruited teams of students and divided them into two groups: one group had the power to choose applicants for an internship, the other group could advise but not select. The powerful participants paid more attention to information that conformed to stereotypes. In other words, having power seemed to make them less inclined to challenge received wisdom.[8]

In a further experiment, the participants were subjected to personality appraisals that evaluated the need for dominance. Those who scored higher were put into a separate group from those who scored lower, and both groups were asked for their opinions as to how to evaluate students for internships. While the students who had scored higher for dominance did not completely ignore information that challenged stereotypes, they still gave it less attention. Dominant people, it appears, use snap judgments and conform to received wisdom more than do the less dominant. Those who need power, and those who have it, think differently. The stereotypes they fall back on can be counteracted—but doing so requires a great deal of motivation and cognitive effort. Power does corrupt, but far more insidiously than even the powerful appreciate.

Frances Milliken, one of the academics responsible for work on organizational silence, did a marvelous study comparing how those in power communicate differently from those who lack power. She found that, like the rich, the powerful are different from other people. Confronted by risky situations, they are more likely to expect positive outcomes. They're so optimistic at least in part because they have—or think they have—the power needed to overcome most adversity. That psychological distance between themselves and others means that they can't think as concretely as other people; inevitably they have to think in far more abstract terms. But what is frightening about Milliken's study is that the combination of power, optimism, and abstract thinking makes powerful people more certain. The more cut off they are from others, the more confident they are that they are right.

Just to add a little spice to what might otherwise have seemed a rather dry linguistic inventory, Milliken chose to focus on the response of officials during and after Hurricane Katrina. Milliken and her team collected a vast array of public statements by officials during the disaster and analyzed the language of each piece according to the amount of power held by its speaker. It must have been a lugubrious process but the conclusions feel real. Sure enough, she found that federal officials—those with the most power and who didn't live in New Orleans—were very much less troubled by events, more optimistic that the crisis would be effectively dealt with, and far less prone to doubt. Psychologically this becomes self-reinforcing: the less they knew, the less curious and anxious they became.

The poster child for this conclusion, of course, must be Michael Brown, the director of the Federal Emergency Management Agency. Although Milliken is wonderfully discreet and doesn't shape her argument around his pronouncements, he was a walking demonstration of her argument. On August 29, the day the hurricane first made landfall in Louisiana, Brown seemed relaxed, reminding emergency services personnel "not to respond to hurricane impact areas unless dispatched by state, local authorities."

Two days later, he received an e-mail from a FEMA colleague: "Hotels are kicking people out, thousands gathering in the streets with no food or water. Hundreds are still being rescued from homes. We are out of food and running out of water at the dome."[9] But Brown, despite the detail he'd received, didn't seem worried as he responded: "Thanks for update. Anything specific I need to do or tweak?"

Four days later, he told TV news anchor Ted Koppel on ABC's *Nightline* that he had been unaware that twenty to twenty-five thousand refugees were stranded at the city's convention center without food or water.

> BROWN: We first learned of the convention center—we being the federal government—today.
> KOPPEL: Don't you guys watch television? Don't you guys listen to the radio? Our reporters have been reporting about it for more than just today.

BROWN: We learned about it factually today that that was what existed . . . When we first learned about it, my first gut instinction [sic] instinct was: Get somebody in there, give me truth on the ground, let me know because if it is true, we've got to help those people.[10]

KOPPEL: But here we are five days after the storm hit and you are talking about what is going to happen in the next couple of days.

BROWN: I just want to say to the American public that they do need to understand exactly how catastrophic this disaster is. And they do need to know that we are going to have every available resource to do everything that we can. We're going to take care of these victims. We are going to make it right. We are going to make certain that the devastation that has been reaped [sic] upon these people is taken care of and that we get their lives back in order.

What's so striking about all of Brown's responses is that they are so remote, so confident, and so extraordinarily abstract. He mentions no individuals, he mentions no fear or hunger in his response. He only speaks about abstract "victims" whose lives someone somewhere is going to get back in order. Koppel's responses, while polite, finally exploded with disbelief—and real detail.

KOPPEL: Mr. Brown, some of these people are dead. They are beyond your help. Some of these people have died because they needed insulin and they couldn't get it . . . You say you were surprised . . . so many people didn't make it out. It's no surprise to anyone that you had at least one hundred thousand people in the city of New Orleans who are dirt poor, who don't have cars, who don't have access to public transportation, who don't have any way of getting out of the city simply because somebody says, 'You know there's a force-five storm coming? You ought to get out.' If you didn't have the buses there to get them out, why should it be a surprise to you that they stayed?

Brown wasn't as far away as it might seem; he was in Baton Rouge, Louisiana. But psychologically he was miles away, not just because he was part of the Washington elite but also because he had been hoping for some time to retire from FEMA. He didn't want to be in his job and, mentally, he was already gone, which is why, three days after the levees broke, he wrote his infamous e-mail: "Last hurrah was supposed to be Labor Day. I'm trapped now, please rescue me."[11] That Brown can make a joke, comparing his metaphorical bondage with the physical and tragic trap the citizens of New Orleans found themselves unable to escape, illustrates how unbridgeable the gulf between them was.

The distance imposed by geography and implicit in power is reinforced by the structures within which work gets done. It's been that way ever since 1776, the year Adam Smith published *The Wealth of Nations* and extolled the glories of the division of labor. While it might take one man a day to make a single pin (or ten pins if he were skilled), he explained, ten men could produce forty-eight thousand by each taking on a separate part of the work. (Today, Smith's observation is commemorated on the British twenty-pound note.) As most manufacture became a good deal more complicated, and more lucrative, than pins, the idea became embedded in industry. The modern American automobile, for example, can contain components designed in the United States, manufactured in Asia, and assembled on Native reserves in Canada before returning to the United States to be completed.[12] Toyota makes engines, carpets, and instrument panels in the United States, headlights and brakes in France, steering wheels in Turkey, airbags in the Czech Republic, wheels in Germany, suspension parts in Spain, and windshield wipers in Italy. Such attenuated processes have multiple aims: to reduce costs, to use the most specialized labor, to provide employment and take advantage of tax breaks. Division of labor has become central to our concept of work: for-profit, nonprofit, government, service, and commodity businesses all seek to use specialized talent to deliver faster, better, cheaper results. As Adam Smith argued, with greater specialization comes greater efficiency and productivity.

But in an established corporation like BP, that meant that the cost-cutters didn't know much about safety. Why should they? It wasn't their department. They had, or claimed to have, very little insight into the consequences of mandated savings; that wasn't their job. Manzoni lacked refining experiences and, according to his executive assistant, Lord Browne showed "no passion, no curiosity, no interest in safety."[13] In theory, there were plenty of other people to look after those details, but the company's internal inquiry shows a concatenation of poor communication among them all.

The division of labor isn't designed to keep corporations blind but that is often its effect. The people who manufacture cars aren't the people who repair them or service them. That means they don't see the problems inherent in their design unless a special effort is made to show it to them. Software engineers who write code aren't the same as the ones who fix bugs, who also aren't the customer-service representatives you call when the program crashes your machine. Companies are now organized—often for good reasons—in ways that can facilitate departments becoming structurally blind to one another.

Nowhere was this more the case than in the U.S. Food and Drug Administration, where (before 2007) one vast bureaucracy—the Office of New Drugs—was responsible for approving drugs, but an entirely different set of individuals—the Office of Drug Safety—was responsible for the safety of drugs once they were on the market. On one level, the separation seems to make sense; after all if the approvals process worked, the Office for Drug Safety shouldn't have anything to do. That is why their funding was so different, with new drug approvals taking nearly 80 percent of the budget.

But there were inherent problems in the structure. The smaller team, responsible for ongoing safety, had less money but was responsible for policing the entire market of drugs being consumed by millions of consumers. Moreover, its funding could be taken as a reasonable indicator of its organizational clout. To overturn an approved drug would always require a great deal of research and data, both of which took money. To cap it all, the safety team didn't even have final authority to withdraw a drug. All they could do was recommend withdrawal—to the very people who had approved the drug in the first place. Without money or clout, they needed to ask colleagues publicly to change their minds. No wonder they met with denial and resistance. In effect, therefore, the monitoring of drugs that had been approved in small-scale trials was abandoned once they were being taken by millions of patients, leaving the FDA effectively blind to the outcome of their own decisions.

The Vioxx scandal in 2004 brought all of this to light. Of course it didn't help that the pharmaceutical company responsible for the drug, Merck, struggled mightily to conceal concerns that the drug could cause heart attacks and strokes. But in this, it seemed like the approvals team within the FDA were their allies, not their watchdog. The only reason the scale of the problem came to light was because Dr. David Graham, associate director of the Office of Drug Safety, was able to collaborate with Kaiser Permanente on a three-year study of the arthritis drug. What he found suggested that many patients were at risk. When he later testified to Congress about how things had gone so wrong, he was at pains to describe the scale of the problem.

"Imagine that instead of a serious side effect of a widely used pre-scription drug, we were talking about jetliners. Please ignore the obvi-ous difference in fatality rates between a heart attack and a plane crash, and focus on the larger analogy I'm trying to draw. If there were an average of 150 to 200 people on an aircraft, this range of 88,000 to 138,000 would be the rough equivalent of 500 to 900 aircraft dropping from the sky. This translates to two to four aircraft every week, week in and week out, for the past five years."[14]

But, despite evidence that Vioxx might be very unsafe indeed, Gra-ham's concerns found no support within the FDA.

"An e-mail from the director for the entire Office of New Drugs was revealing," he later testified. "He suggested that since FDA was 'not contemplating' a warning against the use of high-dose Vioxx, my conclusions should be changed. Even more revealing, a mere six weeks before Merck pulled Vioxx from the market [the Center for Drug Evaluation and Research, the Office of New Drugs, and the Office of Drug Safety] management did not believe there was an outstanding safety concern with Vioxx. At the same time, two to four jumbo jet-liners were dropping from the sky every week and no one else at FDA was concerned."

The same month that Dr. Graham was encouraged to change his con-clusions, the FDA approved Vioxx for children with rheumatoid arthri-tis. The following month, they called Dr. Graham's study "a scientific rumor." But eight days later, Merck pulled the drug off the market.

In his testimony, Graham went to great lengths to explain that Vioxx was not unique. The problem wasn't just the drug—it was the FDA's structure, which seemed to be designed to ensure that problems could not, or would not, be seen. The vast power and funding of one division effectively masked the insights and recommendations of its lesser part-ner. It took an act of Congress—the Food and Drug Amendments Act (2007)—to change things.

Where you put information makes a difference in how visible it is. When, as in the case with Vioxx, important information resides in an underfunded department that doesn't have much power, the organiza-tion becomes structurally blind. Similarly, if large amounts of money are parked in off-the-balance-sheet vehicles, special-purposes entities, and offshore subsidiaries, getting a comprehensive overview of a business becomes impossible. When the banks began to teeter in 2008, one of the biggest problems they faced was that they simply did not know how much money—or debt—they had. The monolithic insurance giant AIG could not answer simple questions about their assets because so many of them had been buried in accounting complexity. After Enron went bust, it turned out that the company had far more money than they imagined; they just couldn't see it because it sat off the balance sheet. Goldman Sachs invented creative derivatives deals in order to help their client, the Greek government, mask the true extent of their deficit—as though merely stashing the debt where it could not be seen would solve the problem. Ernst & Young, together with the London solicitors Linklaters, were accused in 2010 of together having figured out a way—known inside the bank as Repo 150—to hide as much as fifty billion dollars of Lehman Brothers debt, thus rendering their client effectively blind to its own danger.[15] In the desire to boost their balance sheet, such maneuvers willfully blinded their organizations to their own operations and vulnerabilities.

Structural blindness assumes a concrete reality when it takes the form of outsourcing. Corporations, eager to reduce fixed costs and overhead, suddenly realized that they didn't have to employ all the talent they needed. If they could buy it in, then they could eliminate swaths of management while retaining, or even increasing, negotiating power. The markets loved the idea because it looked as though huge areas of expense and exposure were eliminated from balance sheets permanently. Entrepreneurs leapt at the idea because it meant that, instead of working for dreary monolithic organizations, they could set up their own businesses and be masters of their own destiny in a competitive marketplace. At least that was the idea.

In reality, the disaggregation of work has made it harder than ever to connect all of the pieces; in fact, you need huge swaths of management to oversee outsourcing, competitive bidding, partnerships, and contractors. What used to be departments are now outside firms, but someone still needs to get them all to work well together. At least at the FDA, the fight between the approvals people and the safety people was clearly, if painfully, visible. But once you outsource or subcontract work, it loses its visibility.

When he joined in the investigation of the *Challenger* disaster in 1986, this is exactly what the great iconoclast Richard Feynman discovered.

As an outsider, he had little concern for the hierarchies within NASA; in telling the story, he reveled in his contempt for rank and deference. As focused as a cat on a rat as he chased down every conceivable source of information, truthfulness, and insight, he delighted in crashing through barriers and filling in gaps. He eventually, and triumphantly, figured out that a major cause of the disaster had been the O-ring seals, which, in the extremely low temperatures to which they were subjected, must have cracked. But the O-rings, of course, hadn't been made by NASA. They had been made by Morton Thiokol, an aerospace company that had used plastic specially manufactured by the Parker Seal Company. NASA was based at the Kennedy Space Center in Florida but also at the Marshall Space Flight Center in Huntsville, Alabama. Morton Thiokol was based in Brigham, Utah, and Parker Seal in Lexington, Kentucky.

When the Morton Thiokol team became concerned about the low temperatures forecast for launch, they did their best to relay their concerns. But the engineers couldn't raise a red flag until they got support from their management. As subcontractors, they had little leverage; after all, NASA was their customer. Nevertheless, two meetings were called to address concerns. Given the geography, of course, these had to be conference calls; and given the number of people involved, not everyone could attend, or attend both calls. NASA was under political pressure to launch, and Morton Thiokol was under commercial pressure and could never have had the power to stop the launch. In the inquiries that followed the disaster, the sheer difficulty in understanding what had happened aptly reflected the endemic nature of the problem: A director from Morton Thiokol had to turn up—uninvited—at one of Feynman's meetings in order to be able to share what he knew.[16]

More recently, SIGG, makers of trendy aluminium water bottles, discovered that outsourcing their manufacture didn't give them the control their high-end brand needed. SIGG's chic products had developed a substantial following among conscientious consumers worried about the bisphenol A found in many hard plastics. BPA has been linked to diabetes, heart disease, premature puberty in girls, and lower sperm counts in men. The claim that the SIGG bottles didn't pose this hazard was important to their consumers, who wanted a permanent water bottle to reduce waste (good for the environment) and one that was free of BPA (good for the drinker). But, in fact,

SIGG did not manufacture the lining of their bottles; a third party did. And that third party did not tell SIGG what materials they were using.[17] When it transpired that there was, after all, some small amount of BPA in the mysterious liner, the company was publicly trashed by its customers and the CEO lost his job. It's astonishing to think that the company was manufacturing blind; certainly that explanation failed to assuage the anger of their knowledgeable and vigilant customers.

SIGG was making a simple product in Switzerland. There wasn't anything especially stressful, dangerous, or complex about their business. In conditions of great ambiguity and danger, however, the difficulties inherent in the division of labor become pronounced and even fatal. In Iraq, the U.S. military works with some one hundred eighty thousand private military contractors—some building Pizza Huts, some bringing commercial supply-line expertise to the delivery of gas and ammunitions. With so many moving parts, each under separate management and under commercial pressures, dumb but tragic things happen. When Staff Sergeant Ryan Maseth, a decorated Green Beret, was electrocuted taking a shower, a subsequent investigation showed that the contractors concerned had been instructed to fix anything that was broken; nothing in their contract required that they uncover or fix potential hazards. The Army wasn't sufficiently aware of their own electrical problems and the contractor never had their work inspected. They were both blind to each other.[18]

The same kind of confusion reigned over the appointment and use of contractors to supervise and interrogate detainees in Iraq. Investigations into the abuses at Abu Ghraib showed a classic confusion over who answered to whom, with contractors insisting they answered to the military and the military saying they had no control over contractors. It's easy enough to explain this by arguing that, in light of the actions taken at Abu Ghraib, no one wanted to take the blame, but the fact that everyone can deny responsibility fully articulates the problem and the full horror of its consequences.

That same confusion was reflected in the chaos, scapegoating, and finger-pointing that immediately followed the explosion on BP's Deepwater Horizon oil rig. BP, of course, hadn't built the rig; the Deepwater Horizon was built by Hyundai in Korea according to a design from a Texas firm, R&B Falcon, which had been bought by the Swiss operators, Transocean, who had leased the rig to BP. Most of those killed weren't BP employees and therefore were not the responsibility of the British company. Once you outsource critical functions, you may be blind to how the work gets done. The cynical will conclude that that is precisely what outsourcing is for.

It's challenging to recognize that outsourcing has become so embedded in Western economies, that there are no areas in which it is not considered. We outsource our wars now, through private security firms and much of our policing: In the United States and the United Kingdom, the number of private guards is now more than twice the number of public police officers.[19] Current debates over the outsourcing of clinical trials for new drugs to India, China, and other cheap labor markets focus entirely on whether or not ethnic differences will generate different data. But those debates overlook the far bigger issue, which is about the imbalance of power between rich Western pharmaceutical companies and poorly paid, unprotected volunteers half a world away. When a very rich Western firm employs a far less wealthy foreign firm to do clinical trials, what are the pressures upon that dependent business to deliver "good" results? And how convenient is it to the larger company to take those "good" results at face value? Disregarding these inequalities of power is a form of blindness in itself.

Everyone who's ever worked in an organization knows how intensely difficult it can be to prevent silos, to find people who are intellectually able and politically prepared to connect the dots. It takes effort, commitment, and mistakes to overcome the sheer difficulty people have working with each other, negotiating the complex interface between their personal ambitions and organizational goals. But the silos, which should be a metaphor for disconnection, take on a substantial reality when we are talking about separate institutions—be they companies or organizations—with different mandates, goals, power bases, and agendas. When John Snow, U.S. secretary of the Treasury between 2003 and 2006, testified before Congress on the role of financial regulators in the 2008 financial crisis, he explained that part of the problem had been that he couldn't even see the problem.

"Nowhere in our financial regulatory system is there anyone with full accountability and full three-hundred-sixty-degree view on risk and leverage. I saw that in my days at the Treasury Department. I remember in 2005, sensing that there were developments in the debt markets, the sub-prime, and the mortgage markets that needed to be better understood. I took what was deemed to be a fairly extraordinary step and called in all of the substantive regulators of the mortgage market. I asked them to give their considered views on whether or not undue risk was being created. We didn't yet have a housing crisis. We didn't yet have a sub-prime crisis. But I wanted to get their view. But no [*sic*] one of them had that view. They had pieces of the puzzle. It's like the blind man and the elephant. They are all touching a piece of it, but they don't know what the big picture is."[20]

If Snow had difficulty peering through a structural morass of regulation, how much more difficult was the challenge of gaining a holistic view of the market itself? The division of labor, institutionalized into different organizations, had taken the once simplistic task of buying a home and blown it into so many different transactions that, apparently, no one could put the pieces together anymore. That was the conclusion the London School of Economics drew when asked by the Queen of England why no one had seen the banking crisis coming. "The difficulty was seeing the risk to the system as a whole rather than to any specific financial instrument or loan. Risk calculations were most often confined to slices of financial activity, using some of the best mathematical minds in our country and abroad. But they frequently lost sight of the bigger picture."[21]

The mortgage market, comprised of buyers, brokers, primary and secondary funders, and securitizing banks, had spectacularly become the ultimate expression of Adam Smith's division of labor: each institution doing what it was best at, generating products at a faster rate than any individual was capable of, but with a level of complexity no one could any longer understand. Most pernicious of all, financiers had come to see banking as its own universe, separate and distinct from the rest of society, so siloed by its wealth and abstractions that they could not even perceive public outrage when the banking failure destroyed jobs, businesses, and funding for all those activities—education, health, the arts—that knit society together.

We don't see things that are too far away, that are too distant from our own experience, too separate from our own concerns, or simply too complicated to assemble. But we also don't see things that are too far away in time, be it the past or the future. One of the reasons it has proved so hard for climate-change activists and negotiators to gain traction must be that the threat feels so far away in time—well after the heads of state responsible for it will have left the stage. Fear of change, of conflict, the pull of inertia, all of these help us to remain blind to something so far away in the future that it's very easy to ignore it day after day.

Similarly, the past recedes from view unless we find ways to memorialize it and keep it within our lines of sight. In Libby, Montana, Gayla Benefield and Gary Svenson used to make wooden crosses every year, each one painted with the name of a victim of asbestosis. Some in the town complained; they didn't want their loved ones' names used in a campaign. So Gary has built a pergola down by the river and intends to raise money by selling small medallions, each engraved with the name of someone lost to the dust of the vermiculite plant. That way, he says, people can choose to have their kin memorialized or not. He wants the town to remember, and visitors to the town to learn, what happened there. But already another, bigger, pergola has been set up next to his, as though to make sure his doesn't get all the attention.

In Texas City, one man carries with him a searing memory of the explosion. Dave Senko supervised the contractors who were killed but he was at another site on the day of the accident. Today, his hands shake as he talks about the friends he lost. Many of them had wanted to quit the project, he says, because they didn't feel safe working at the site. But Senko had persuaded them to stay. He misses these men and carries them on his conscience. BP, he told me, wouldn't have a memorial to them on the site; they weren't BP employees. So he waged a one-man campaign to get a memorial at the offices of the contracting firm that had employed the men. They eventually gave in.

"What is on the memorial?" I asked him.

He was too upset to speak. I waited. Silence. Then he handed me his phone; on it was a picture of a small stone slab. All it says is: MARCH 23, 2005. No names. No description. After he'd pestered his company a little more, Senko was able to add a light and a small pear tree. He goes there some evenings to check that it's still there and that the light still works. One time, the security guard came over and asked him to move. He was outraged and said the guard could call the police if he wanted to. Senko wasn't moving.

"Remembering is important," he said. "It matters. If you can't see these things, they'll just keep happening."

Why do we build institutions and corporations so large and so complex that we can't see how they work? In part, it's because we can. Human hubris makes us believe that if we can imagine something, we can build it, and if we can build it, we can understand it. We are so delighted with our own ingenuity and intelligence and it gives us a sense of mastery and power. But the power is problematic as it takes us farther and farther from the reality of what we have built. Like Daedalus, we build labyrinths of such cunning complexity that we cannot find our own way out. And we are blind to the blindness these complex structures necessarily confer. So we forget all about it.

10

DE-MORALIZING WORK

IDEAS AND EVENTS enjoy a funny relationship. Sometimes they seem to develop in lockstep, like Rousseau and the coming of the French Revolution. At other times, ideas emerge as a critique of prevailing social moods or trends, as when the Romantic idealization of sentiment grew out of the Industrial Revolution. That contentious relationship is analogous to what happened at the turn of the last century, when so much public energy suddenly centered on money. As the Western world experienced a financial bonanza, with global markets reaching new highs daily and consumers avid for each new avenue of expenditure, along came a bunch of psychologists and economists with a challenging message: money doesn't make people happy.

What? In the middle of a consumer explosion, when ten-thousand-dollar handbags flew out of stores and people bought homes whose garages were larger than their houses had been, how could it be that money didn't make us happy? But that's what positive psychologists like Martin Seligman and economists like Richard Layard were saying. And to prove it, they could show that despite increases in gross domestic product, overall life satisfaction hadn't gone up. And the richest countries weren't the happiest.

The data, and its corollaries, caused a big stir, as they should have.

After all, if GDP growth didn't make people happy, why were all Western economies pursuing it so ferociously? Wasn't happiness itself a more meaningful goal? If it was, then how would it be measured? And if money couldn't increase it, what would? At that point, a lot of thinking stalled. Hmm. If money wasn't going to make people happier, how could a government, or political movement, measure its success?

In companies, the money-vs.-happiness debate was a bit of a poser too. Some CEOs thought they saw a light at the end of the tunnel: Did this mean they didn't have to pay their employees so much? Not surprisingly, nobody was volunteering to take pay cuts on the grounds that they thought it would make them feel better. Did it mean that shareholders wouldn't be so insistent on growth or dividends? If there were any shareholders who thought they would be happier with less, they were a consistently silent minority—with plenty of stocks to choose from.

The reason the argument started to peter out was simple. Just because money can't make people happy doesn't mean that we aren't motivated by it. We are. In a 1953 experiment, patients were asked to hang on horizontal bars for as long as they could; most could take it for about 45 seconds. When subjected to the power of suggestion and even, in some cases, hypnosis, they could stretch to about 75 seconds. But when offered a five-dollar bill (which today would be worth about thirty dollars) the patients managed to hang from the bars for 110 seconds. Anything that allows you to increase your performance by 250 percent is pretty motivating.[1]

Nor was that some weird anomaly of 1950s America. More recent studies have shown that the mere idea of money can make people persevere more and work longer.[2] Another study showed that money changes what we remember. In that experiment, volunteers were shown a selection of images, each accompanied by a price. Remembering one picture was worth five dollars; remembering another was worth merely ten cents. Testing their subjects the next day, the researchers found that their participants were far more likely to have remembered the high-price scenes.[3] Much of this motivation may not even be conscious; humans tend to adapt the degree of effort they expend according to the magnitude of reward they expect.[4]

Serious students of motivation such as Daniel Pink argue that money may make us work harder but it doesn't make us work smarter. Citing experiments conducted by psychologist Dan Ariely, Pink argues that money inhibits creativity and problem solving, the kind of higher-order thinking on which developed economies depend.[5] The problem is that knowing that money doesn't make us smarter may not stop us wanting it.

We want money for a very good reason: it makes us feel better. A fascinating series of experiments by a team of Chinese and American researchers put volunteers through their paces in a Cyberball game in which they were slowly but surely socially excluded, with the result that they registered distress. But then, in their distressed condition, they were made to count money and their mood lifted. As a control, some were asked to count paper, just to ensure that it wasn't the re-petitive task of counting that had the ameliorative effect. Paper, it turned out, wasn't an analgesic, but money was. Simply counting the money made people feel stronger.[6]

What held true for psychic pain turned out to be true for physical pain also. Students submerged their hands in very hot water: 109.4°F (43°C) for ninety seconds, 122°F (50°C) for thirty seconds, and then again 109.4°F for a minute. The pain they experienced was lower after counting money than after counting paper. And while it might be tempting to dismiss the results as indicative of loan-depleted American students obsessed with cash, the students who volunteered for the experiment were Chinese and were rewarded only by gaining course credits for their participation.

Money does motivate us and it does make us feel better. That's why companies pay overtime and bonuses. It may not, in and of itself, make us absolutely happy—but, just like cigarettes and chocolate, our wants are not confined to what's good for us. The pleasure of money is often short-lived, of course. Because there are always newer, big-ger, flashier, sweeter products to consume, the things we buy with money never satisfy as fully as they promise. Psychologists call this the hedonic treadmill: the more we consume, the more we want. But we stay on the treadmill, hooked on the pleasures that, at least initially, make us feel so good.

What all this has shown is that money may be the richest area ever discovered for the study of unintended consequences. From which it should follow, but rarely does, that managers and compensation com-mittees need to be tremendously thoughtful when deciding how to apply such a powerful, even irrational, motivator. Because money has a more complex influence on people than just to make them work longer.

"Money certainly changes the way you think," says David Ring. He's an internationally renowned orthopedic surgeon at one of the top hospitals in the United States. Ring is tall, handsome, and, for the most part, silent—except when he starts talking about his work, which is when he really comes alive. He loves what he does, but he doesn't love the role that money plays in medicine.

"Doctors who own stakes in testing labs order more tests; I've experienced' that firsthand. Colleagues working in surgical centers that they own—they take the money, the government pays the facility fee, and they get some of that money. Now, if you're doing that kind of case, the way to make money out of that is to spend less. So if you're working at your own surgical center, you will treat a fracture with pins. Then the same doctors will go to treat the same kind of case but this time they're in a hospital, so they'll use an expensive plate. They will tell you that with a straight face. They bypass questionable ethics. Some of it is conscious and some of it I'm sure they just don't see."

Could that mean, I asked him, that money might influence a diagnosis?

"Change diagnosis? I think so. The minute you see dollar signs in your patient's eyes, it changes how you think. You have to learn not to look at their insurance—get as far down the diagnostic path as you can before you know their income. It's impossible not to be swayed by the profit motive. I'm an academician and devoted to things that don't earn money but I watch people come in on my path and gradually get off of it. First, they just want to do well in their practice, just to be good surgeons. After a few years, they start to realize that what they do determines how much money they make and they start to learn a new game. The old game was: diagnose well, communicate well, do the surgery well. The new game becomes: make money. They don't really see the game change, they're blind to it. But it changes.

"Arthroscopy for arthritis, that's a classic example. You definitely don't cure osteoarthritis with arthroscopy. There was one brave guy in a Veterans Administration hospital in Texas who did a pilot study comparing knee arthroscopy with washing the knee and with cleaning the knee out. All three treatments were equally effective! But there's a lot of money in arthroscopy. So the response of American orthopedic surgeons was very defensive. It is a willful blindness: You bypass curiosity and scientific knowledge and concern for your patient and go straight for profit motive and preserve your position."

Ring is a vocal critic of the role that money plays in medicine. But that doesn't mean he feels himself to be immune to its influence.

"You could say that I'm really high-minded because I'll fly to Sheffield to teach or do research in my free time—but I still get caught up. You can see the temptation, especially in Massachusetts where there is only one good payer, workers' comp. It is devilishly good. You can make so much out of one case. So I can make a lot of money—ten times what I can make from Medicare or an HMO. It is so tempting; with just a few workers' comp patients, you've made your year's income in a month. If this is the going rate, why should I be the sucker?"[7]

What is so striking about Ring's perspective is not just that he's so forthright but that, unlike most of us, he is highly conscious of the influence that money has on him, as well as on his colleagues. Money is not making these doctors less motivated; they're as motivated as ever—maybe even more so. What money changes is their behavior.

In a series of experiments carried out in 2007, participants got to play the board game Monopoly (or were forced to, depending on your view of the game). Some came away with four thousand dollars of play money, some with two hundred dollars, and some with none. They were then taken across the lab, ostensibly to another room for another experiment. But on their way, they encountered a woman who spilled a box of pencils. The volunteers who had made the most money from the Monopoly game turned out to be the least helpful, picking up the fewest number of pencils. In another version of the experiment, volunteers encountered a colleague who seemed to be highly confused about a task. The participants who were not thinking about money spent 120 percent more time helping their colleague than those who had money on their minds.[8]

Then the researchers wondered whether they were just asking for a form of social interaction of a kind that the money-primed participants weren't very good at. So they designed an opportunity to do something that was easy and money-related: donate to the university student fund. Each student volunteer had been given eight quarters, two dollars, for taking part in the experiment. But the participants who had been reminded of money donated only 39 percent of their payment (on average) to the student fund. Their peers, who were not so conscious of money, donated 67 percent.

But the volunteers who had money uppermost in their minds weren't entirely without values. When they were given difficult or impossible tasks to perform, they worked 48 percent longer before asking for any help. They persevered—but they persevered alone. The researchers concluded that, while money was great at motivating individual effort, it carried with it significant negative social side effects. In the conflict that we all experience—between our interest in ourselves and our concern for others—money appears to motivate only our interest in ourselves, making us selfish and self-centered.

A further set of experiments confirmed this insight. When reminded of money—by screen savers, posters, or watercolors—participants put greater physical distance between themselves and others. Given the choice, they were also more likely to want to work alone and to prefer solo leisure activities. Small reminders of money produced large changes in behavior, making people less social, less connected to others. They were more motivated than ever but more isolated, less helpful, and less concerned for their fellow man.[9] Over time, the researchers concluded, the mere presence of money elicits a market-pricing orientation toward the world. Money makes people feel self-sufficient, which also means they don't need or care about others; it's each man for himself.

The most striking live demonstration of this phenomenon in recent years has been Guy Hands, a former executive at Goldman Sachs. Today, he heads up his private equity firm, Terra Firma, best known for its acquisition of the music business EMI. Hands is demonstrably successful and has made enough money to be very comfortable. Nevertheless, in his desire to preserve his assets and avoid paying tax, he has left his native United Kingdom and never visits his school-age children, who remain in England with their mother. Neither has he visited his mother and father there. "I do not visit my parents in the United Kingdom and would not do so except in an emergency," he said.[10]

Few of us are likely to worry about taxes to the degree that Guy Hands does, but that doesn't mean we are immune to the impact of money on our motivation. Performance-related pay, performance bonuses, and all kinds of incentive plans are designed to elicit harder work and perseverance from the workforce. But the unintended social consequences of such plans are far from straightforward.

"Every branch office had its own incentive scheme," Paul Moore told me. Between 2002 and 2005, Moore was head of group regulatory risk at HBOS, the largest mortgage lender in the United Kingdom. "I remember one in particular: Every Saturday, once the office closed for the day, the sales staff would all get together. And the sales advisors who'd beaten their targets, they got cash. But if you'd failed to beat your target, you were given a cabbage. Cash or cabbage, in public, every Saturday."

The ritual humiliation of employees was just one aspect of the company culture that alarmed Moore. To him, it signified that money had obliterated all other motives within HBOS, even concern for employees' respect for each other, and for their customers.

"When we were doing a review," Moore said, "one woman in Scunthorpe told me: 'We hit our targets but we have never hit our sales targets ethically.' What she meant by that was that the pressure to hit targets was so great that they were all anybody thought about. So there was a culture of bullying in HBOS, focused on sales numbers. I don't think people had started that way; it's what working for the company turned them into. The management just didn't think carefully enough: If you demand a sales increase of ten percent, and then only allow a cost increase of three percent, then you are going to get some highly improper sales and some very antisocial behavior. And that's what happened."

Moore's job was to look for all aspects within a company's processes and procedures, as well as within its balance sheet, that exposed it to risks. This meant, inevitably, spending a great deal of time poring over balance sheets. But for Moore, the greatest exposure didn't lie in the numbers. It lay in the people, the culture, and their incentives. He came to see that the firm's management—the CEO and his executive teams—were so driven by earnings (and by their own compensation, which derived from earnings) that they couldn't, and wouldn't, see the impact that the company's culture had on individual morality or on the wider society that the company served.

When he shared his insights with the CEO, Moore was fired. He was later vindicated when, in September 2008, the bank collapsed. Testifying to the UK Parliamentary Select Committee six months later, his rage was still palpable.

"Anyone whose eyes were not blinded by money, power, and pride, who really looked carefully, knew there was something wrong: that

economic growth based almost solely on excessive consumer spending, which was based on excessive consumer credit, which was based
on massively increasing property prices which were caused by the very
same excessively easy credit, could only ultimately lead to disaster. But
sadly, no one wanted or felt able to speak up for fear of stepping out of
line with the rest of the lemmings who were busy organizing themselves to run over the edge of the cliff behind the pied-piper CEOs
and executive teams that were all being paid so much to play that tune
and take them in that direction."[11]

A survey of 563 risk managers subsequently undertaken by Moore,
in conjunction with the Cranfield University School of Management,
cited culture and remuneration practices as two of the chief causes of
the banking failure. These most hard-nosed and numerate of executives didn't think regulation or economic models were chiefly at fault,
and they were entirely dismissive of the idea that banks had failed
due to "global circumstances beyond anyone's control."[12] What went
wrong, they thought, was the culture: people's attitudes to money. Pur-
suit of profits had effectively displaced concern for people. "A constitution for knaves may produce knaves" is how one economist described
what happens when money becomes the chief motivator.[13]

One of the first people to identify the strange and often unintended
consequences of money was the British social scientist Richard Titmuss. Born in 1907 to a Bedfordshire farmer, Titmuss moved with his
family to London where, at the age of fourteen, he went to work in his
father's transport business. When his father died a few years later, Titmuss moved to an insurance firm; because he had become the family's
major breadwinner, a serious salary and a permanent position were
crucial. Working in insurance taught Titmuss a great deal about how
people lived, moved, worked, or lost their jobs. He had boundless
energy and deep curiosity about how the world worked. Why did
people behave as they did? Why was there so much inequality?

Self-taught and highly motivated, Titmuss eventually left the dusty
world of insurance to work on social policy; by the time the Second
World War was over, he was well known and highly regarded. Despite never having attended a university, Titmuss became professor in
social administration at the London School of Economics. He was,
demonstrably, a man who knew a lot about motivation.

Much of Titmuss's academic work informed the postwar development of the welfare state and the creation of the United Kingdom's

National Health Service. To all intents and purposes, he was a good, old-fashioned policy wonk: embroiled in the minutiae of social legislation and politics, a man who never really lost his passion for statistics. And then, three years before he died, he published a book that blew up the world of economics. *The Gift Relationship* argued that money didn't always motivate people; in fact, paying people could undermine their moral motivation. Using the example of blood donation, Titmuss showed that paying donors made them less willing, not more willing, to donate blood and that the blood supply was more likely to become contaminated when donors were paid. The book caused a sensation worldwide because it dared to challenge the two fundamental tenets of modern economics: first, that individuals make rational economic decisions and second, that individuals are motivated only by self-interest. If people did less when offered more, what could that mean for economics?

Titmuss died before he could follow up his argument, but his book, and the questions he posed, continued to infiltrate and disrupt economic thinking. The idea that we make economic decisions rationally came under a lot of fire, with an army of behavioral economists demonstrating that biases and cognitive shortcuts interfere with our reasoned decision making. And evidence mounted that money and behavior might have a more complicated relationship than was allowed for in the popular economic models of the time.

One of the most interesting studies came out of Switzerland, where two economists wanted to test their theory (derived from Titmuss's work) that, far from enhancing our motivation, money might destroy it.[14] In 1993, they visited two communities in central Switzerland designated as potential sites for nuclear waste storage, and asked 305 residents whether they would be willing for the storage facility to be located in their neighborhood. More than half of their respondents (50.8 percent) said that, if asked, they would vote in favor of having the facility in their community. This wasn't because they were enthusiastic about nuclear waste: Nearly 40 percent believed there was a chance of a serious accident and nearly 80 percent believed that many local residents would suffer long-term effects from it. But they thought, if the storage facility was necessary, it might as well be in their area. In other words, their sense of a common, social good overcame their individual reservations.

What was most interesting, however, was what happened when the two economists offered to pay residents to house the nuclear waste store. The amount offered wasn't trivial: between \$2,175 and \$6,525 per individual per year—near or above the community's median monthly income. But now the level of acceptance *halved*. The economists tried raising the amount of compensation offered to see if that could influence their respondents. Only *one* person who had declined the first offer was prepared to accept anything higher, and only 4.9 percent said that the amount of the compensation mattered. You might have thought that, with two reasons to support the project, commitment would be higher. After all, now the Swiss residents could do good *and* make money. But that isn't the way it worked. Just as in the lab experiments, the mere prospect of money reduced people's sense of connectedness to the community.

Nor was this some weird Swiss peculiarity: an experiment in Nevada reported similar findings when pay diminished the respondents' sense of commitment to one another. Subsequent studies reinforced these findings.[15] When there was no penalty for lateness when collecting their children from a daycare center, parents were rarely late. But once they were fined for being late, the possibility of losing money didn't make them more punctual—it made them less so. Nor could their previous punctuality be revived; when fines were withdrawn, they still didn't care as much about being on time. What had started as a social relationship had been reduced irrevocably once money was introduced.

What these group studies showed was just what the lab experiments with individuals had gleaned: Money blinds us to our social relationships, creating a sense of self-sufficiency that discourages cooperation and mutual support.

Nobody yet quite understands why money works the way it does. Economists have speculated that motivation may work in ways similar to cognitive load.[16] Just as there is a hard limit to how much we can focus on at one moment, perhaps we can be motivated by only one perspective at a time. When we care about people, we care less about money, and when we care about money, we care less about people. Our moral capacity may be limited in just the same way that our cognitive capacity is.

We're at the raw edge of brain science here. A number of fMRI experiments have attempted to understand what happens when the brain makes a moral choice. Some have looked at the brain as it decides between two conflicting options; others have tried to see the difference between a utilitarian decision (do I take the bus or the train?) and a moral decision (should I lie?)[17] The findings are unclear. Certainly moral choices occupy a great deal of brain capacity, and they seem to employ autobiographical memories (which implies empathy) and social awareness. But no one knows how to trace motivation, at least not yet. It seems to sit on the cusp between brain and mind in a relationship that is endlessly fascinating but still obscure.

Empirically, however, we do know that one incentive—money—seems to crowd out our more social motivations. Since the mere presence of money evokes a market-pricing orientation, people become commodities and every commodity has a price. That would explain why, when senior managers at Countrywide would gather to look at the company three years out, they could have such extraordinary discussions.

"A lot of us on the operations side and risk management side would have meetings which led to a discussion of sub-prime mortgages," Catherine Clark recalled. "The sales people got such high commissions, they wouldn't stop. We kept asking: What happens in three years' time? And the only answer we got was from the guy in charge of all the back-office servicing: He said the technology infrastructure would not keep up with all the foreclosures."

What is so memorable about the scene Clark paints is that there aren't any real people in it. There are just sales—and a looming I.T. problem. Nobody can see that the I.T. problem represents thousands of families losing their homes. By the same token, when we learn just how many investors identified early the looming failure of the banking industry, the remarkable element is not that these bright individuals had such foresight, but that their only thought was to cash in on it.[18]

At a time when BP was so focused on cost-cutting, mergers, and acquisitions, it's perhaps not surprising that market thinking predominated. In 2002, the company was on a very aggressive growth path, about to deliver one of the strongest financial performances in its history. That's when some members of the Health and Safety Team got together to run a course. Part of the training involved an analysis of the decision whether to place contractors at Texas City in temporary trailers, permanent trailers, or permanent buildings. But that isn't how they chose to think about the cost-benefit analysis. Instead, a PowerPoint presentation shows an analogy with the Three Little Pigs. Each trailer option is designated a straw house, stick house, or brick house—with, for good measure, a fourth option, which is a blast-resistant house. The slide is decorated with little pigs and this is BP's cost-benefit analysis:

Frequency: the big bad wolf blows with a frequency of once per piggy lifetime

Consequence—If the wolf blows down the house, the piggy is gobbled.

Maximum justifiable spend (MJS)—A piggy considers it's worth $1,000 to save its bacon

1.0 piggy lifetime × $1,000/piggy life = $1,000

Which type house should the piggy build?[19]

In making their decision about what kind of trailer to build, the BP executives had to calculate the value of a life ($1,000) times the number of people in a trailer, the cost of a trailer, and the likelihood of a fatal accident in which a "piggy" might be killed, or "gobbled." You have to ask how this analogy helped them toward a moral decision. I often wonder how BP employees responded to this presentation. I hope somebody was appalled but I can imagine a fair amount of laughter as the metaphor was teased out. It isn't clear from the presentation whether this was a training exercise, a decision process, or both. What is clear is that human beings weren't under consideration. The Texas City contractors were animals, with a market value. And they were, ultimately, allowed to work and die in houses of straw.

It would be wrong to say BP is the only company in the world that thinks this way. Many have been shown to: Ford, when it calculated the costs of reinforcing the Pinto's rear end, as compared to the cost of lost lives; A. H. Robins, when it chose not to recall the contraceptive Dalkon Shield; W. R. Grace when it chose bankruptcy as a means of shaking off the dust of Libby, Montana. And when the archbishop of Dublin, Kevin McNamara, took out insurance against claims resulting from priests abusing children, what was he doing but placing market concerns over social ones? He could have removed accused priests from their ministries and tried to get them help; he might have launched a thorough investigation, imposed a child protection policy, or alerted other bishops—but he turned a blind eye to people and focused instead on protecting the Church's assets. In treating people as less important than things, work becomes both demoralized and demoralizing and we become blind to the moral content of our decisions.

Money and willful blindness make us act in ways incompatible with what we believe our ethics to be, and often even with our own self-interest. Driven by our desire to see ourselves as good, we value money because it appears to be the external proof that we are good—and much of society reads it just the same way. So the problem with money isn't fundamentally about greed, although it can be comforting to think so. The problem is that we live in societies in which mutual support and cooperation are essential, but money erodes the relationships we need to lead productive, fulfilling, and genuinely happy lives. When money becomes the dominant motivator, it doesn't cooperate with, or amplify, our relationships; it separates us from them. The farther removed we become from our neighbors, the more siloed in our self-sufficiency, the easier it is to treat people as things, to turn a blind eye to the human costs of toxic cultures and to make immoral decisions.

This isn't caused by money alone. All the other organizational forces of willful blindness—obedience, conformity, bystander effects, distance, and division of labor—combine to obscure the moral, human face of work. Money keeps us very busy, often too busy, to see clearly and work thoughtfully. It keeps us silent, too, fearful lest debate or criticism jeopardize salaries. Money reinforces and often appears to reward those core, self-identifying beliefs that blind us to alternatives and to argument. You could say that if we are just obeying orders, fitting in, diffusing responsibility for people who are a long way away and, anyway, may not be our concern at all—then money is the final incentive to keep looking away. The fact that money tends to be addictive—the more we have, the more we feel we need—merely ensures that the cycle is rewarded and perpetuated. To paraphrase Edmund Burke, all that evil needs to flourish is for good people to see nothing—and get paid for it.

No one visiting Stanford University could fail to be impressed by its sheer scale or its wealth. Over twelve square miles, it's ten times larger than Vatican City or Monaco, and the vast avenues of palms leading to fountains and Spanish courtyards are reminiscent more of Renaissance papal power than twenty-first-century cutting-edge research. Such lavish public buildings feel brash in their confidence, but their rooms harbor perpetrators of doubt and skepticism. At the heart of the campus, ensconced in an unremarkable linoleum-floored, book-lined room, sits Albert "Al" Bandura. In many respects, Bandura is the grand old man of psychology: its most cited living author, the father of social learning theory, and one of the first people to argue that children's behavior derived not just from reward and punishment but from what they observed around them. That this seems such an obvious thought to us nowadays is testimony to how profound Bandura's impact has been on our thinking. The very phrase "role model" would scarcely exist without him.

Bandura's own upbringing and life demonstrate many of the themes which distinguish his work. Born in the town of Mundare in northern Alberta, he grew up as part of a community of Eastern European immigrants who, in the very act of immigrating, demonstrated a profound capacity for changing their lives. His parents created, from scratch, a workable farm. During the Depression, the family kept cattle alive by feeding them pieces of their home's thatched roof.

Aware that growing up in what was a tiny hamlet limited the young Bandura's experience of the world, his parents insisted that he go further afield and learn other crafts; he credits his experience in Edmonton learning to make furniture with giving him the capacity to put himself through the University of British Columbia. His entire career has focused on, but also exemplified, the capacity of human beings to mold and change the way that they experience the world.

Much of Bandura's work has so seeped into public consciousness that we are barely aware it is there, and his work has attracted scores of awards, honors, and distinctions. But today, at the age of eighty-five, this hasn't stopped him working, nor has it rendered him complacent. For all his eminence, he's an engaging and accessible man whose mild manner belies a tenacious mind. And one of the issues he has wrestled with for years is the process by which individuals lose sight of morality in their need to preserve their sense of self-worth.

"People are highly driven to do things that build self-worth; you can't transgress and think of yourself as bad. You need to protect your sense of yourself as good. And so people transform harmful practices into worthy ones, by coming up with social justification, by distancing themselves with euphemisms, by ignoring the long-term consequences of their actions."[20]

One of the most prominent ways in which people justify their harmful practices is by using arguments about money to obscure moral and social issues. Because we can't and won't acknowledge that some of our choices are socially and morally harmful, we distance ourselves from them by claiming they're necessary for the creation of economic wealth. Nowhere is this more dangerous, he argues, than in our attitudes toward the environment and population growth. The easiest way for those who resist calls to curb population growth, and who oppose environmental controls, is to represent themselves as the good guys because they just want to make everyone better off.

"To defend their positions, they can't say, 'Sure, we're the bad guys and we want to rape and pillage the planet,'" Bandura told me. "They have to vindicate harmful practices that take such a heavy toll on the environment and the quality of human life; they have to make out that what's harmful is, in fact, good. And one way they do that is to use the notion of nature as, in fact, an economic commodity. So they see nature in terms of money and market value, rather than its inherent value."

That's why, Bandura argues, those who claim to love nature can also support, for example, drilling for oil in Alaska. They can't see themselves as destroyers, so they position themselves as the rational liberators of natural wealth. In this vein, Bandura quotes Newt Gingrich: "To get the best ecosystem for our buck, we should use decentralized and entrepreneurial strategies."[21] Similarly, when China signed a multi-billion-dollar deal with the Indonesian government to clearcut four million acres of forest, in order to replace it with palm oil plantations, a clan elder could not conceive of himself as doing the wrong thing. "As he put it succinctly, 'Wood is gold.'" It is, says Bandura, the economic justification that makes the environmentally damaging decision possible. Seeing nature as just a source of money blinds such decision makers to the moral consequences of their decisions.

Bandura has spent a lifetime dissecting the moral disengagement required for the perpetration of criminal and inhuman acts—through the tobacco industry, the gun lobby, the television industry, and implicit in environmental deregulation. He has a deep understanding of the forces at work which encourage employees to be blind to their collusion in these processes. But nothing enrages him more than the economic justifications used to defend continued population growth.

"I went to a conference in Germany," Bandura recalled, "where a young African woman spoke about the tremendous difference that birth control and health education had had on her community. The fact that she and her peers now had control over the number of children that they conceived and raised had transformed their lives. And she spoke of this very eloquently. And there, in that audience of well-heeled Europeans, rich Westerners, *she was booed!*"

When he recovered from his shock, Bandura analyzed what was going on in the minds of the audience. What drove them, he reasoned, was their recognition that Western birthrates won't pay for the pension requirements of the elderly; if the West doesn't produce more children, it can't produce the wealth needed to look after parents when they retire. Therefore, even though consumption and environmental degradation are clearly linked, the needs of the market trump the needs of the planet.

Nor was this a purely Western phenomenon. The need for money effectively positions infants as moneymaking machines.

"In some countries," Bandura writes, "the pressure on women to boost their childbearing includes punitive threats as well. The former prime minister of Japan, Yoshiro Mori, suggested that women who bore no children should be barred from receiving pensions, saying 'It is truly strange to say we have to use tax money to take care of women who don't even give birth once, who grow old living their lives selfishly and singing the praises of freedom.' In this campaign for more babies, childbearing is reduced to a means for economic growth."[22] In this mind-set, children are nothing more than moneymakers in the eyes of politicians, who are merely crunching the numbers, blind to the moral, environmental, or humanitarian consequences of their policies. Market thinking has obliterated moral thinking on a grand scale.

So persuasive (and pervasive) has the economic argument in favor of population growth become, says Bandura, that all of the major non-governmental organizations have had to stand aside from it. "Fear of alienating donors, criticism from the progressive left and disparagement by conservative vested interests claiming that overpopulation is a 'myth' served as further incentives to cast off the rising global population as a factor in environmental degradation. Population growth vanished from the agendas of mainstream environmental organizations that previously regarded escalating numbers as a major environmental threat. Greenpeace announced that population '*is not an issue for us.*' Friends of the Earth declared that '*it is unhelpful to enter into a debate about numbers.*'" The fear of losing money disabled those very organizations best placed to understand the ultimate consequences of thinking only about money.

What money does, Bandura argues, is allow us to disengage from the moral and social effects of our decisions. As long as we can frame everything as an economic argument, we don't have to confront the social or moral consequences of our decisions. That economics has become such a dominant, if not the prevalent, mind-set for evaluating social and political choices has been one of the strangest yet most defining characteristics of our age. As long as the numbers work, we feel absolved of the harder, more inchoate ethical choices that face us nonetheless. We appear to have gone from having a market economy to being a market society (if that isn't an oxymoron). Our obsession with economics could be seen as one long sustained phase of displacement activity.

Money is just one of the forces that blind us to information and issues which we could pay attention to—but don't. It exacerbates and often rewards all the other drivers of willful blindness: our preference for the familiar, our love for individuals and for big ideas, a love of busyness and our dislike of conflict and change, the human instinct to obey and conform, and our skill at displacing and diffusing responsibility. All these operate and collaborate with varying intensities at different moments in our life. The common denominator is that they all make us protect our sense of self-worth, reducing dissonance and conferring a sense of security, however illusory. In some ways, they all act like money: making us feel good at first, with consequences we don't see. We wouldn't be so blind if our blindness didn't deliver the benefit of comfort and ease.

But in failing to confront the greatest challenge of our age—climate change—all the forces of willful blindness come together, like synchronized swimmers in a spectacular water ballet. We live with people like ourselves and sharing consumption habits blinds us to their cost. Like the unwitting wife of an alcoholic, we know there's something amiss but we don't want to acknowledge that our lifestyles may be killing us. The dissonance produced by reading about our environmental impact on the one hand, and continuing to live as we do, is resolved by minor alterations in what we buy or eat, but in very few significant social shifts. Sometimes we get so anxious that we consume more. We keep

too busy to confront our worries, pursuing a kind of wild displacement activity with schedules that don't allow us to be as green as we'd
like. The gravitational pull of the status quo exerts its influence and
global conferences end when no one has the stomach for the levels of
conflict they engender. In our own countries, no politician shows the
nerve for the political battles real change would require.

We're obedient consumers and we might change if we were told to,
but we're not. We conform to the consumption patterns we see around
us as we all become bystanders, hoping someone else somewhere will
intervene. Our governments and corporations grow too complex to
communicate or to change and we are left just where we do not want
to be, where our only consolation is cash.

This is willful blindness on a spectacular scale and it would leave us
abject with despair, were it not that all around us are individuals who
aren't blind. That they can and do see more, and act on what they see,
offers a possibility that we can be willfully sighted, too.

11

CASSANDRA

I cannot leave the truth unknown.
— Sophocles, *Oedipus*

I WASN'T SURPRISED," said Cynthia Thomas. "I'd been saying for months that something like this was bound to happen. It was so obvious. You push these boys too far, what's in their heads is so awful and so violent. Of course you're going to have problems with violence."

On November 5, 2009, U.S. Army Major Nidal Malik Hasan shot and killed fourteen people on Fort Hood military base. Cynthia Thomas was deeply upset, but she understood what had happened. Earlier that year, she had started the Under the Hood Cafe to offer soldiers a refuge from the base, a place to hang out where they could find comfort and, if they wanted it, psychological, psychiatric, and legal help.

"This stuff happens, on a smaller scale, all the time: soldiers killing someone or stabbings, shootings. All the time. People don't understand. We can have two weeks and there will be three, four, five violent incidents. And people don't see them. The violence. Everything is just all the time. A soldier snapping and doing this is not surprising. People don't want to see it, they don't want to hear about it. But it's here. It will go on happening."

Cynthia Thomas is a Cassandra. In ancient Greek mythology,

Cassandra was royalty, the daughter of King Priam and Queen Hecuba. Besotted by her beauty, Apollo fell in love with her and gave her the gift of prophecy. But when she spurned him, he retaliated by adding to her gift of prophecy the fate that no one would believe her. So the Trojans ignored her when she warned them not to bring in the great wooden horse left by the Greeks. And it was Cassandra who warned Agamemnon of Clytemnestra's murderous rage on his return from war. Cassandra must have known she was doomed to die then, too, because that was her unique gift: to see what others did not.

The savage irony of Cassandra is that, as we read her prophecies, we know that they are true, but no one else does. As such, she is one of the first characters in literature to offer readers that invaluable plot device, superior knowledge. Believing Cassandra, when everyone else derides her, we see simultaneously two contradictory points of view. We learn that any situation can contain truths that we may not be able to see but that are, nonetheless, visible. And she teaches us that sometimes it is the despised who know most.

But Cassandra captivates our imagination also because she embodies that baffled rage that we all feel when no one else can see what we see. The epitome of frustration, because she is doomed always to be right, Cassandra shows us that the truth is knowable but won't necessarily set us free.

The world is full of Cassandras, individuals whose fate it is to see what others can't see, who are not blind but compelled to shout their awkward, provocative truths. That's why, after any industrial or organizational failure, individuals inevitably surface who saw the crisis coming, warned about it, and were mocked or ignored. In Libby, Montana, Gayla Benefield was a classic Cassandra, insisting that there was something wrong with the town, even when all around her didn't want to know anything about it. But when you meet Gayla, she has none of the wild eyes or inspired fury of the classic portrayals of Cassandra; she's a middle-aged mother and grandmother who blends right into her surroundings. Nothing physically marks her out as a rebel or nonconformist, but she seems, from an early age, to have seen things that others did not.

"In high school, I remember our teacher wanted us to have silhouettes taken behind a sheet. And there was just something about it that made me uneasy. I didn't know why it wasn't right but I knew it wasn't." Gayla paused for a moment, reaching for the facts, trying to make sure she captured an accurate memory. Then she laughed. "Maybe it was just that I wasn't going to take off my false boobs! Whatever it was, I led the walk out."

Taking a stand seems to have become something Gayla did easily. She felt comfortable being different, even when it meant being pilloried or left out.

"I took mechanical drawing in high school—no girl ever had done that at our school, but I didn't know why. I remember, I was sat in a far corner away from the boys."

That childhood experience of difference and exclusion, along with no small degree of endurance, stood her in good stead when, from 1974 to 1999, Gayla figured out that her neighbors were dying of asbestosis. She had to be curious enough to notice the number of people using oxygen tanks. She had to be good at recognizing patterns. She had to be resourceful enough to dig up information and keep examining what she found, even when, for those twenty-five years, everyone told her to ignore it. Where did that drive come from?

"My grandfather was a Russian immigrant who ended up in eastern Montana. He taught me not to fight the system, but always to question it. He was the best American you could ever find. He was always trying to find a better way to do things. I never danced to a different drummer but I questioned. I've always questioned. I've brought my kids up to question. I wasn't a blind follower. Never have been."

Cassandras are often also whistleblowers, determined not just to see what others don't see, but to act upon it, trying to alter fate. Both see things that others don't see because they are questioners, driven to ask: What is really happening? Does it have to be that way? Am I missing something? Is there some other explanation or solution? They're driven, dedicated, often quite obsessive truth seekers—even (or sometimes especially) when no one agrees with them. But that is almost the only generalization you can make about these extremely and willfully sighted people.

The world contains millions of Cassandras, in all walks of life and all of them different. Academics have struggled to find identifying qualities they all have in common, but to no avail. It used to be thought that whistleblowers were more likely to be women because, as newcomers to most institutions, they didn't have the same stake in the status quo. It was a nice theory but turned out not to be true.[1] There doesn't seem to be any correlation between age or years of service, and neither pay nor education level turn out to be good predictors, either. Religion doesn't seem to play a definitive role; while all Cassandras have a pronounced sense of right and wrong, as many derive their morality from history or personal experience as from any formal faith. And despite the fact that these troublesome truth tellers are sometimes thrown into jail or sent for psychiatric assessments, there seems to be no evidence that, as a group, they are crazy.

What we do know is that society needs people like Gayla Benefield: individuals willing to ask awkward questions, trace tricky connections, and challenge embedded assumptions. Because although it's fiendishly difficult to size the level of threat, corruption, and crime within organizations, no attempt to do so has ever emerged with good news. In the United States, in 2000, the Ethics Resource Center in Arlington, Virginia, found that a third of public and private employees had personally observed misconduct. A far higher percentage—80 percent—of directors of internal auditing said they had observed wrongdoing by their organizations. And when Harry Markopolos testified before a U.S. Senate committee in 2009 about the Madoff fraud, he argued that "white-collar criminals cause far more economic harm to this nation than armed robbers, drug dealers, car thieves and other assorted miscreants put together. These fraudsters steal approximately five percent of business revenues annually, dwarfing the economic losses due to violent crime, yet not nearly enough federal law enforcement resources are devoted to catching them."[2] Thomas Gabor, a criminologist at the University of Toronto says the situation in Canada is even worse.

"Canada has been very delinquent in dealing with white-collar crime, even worse than the U.S.," says Dr. Gabor. "There's no public pressure to prosecute white-collar crime. In Canada, there's a real preoccupation, sometimes excessively so, with social crimes and people falling through the safety net. But one of the problems is that, to combat white-collar crime, you need a dedicated program, attorneys with expertise in that area, and you have to be prepared to spend millions of dollars and interview thousands of people. It could be that one reason no one wants to tackle it seriously is precisely because it is so pervasive."

Other kinds of threats and disasters, too—the *Challenger* explosion, the poorly coordinated response to Hurricane Katrina, climate change— can only happen when individuals and organizations turn a blind eye to what they know. In the United States, vast amounts of federal legislation have been introduced to try to protect whistleblowers. The first of these, in 1912, protected federal employees who wished to offer information to Congress, and much subsequent legislation has been focused on ensuring that government employees in particular are protected. The Whistleblower Protection Act (1989) and the No Fear Act (2002) seek to protect federal employees from retaliation and the loss of their jobs, while the False Claims Act, passed during the Civil War, sought to elicit help from ordinary citizens against contracting fraud. That law offers a percentage of the settlement to the whistleblower and, since Congress reinforced the act in 1986, the Justice Department has recovered more than twenty billion dollars. (It is on this act that the Madoff whistleblower, Harry Markopolos, hopes to build his new business investigating fraud.) The Office of Special Counsel was also created in 1979, specifically to investigate complaints by federal whistleblowers.

They are not cynics, but almost always start as optimists, not nonconformists but true believers. They are not, typically, disgruntled or disappointed; they're not innately rebels but are compelled to speak out when they see organizations or people that they love taking the wrong course. When Gayla Benefield first began piecing together the puzzle of ill health in Libby, she expected her findings to be the start of something wonderful.

"In my heart of hearts, I felt that by bringing W. R. Grace to task, they would come back and say: What did we do? What can we do to heal you? How can we put it right?" She shrugged and gave a sad, small smile. "That is the dreamer part of me."

Such naïveté is common. When Pat Lewis designed his risk model for Bear Stearns, or Paul Moore drew the board's attention to risks within HBOS, they did so as committed employees trying to contribute to stronger businesses. They might have expected to be treated as heroes, certainly not as pariahs. And when Sherron Watkins wrote to Enron chairman Ken Lay, she thought he would welcome her questions and appreciate that, far from trying to wreck the company, she was trying to save it.

"I'd been so loyal!" Watkins recalled. "I thought his first response would just be to want to get to the truth, to know what was going on in his company! It was the sense that, if you tell the captain the ship is sinking, he is going to man the lifeboats."

The letter Watkins wrote, detailing accounting problems she could not resolve and risks she believed Lay did not know about, did not go to the press; she wrote to Lay as the person she believed was most likely to fix the problems she'd identified. And Watkins never went public. Only after the company had collapsed did investigators find her letter.

"I thought good would prevail, that we'd unwind some deals, restate earnings, that they'd be grateful to me for identifying the problems. I only found out later that Lay almost instantly took legal advice about whether he could fire me!"[3]

When Harry Markopolos first started examining Bernard Madoff's investment strategies, it wasn't with a view to discovering criminality. The last thing on his mind was identifying systemic failures in the Securities Exchange Commission. Markopolos explored Madoff because he wanted to see if he could copy him, not bring him down.

In many instances like this, what enables Cassandras to see what others don't is a tremendous eye for detail. They don't allow distance or theory to obscure the nitty-gritty of what they are doing; in fact, they relish it. They don't wrap themselves up in dogma, but relish facts and arguments. In just the same way that Alice Stewart immersed herself in all the domestic detail that might explain childhood cancers, Cassandras typically like getting down to the bare bones of otherwise abstract problems.

That's what James Hansen did in the late 1970s. Having completed his Ph.D., writing on the atmosphere of Venus, he was a geek, not a dissident, buried in his data and oblivious to the student riots that surrounded him. Soon Earth's atmosphere became more captivating than Venus's, as he grappled with the detail of chlorofluorocarbons and the ozone layer. One of his key interests, he wrote, was "radiative transfer in planetary atmospheres, especially interpreting remote sounding of the earth's atmosphere and surface from satellites." In 1981, he published a paper predicting that the following decade would be unusually warm, and the decade after that warmer still. He was right, and he kept being right, but his work was full of detail and caveats, identifying areas of ignorance and uncertainty that would constitute a lifetime's work.[4] He had not set out to prove or disprove theories of climate change; his work didn't begin with ideology. He started with detail and merely kept following where the data led him.

It's also what Daniel Ellsberg did. He was perhaps predisposed to be skeptical of authority; at the age of fifteen, Ellsberg lost his mother and sister when his father fell asleep while driving. "I think it did probably leave an impression on me, that someone you loved and re-

spected could fall asleep at the wheel and they needed to be watched."
It was detail, not dogma, that turned him finally against the Vietnam War. After working for Robert McNamara at the Department of
Defense, Ellsberg insisted on going to Vietnam and seeing for himself, firsthand, the reality of government policy. On his return, he
read the seven thousand pages of the Pentagon Papers and learned in
immense detail of the many times the public had been misled by ad-
ministrations that said one thing while doing another.

Detail, facts, and research drove Sheila Bair, too, when, in 2006, she
was appointed to head the Federal Deposit Insurance Corporation—
the government insurance company that guarantees some eight hundred thousand American banks. Bair had been worried for some time
about the amount of debt that banks were carrying. She had watched
the growth of sub-prime mortgages with alarm and now she wanted
to find out what was really going on. What she did was simple: She
bought a database of sub-prime loans and studied it, something any
federal regulator could have done.

"We just couldn't believe what we were seeing. Really steep payment
shock loans and sub-primes . . . Very little income documentation, really high prepayment penalties."[5]

Without the beguiling fog of ideology, and with the gruesome details right in front of her—data about real people buying real loans for
real houses—she was in no doubt about what was going on around
her. In March 2007, she issued a cease-and-desist notice to shut down
one of the worst sub-prime offenders, Fremont Investment and Loan.

From an entirely different vantage point, Aaron Krowne gained the
same insight. Krowne wasn't a financier, far from it. He was a computer science and math graduate working as a software developer.
Fascinated by economics since the dotcom bubble, he was just a keen,
smart observer who liked asking himself questions about what he saw
around him.

"I have a strong moral sense from my father and I learned you collect the data, form a hypothesis, and try to confirm or disprove the
hypothesis. You don't impose your views on a priori findings; you
present what you find even if it isn't what you want. Because it is important for all our lives and the well-being of society. I just felt a need
to say something and speak up."

What gave Krowne something to speak up about was his experience
in 2005 when he tried to buy a home.

"I was in a situation where I had to leave the apartment I was in or buy it. The owner wanted to sell, so I looked at the buy versus rent fundamentals and made a chart of the price for that kind of unit over ten to twenty years. And it spiked up just like a bubble! Everyone was saying you have to buy! But I said: Look at the fundamentals. I'd have had to get an exotic loan to come out ahead monthly and I just didn't feel comfortable after such a rapid run-up. So I declined and had to move."

Toward the end of 2006, Krowne noticed a lot of sub-prime lenders going under. He thought that the bubble he'd spotted was about to pop, so he launched a little Web site to ask hard questions about what was going on, why, and who was responsible.

"It started as just a single page, with seven or eight lenders on it. I called it Implode-o-Meter for a little humor, the whole thing was so ridiculous. I posted it on some economic blogs I frequented and it caught on. Traffic steadily increased and it got picked up actively by newsletters and a few months later by Bloomberg TV and CNBC. By March 2007, it was pretty well ensconced as the biggest site for the mortgage industry itself, with everyone sending in tips and information."

The site was fed by the industry it reported on, so Krowne was getting live, firsthand, unmediated information from hundreds of sources across the industry. His site demonstrated that the knowledge was out there.

"Ninety-nine percent of the information that we got—tips from people in the companies—proved correct. People out there *knew* what was going on in their organizations. We'd get a lot of vociferous denials from management—but the angrier they got about leaks, the more true the leaks turned out to be. There were very few instances where the problem was a disgruntled employee making things up. We did all we could to verify the information, at risk to ourselves, but the information we got was usually very honest. There is a phenomenon where whistleblowing is almost always accurate; otherwise why take the risk?"[6]

Krowne wasn't a banking insider or a policy wonk or even an economist. He was just a guy on the ground who looked around and asked himself questions about what he saw. Being an outsider may have been an advantage, giving him a less biased perspective on what he heard and saw. Most Cassandras are outsiders, either by accident of birth, or life, or by dint of what they see that sets them irrevocably apart.

"When my relatives heard I was working at a bank, they thought I was going to be a teller!" Frank Partnoy laughs now at what he considers, nevertheless, to have been a significant advantage when he became a Wall Street investment banker.

"I grew up in Kansas and didn't have the built-in blinders that someone with more pedigree might have. My parents didn't go to Harvard or Yale. And maybe to me the stakes seemed lower. To many people, once you're at Morgan Stanley and have climbed the mountain, the idea of leaving it behind is unthinkable. For me, it wasn't such a big deal."

In *F.I.A.S.C.O.*, Partnoy unsparingly chronicles his growing enthusiasm and then disgust with the trading world he moved in. Not being from that world helped him to see what kind of world it was—and what the costs of conformity would entail.

"Everyone I knew who had been an investment banker for a few years, including me, was an asshole. The fact that we were the richest assholes in the world didn't change the fact that we were assholes. I had known this deep down since I first began working on Wall Street. Now, for some reason, it bothered me."

Partnoy left and wrote first about his own experiences and then, in *Infectious Greed*, about the rampant explosion not in derivatives but in financial disasters caused by derivatives. He predicted that there would be more, and this was early, in 2003. (In 2002 he had also tried to explain to Congress that Enron had collapsed not because of a few bad men but because of derivatives, but no one really paid attention then, either.) Then in 2006 he was back in Washington, warning about the structural problems inherent in credit ratings agencies like Moody's. Apart from having a strong stomach for unpopular positions, why could he see what others did not?

"I am the sort of person who wakes up every morning, I wipe the slate clean and everything is up for grabs and I am constantly questioning everything. I think also there's something about my educational experience at Yale Law School. Those three years are so focused on questioning everything; that's what Yale Law School is by design—an institution whose constituents are trying to make the world a better place all the time. It seems to generate a lot of people who don't wear blinders and try to keep them off, almost religiously."

Partnoy left banking to work in academia, a world, he says, where prestige, intellectual respect, is the equivalent of a bonus. You can't use prestige, he says; you can't spend it. It just makes you happy. But he's not only a professor; as well as academic papers, he also writes popular books about finance and history and he testifies before Congress. He is never exclusively wedded to one mind-set, but always traveling between perspectives. It's what Hannah Arendt called "thinking without a banister."

"Even within my profession, I think people climbing the ladder are constrained. So you have to make sacrifices not to be constrained. For me freeing myself from those constraints is what gives me happiness and gives me freedom. When you are a teenager, or in college, you're always reexamining your life. But when most people graduate, they stop doing that and I wonder why. Is it that it gets too draining to keep questioning your life?"

This highly unconstrained travel, between points of view, is hard work and it can be risky, not just because it can take you off of well-established career paths, but because it provokes questions that, as a Cambridge professor once sternly reminded me, "one is not invited to ask." Questions that one is not invited to ask make everyone uncomfortable, not least because they don't easily lend themselves to prepared answers. But in the intersection between disciplines, real insight can be gleaned.

Although ensconced inside an establishment newspaper—the *Financial Times*—Gillian Tett was, in her own way, an outsider: a pretty, slight, blonde woman working in structured finance. That she has a gentle lisp and a Ph.D. in anthropology definitely set her apart from mainly male, macho bankers. In 2006, when she and her team became seriously alarmed by what they saw in structured finance, they tried to point out the dangers. It was, she says, a lonely endeavor, too boring and technical, too much nitty-gritty, and bad news to boot. But she credits some of her insight not to her outsider perspective but to her training as a social anthropologist.

"Anthropology is a brilliant background for looking at finance," she said. "You're trained to look at how societies or cultures operate holistically, so you look at how all the bits move together. And most people in the City [of London] don't do that. They are so specialized, so busy, that they just look at their own little silos. One of the reasons we got into the mess we are in is because everyone failed to ask hard questions: Why are credit cards so cheap? Why can I get such a big mortgage? The silence suited everyone! Who had incentives to see? No one. What was missing in banking was the wider perspective, the context. But that didn't happen in finance. It wasn't in anybody's interest to look further."

That absence of holistic thought, Tett believes, allows us all to become narrow and deep. Buried deep at the bottom of our riverbeds, we are blind to connections and dependencies. We see only what we know and like and are lulled into a sense of mastery by our isolation from challenge. That feels comfortable, of course, until different perspectives bring unwanted and unwonted challenges.

"One of the most powerful people in the U.S. government at the time stood up on the podium at Davos and waved my article, the article that predicted the problems at Northern Rock, as an example of scaremongering."[7]

The fragmentation of the banking world, together with its sheer complexity, she argues, encouraged financiers to regard banking as its own world, distant and detached from the rest of society. This became very clear when she was summoned one day to Canary Wharf—a major business district of London which is, she was at pains to point out, an island.

"So I was called to Canary Wharf by this banker who said: 'I don't know why you keep saying [collateralized debt obligations] and structured finance are opaque and murky. It's all on Bloomberg terminals; it's right there.' But what, I asked him, what about the people who don't have Bloomberg terminals? He looked at me as if to say: There *are* people out there without Bloomberg terminals—and we're supposed to care about them? He had just retreated to his Bloomberg cyber village.[8] They had become like the inhabitants of Plato's cave, who could see shadows of outside reality flickering on the walls, but rarely encountered that reality themselves. The chain that linked a synthetic [collateralized debt obligation of asset-backed securities], say, with a 'real' person was so convoluted it was almost impossible for anybody to fit that into a single cognitive map."[9]

Being able to draw a cognitive map requires traveling well outside of our immediate knowledge and safety. It means meeting people not like ourselves, in industries and neighborhoods far from our own, and, when we're there, having the confidence and curiosity to keep asking questions. Robert Shiller, the Yale economist who so famously warned about the property bubble and impending financial collapse, says that his work is deeply informed by his wife, who is not an economist at all but a clinical psychologist. Drawing our cognitive map calls on a breadth of experience, either from different disciplines or different life experiences.

At first sight, there's nothing remotely unconventional about Roy Spence. He's enjoyed a highly successful career running a Texas advertising agency whose clients have been some of the business legends: Sam Walton of Walmart, Herb Kelleher of Southwest Airlines. Spence's company does what all ad companies do and Roy is like successful executives you meet everywhere: handsome, energetic, polite, punctilious. Just an ad guy, you might think.

But Roy was one of the few people to turn down business with Enron. And he seems to be one of those people who can tap into the zeitgeist and see things that others don't. Was it being in Texas, when the rest of the ad world is based in New York, that gave him his particular take on events?

"It helps," he agreed. "It helps that if you come home from Manhattan with your head stuffed full of nonsense, everyone here will tell you."

But much more important, he felt, was his experience growing up with his sister, Susan, who was born with spina bifida.

"When I used to push my sister to school, I thought I was crippled. If you come from a place that is vulnerable to start with, it's out in the open: We have something different going on here. That changes who you are and how you look at things. When you're out there, you see yourself being looked at and you become the watcher, too. You start to see how other people see. And the vulnerability of other people, too."

He paused for a second, remembering his sister.

"People thought my sister was different. Well, she was: she could never walk. But people couldn't see beyond that. You saw how blind they were. And it makes you think: If they're missing so much about me and about her, what am I missing about them?"

The image of the young Texan boy pushing his sister to school, scrutinizing faces while trying to imagine the thoughts behind them, is striking: simultaneously he sees through his own eyes, his sister's eyes, and the eyes of those watching him. The dialogue he has with himself about those different perspectives is one definition of thought.

What Roy describes is akin to empathy but goes far beyond it. He doesn't see through the eyes of power, but through the eyes of the vulnerable.

"I am married to a soldier," says Cynthia Thomas, proprietor of Under the Hood. "But you shut your feelings down in the military to survive. They all choose to bury their heads in the sand because it is easier that way. It is drilled into your head that you have to be supportive. And you believe that the military will take care of them if something happens. So you are in this bubble where you can't really see what's going on."

For years, Thomas says, she lived in that bubble. She took it for granted that the military would look after her husband and their family, that nothing would go wrong, that they were okay. And she was surrounded by other wives and families who did exactly the same thing. But then, as the Iraq War wore on, she started to see events from a very different perspective, the perspective of powerlessness.

"Tim was wounded in 2005 and came back on life support. In 2007, he was redeployed even though he was not supposed to be. He had brain injuries, fractures on his pelvis. His doctor said he won't be able to save himself if he gets shot at. But they didn't care, they redeployed him anyway. And then my stepson called and said he was joining the Marines. The bubble popped. I thought—oh my god, after everything that happened, these wars are going to be endless and our kids will be fighting them. That moment, I thought, if I don't do something or try to, this will go on forever. And I was upset but I finally did something, I opened up to human beings."

Seeing life through the eyes of young vulnerable men, in a world where most mass media only charts the progress of the powerful, showed Thomas a world of suffering she had been blind to. Thomas's mantra now is that, in war, there are no unwounded soldiers; and she has opened her coffeehouse to tend to all of the wounded. Anyone can come in, regardless of political opinion. It was her openness to them that allowed her to see how dangerous life was becoming for the soldiers of Fort Hood. The soldiers aren't getting the help they need, she says, because once diagnosed with post-traumatic stress disorder (PTSD) they aren't supposed to be redeployed.

"There's real pressure here not to diagnose it. We have soldiers on fifteen medications and they have an adjustment disorder, a mood disorder, you can call it anything but PTSD because they know if they have PTSD, they can get a medical discharge and the government would have to pay them for being disabled and that's a lot of money. The military is a business; if your employee can't do his job, you get rid of him. So you just have this tension building, boys needing help and everyone refusing to see they need help."[10]

At first, it was hard for Thomas to find a site for her coffeehouse; just having that physical presence would raise issues that most of the town preferred to overlook. Killeen is a tight-knit military community, and many fear getting in trouble with Command; everyone hopes that trouble will pass them by. But Thomas sees what others won't because she looks with the eyes of the most vulnerable.

"Just looking around this community and seeing the cost of the war, it is so hard on a daily basis. Walking around on post and looking at really young faces—eighteen, nineteen—they're babies! Oh my god, they don't grasp the severity of it. Nobody understands. You can't describe it. We have boys coming back so young and their lives are ruined. No one knows the cost of war. They don't want to think about it. They'd have to look in the mirror and say, this is what we did."

For Thomas, being able to look in the mirror and see clearly has become a fundamental part of who she is. You can almost hear the dialogue she has with herself, asking whether she's done enough, seen enough, said enough. Given a formal culture of obedience, this isn't necessarily what you would expect from an Army wife, but there are many in the Army who think long and hard about what they will, and will not, do.

"I've always felt people in the military generally would go out of their way to help, far more than people not from a military culture," Lawrence Rockwood told me. "My mother, father, right back to my great-great-grandfather had been in the military and that's what I'd grown up with. That's why, when I went to Haiti, I couldn't understand why everyone seemed to be turning a blind eye. It was like their compassion switch, their ability to see what was going on, had been switched off."[11]

Captain Rockwood was one of twenty thousand troops sent to Haiti in 1994, on a mission to oversee the peaceful transfer of power to democratically elected president Jean-Bertrand Aristide. An intelligence officer, his job was to develop informants in order better to protect the incoming government. But his informants kept ending up dead or imprisoned. Every day, reports of beatings, rapes, kidnapping, and murder—some in graphic detail—crossed Rockwood's desk. Much of this seemed to be taking place in Haitian prisons and Rockwood knew that the departing regime would, if it could, use its last days in power to eliminate its political opponents. He repeatedly wrote up his reports, detailing systemic human rights abuses and requesting permission to visit the prisons to document who was there.

But Rockwood's reports on human rights violations never seemed to make it into the Daily Intelligence Summary, designed for high command. When he protested, his superior officer told him, "One hundred percent of what you hear, don't believe, and fifty percent of what you see don't believe." Orders to be blind seemed strange to the experienced intelligence officer, who had been deployed to Haiti on a humanitarian mission. Rockwood grew more and more distressed at the knowledge he had. He wanted to visit the prisons and document who was there; it was the only way he could think of to protect the inmates.

"I figured that, if they knew we had a list of names, they might stop eliminating people. Their actions would be more transparent and they would face prosecution if it could be shown that so-and-so was in the prison on this date when the U.S. went in—and then he disappeared. That was the best way to protect them. And I had a lot of informants—people going in and out of the jail—who did know what was going on."

"For ten days I turned myself into an absolute nuisance, going to five or six different groups making a nuisance of myself, asking permission to visit. Finally I was told it wouldn't happen for a week. That's what I found unacceptable: that a decision was being made that would lead to the unnecessary deaths of noncombatants."

Rockwood decided he couldn't wait another week. He would go and look for himself. He knew this was a career-ending move but he did not feel that he could fulfill his military duty if he did not see for himself what was happening. When he got to the prison, his worst fears were confirmed.

Rockwood was subsequently given psychiatric evaluations (which he passed) and told to resign or face a court-martial for disobedience. He chose to be court-martialed. He refused to resign. What, I wondered, had made him so determined to see for himself what was going on?

"I felt I had to act. I had to justify my position: there is a line you will not cross. When I was a boy, my father was in the military and he took me to Dachau. He taught me that there are times you must take a stand. You must know there's a line you do not cross, times that it is more important to do the right thing than to obey orders and stick with your team. And I thought about Nuremberg and orders that should not be obeyed. And how important that rule was."

A sense of history, of patterns, helped Rockwood to see what was at stake. But it wasn't until many years later, when Universal Studios got it wrong, that Rockwood understood what else had made him insist on seeing what others wanted him to ignore.

"They wanted to make a movie about me, but I'm so glad it never got made," he laughed. "Because, in the movie, what motivated me was I came in contact with a young Haitian boy and he gets killed and that is supposed to justify what I do. But that was horrifying! I don't need to have a relationship with someone to know that the Haitians are human! There doesn't need to be a personal connection for compassion to be turned on. Can I only be compassionate when these people are like me? That's what really motivated me. And what was so strange and what upset me so much was that, because these people were not like me, I wasn't supposed to care about them. I was just supposed to look away."

That Rockwood succeeded in looking beyond the sides of his riverbed, could see people not like himself and see that they mattered, shows that we don't have to be blind. The expectations of a culture of obedience were overcome by compassion. And that determination—to side with the powerless—has stayed with him. Today he nurses heroin addicts, another group, he says, society would prefer not to see.

Rockwood felt a passionate dedication to what he perceived to be his military mission; he simply saw no conflict between his obligation to the Army and his obligation to Haitians. After Hurricane Katrina, Maria Garzino felt that same commitment when she saw the people of New Orleans on television.

"The looks on their faces: that hopelessness thing," Garzino recalled. A member of the Army Corps of Engineers, she had recently come back from Iraq and what she saw on television seemed horribly familiar.[12]

"You look at the faces of individuals and they know they have a good chance of being dead very soon. And they're pleading for help that should be there. And you realize, it isn't coming. It didn't come. The failure was something beyond an inadequate response. It was a break in trust. When someone doesn't do their best, your trust is gone. How do you restore it? I volunteered to go down to New Orleans in any capacity because I wanted people to understand that the Army Corps cared deeply. All I could guarantee was that I would do my best. That's the only way we could restore trust."

Garzino was experienced in emergency work and she loved it. After begging and conniving to be sent to New Orleans, she was made pump team installation leader, assigned to install new pumps that were supposed to protect the city for the next fifty years.

"Pretty quickly I realized something was wrong. Working with contractors on emergency work is very fast paced so you need a relationship of trust. The first things that are said are: this is a twenty-four-seven project, we are going to help each other, that's the deal. Failure isn't an option. Forthright disclosure is essential; you have to be direct and honest. But I was noticing that contractors didn't want to say anything, they were hiding things and it was hard to get information."

Garzino kept pressing for the information she needed and hoping for the best. But she didn't understand how MWI, Moving Water Industries, had got the contract for pumps that appeared to be ill-suited to their task.

"My problem is, this seems to be good-old-boy network, where they only tell me what they think I need to know. This is not a good candidate for partner of the year. Delivery dates were short. We have only a few months to get the pumps in place. NOAA [The National Oceanic and Atmospheric Administration] is predicting three or four storms that year that could hit the area, so we have to get this done. Then the schedules slipped. That was unacceptable."

As Garzino relayed the detail of her story to me, she struggled to stay calm. Her frustration with a firm that didn't seem to care about deadlines or quality or the life-and-death nature of the job distresses her to this day.

"We started testing and the pumping systems fell apart each time we turned them on. Very concerned is an understatement. When you turn these pumps on, they blow their guts out—in very different ways. The head people would bypass me and call New Orleans and get lesser requirements. So they tried to reduce the specification. Well—why even bother testing? It was so ridiculous, they never made it through testing. The final test was laughable—they just did away with testing the pump assembly and said 'Hopefully they will hold together long enough.'"

Garzino finally cracked when she heard the people of New Orleans being assured that the pumps would keep them safe. She knew no such guarantee could be made. Being very careful to follow fastidiously the chain of command, in 2006 she began to press for a process of review. When she couldn't get any satisfaction, in 2007 she went to the Office of Special Counsel, part of the Department of Justice charged with investigating whistleblower complaints by federal employees.[13] The OSC insisted that the inspector general of the Department of Defense investigate her concerns. While that report upheld many of her complaints, it nonetheless concluded there had been no serious violations. But Garzino would not be deterred and she submitted highly detailed counterarguments. She was emotional about her campaign but she knew it was the nitty-gritty engineering detail that proved her argument.

"Two A.M. I'm replying to e-mails. I have a twelve-foot-tall pile of documents on my desk. If you paid me for the work I did on this," Garzino recalled ruefully, "I could retire right now. Every night. Every weekend. If you realize you won't give up, then you must do the best job you can."

The inspector general was told to look again, but again came back saying the pumps were safe. In an unprecedented move, the OSC then decided to appoint an independent engineering expert to analyze all the available information. His report entirely vindicated the years of Garzino's effort, finding that the pumps installed in New Orleans did not protect the city adequately and that the Army Corps of Engineers could have saved $430 million in replacement costs by buying proven equipment.

"Everything I said was affirmed; it was the greatest day of my four years in this thing. It absolutely justified the pain."

Pitting herself against the Army Corps, against a powerful contracting firm, made for a long and frightening battle. Why, I kept wondering, hadn't she given up? A passionate love of engineering (coupled with a hatred for bad engineering) was part of the answer. So too was a determination to finish what she had begun and a serious commitment to public trust. But key to Garzino's determination was her sense that someone had to stand up for the people of New

Orleans who had already been so badly let down.

"There was a day we drove down to where the pumps were going to be installed. I remember there was a lot of debris around, they were changing the road to allow heavy construction traffic to get through. And they raised the body of an eight-year-old girl. And no one would look. No one wanted to acknowledge what had just happened. But that is what needs to be at the forefront of your mind! Let's talk about this! But they couldn't even look that in the eye. People don't want to look at a really bad thing. One reason this stuff is allowed to happen is because people don't want to look at it and acknowledge it. There were a whole lot of people there that day but no one talked about it."

For Rockwood and Garzino, seeing what everyone wanted to deny and acting on that knowledge was an intrinsically necessary act. Both had a strong sense of duty, not just to their organization but to what that organization stood for. For Joe Darby, who handed in the photographs of Abu Ghraib, the decision was just as taxing but just as clear.

"After about three days, I decided to hand the pictures in. You have to understand: I'm not the kind of guy to rat somebody out. I've kept a lot of secrets for soldiers. In the heat of the moment, in a war, things happen. You do things you regret. I have exceeded the proper use of force myself a couple times. But this crossed the line to me. I had the choice between what I knew was morally right and my loyalty to other soldiers. I couldn't have it both ways."[14]

Darby too was able to think beyond his friends and his colleagues and see that there were other people, very different from himself, who mattered.

"One of the things you have to understand is the mentality of where I grew up, in western Maryland. It's a small town, and there's not a lot of work. So most people are either in the military, in the Reserves, or they're related to somebody who is. They're good people, but I knew they weren't going to look at the fact that these guys were beating up prisoners. They were going to look at the fact that an American soldier put other American soldiers in prison. For *Iraqis*. And to those people—who basically are patriotic, socially programmed people who believe whatever they're told—the Iraqis are the enemy, and screw whatever happens to them. Ignorance is bliss they say but you can't stand by and let this happen."

Cassandras and whistleblowers show us that the forces that enable willful blindness can be overcome. That this can happen feels heroic but rarely feels like heroism in real life. Men like Lawrence Rockwood and Joe Darby, women like Cynthia Thomas and Gayla Benefield see through the eyes of the powerless, and what they see changes who they are and clarifies what they feel is right. But this change and clarity come at a high cost, because their full-sightedness explodes the status quo.

Because the confrontations between Cassandras and the rest of the world are so profound, they are reflected back to us in stories; the conflict between a passion for truth and the desire for illusion has been a mainstay of drama since Oedipus. Whether it's Hickey, smashing the myths that sustain the bums of Harry Hope's bar in *The Iceman Cometh*, or Gregers Werle determined to excavate family secrets in *The Wild Duck*, or Emilia revealing to Othello the folly of his jealousy, the bearer of truths have to be punished. All of these dramas of revealed truths—and they're all tragedies—can be at times almost unbearable to watch as one truth dismantles multiple illusions. Cassandras may see the truth, but they inspire fury because those truths were so energetically and necessarily hidden, and because their revelations demand change. We side with the truth teller but, in the comfort of the theater, we don't have to bear the cost.

In the real world, the cost of being a Cassandra is more ambiguous. In one study of whistleblowers, 30 percent of them had been removed from their offices by men with guns—that is how dangerous they were deemed to be.[15] Most weren't surprised to lose their jobs but were disappointed by how hard it was to find employment subsequently. After a brief flurry of publicity, Sherron Watkins found that, in Houston, most employers were wary of someone with a reputation for being outspoken. Maria Garzino often found herself sitting at her desk with nothing to do. For years, Gayla Benefield had to endure the open hostility of her neighbors, while for Frank Partnoy and Cynthia Thomas perhaps the hardest part is explaining why they've stepped out of their presumed roles. Joe Darby was excoriated by his neighbors when he came home. Once Secretary of Defense Donald Rumsfeld named him on television, he had to relocate and assume a new identity. His old friends weren't proud that he had held America to a higher standard; for him to have looked beyond them was just a form of betrayal.

"He was a rat, he was a traitor, basically he was no good," said Colin Engelbach, commander of the VFW post in Darby's hometown.

"His actions were no good, borderline traitor. Do you put the enemy above your buddies? I wouldn't."[16]

But not all Cassandras are punished. Though many have had to wait to see their prophecies validated and to earn respect for their foresight, courage, and perseverance, they have all found themselves more powerful with the truth than without it. The mother who discovered child abuse in her family found in herself a stronger, more capable parent than she had known she could be. The executive who dared to resist the power of silence in a meeting can look back at a problem fixed instead of buried. The bystander who wasn't passive, the soldier who could not obey, all take as their reward a comfort in knowing that they did what they could and did not choose to look away. Hannah Arendt says that such individuals gain the knowledge that, whatever else happens, they can live "together with themselves," continuing in their minds a dialogue that is neither incriminating nor soporific but dynamic and alive.

The greatest shock, for Cassandras and whistleblowers alike, is their revised view of the world. Having started as conformists and loyalists, they emerge from their experience wary of authority and skeptical of much that they see and read and hear. Seeing the truth, and then acting on it, changes their vision of life. This independence of mind can instill a profound sense of isolation. But setting themselves free from consolatory fictions can also reveal new allies and soul mates and inspire a vibrant and purposeful identity.

"I don't regret any of it," says Joe Darby. "I made my peace with my decision before I turned the pictures in. I knew that if people found out it was me, I wouldn't be liked. But the only time I have ever regretted it was when I was in Iraq and my family was going through a lot. Other than that, I never doubted that it was the right thing. It forced a big change in my life, but the change has been good and bad. I liked my little quiet town, but now I have a new place, with a new job and new opportunities."

Cynthia Thomas's commitment to running the coffeehouse absorbs her night and day. She used to be the one in her family who stayed in touch, brought everyone together; now she's too busy to take a day off. She says her parents are supportive—they're from the military too—but still don't quite understand. But having seen what she's seen, she can't go back.

"I always used to say 'I don't know what I want to be when I grow up.' And now I know. I found myself in this cause and I am not the same person anymore."

For all the punishment and pain they sometimes endure, those who struggle to see share a core belief that seeing the truth matters and will have an impact. The most telling quality of Cassandras is that they believe they can have an impact, that change can happen when the truth is confronted, not ignored. Nobody I've spoken to has articulated that more clearly than Sherron Watkins when she talked about meeting the FBI whistleblower, Coleen Rowley, and the MCI World-Com whistleblower, Cynthia Cooper.

"Cynthia Cooper of WorldCom, Coleen Rowley of the FBI, and I were all together because we had been on that cover of *Time* magazine. And we were talking about what made us do what we did, and did we have anything important in common. So, we are all three women. We're also first born. We're also women of faith. We're also breadwinners for our families. But I think the most telling thing about us is that we grew up in tiny towns with less than ten thousand people. And in that small kind of town, there is the sense of, oh goodness, that tree fell down and knocked down that little shed, let's go call the city, or, there's trash in that vacant lot, better pick it up. There's that sense that your actions matter. What you do matters."[17]

12

SEE BETTER

LEAR: Kent, on thy life, no more.
KENT: My life I never held but as a pawn
To wage against thine enemies; nor fear to lose it,
Thy safety being motive.
LEAR: Out of my sight!
KENT: See better, Lear!
—*King Lear*, Act I, Scene 1

CASSANDRAS SHOW US that we don't have to be blind. They are inspiring individuals because they believe in the possibility of change. Unafraid of conflict, they are more interested in exploring ideas than in defending them. These are people capable of a rich dialogue with themselves, who aren't isolated by power, and for many of whom a sense of history delivers an enriched sense of the future. They listen carefully to silence but don't succumb to it. As such, they clearly demonstrate that, while willful blindness may be part of the human condition, it need not define who we are.

Many people, admiring Cassandras from a distance, hesitate to step into their shoes. The role looks too demanding, the costs too high. But most of us also don't wish to go through life blind. We don't want to collude in what we know to be wrong, and however much we may enjoy the comfort of confirming friends and affirming institutions, we would also like to think we had some influence over what we see and what we edit out. Alerted to how willful blindness works, we may be more attuned to it and determine to be on our guard. But old habits die hard; the riverbed is deep and we can't shake off millennia of neurobiology and a lifetime of cultural comforts.

What we can do is ask the question, what are the conditions required for willful blindness to flourish? How far might we be able to mitigate those conditions, to make it easier to hear the quiet voices at the back of our minds begging for attention? Could we develop new habits that might keep us more aware?

We can start by recognizing the homogeneity of our lives, our institutions, neighborhoods, and friends, putting more effort into reaching out to those who don't fit in and seeing positive value in those that prove more demanding. Looking at any of our major institutions— from Congress to corporate boards, think tanks and churches—that homogeneity suddenly looks like a weakness and a risk. Diversity, in this context, isn't a form of political correctness but an insurance against the internally generated blindness that leaves these institutions exposed and out of touch. The very fact that these groups feel comfortable should ring alarm bells.

By the same token, we have to acknowledge our biases. Whenever I discuss bias in groups of business leaders and educators, far from being disturbed by the findings of Implicit Association Tests, they're rather relieved. Men are glad to hear that bias isn't their fault, women and members of religious or ethnic minorities feel their suspicions have been validated. Maybe they're reassured to learn that they can't help being biased and that it isn't personal. What those findings do mean, however, is that once we've acknowledged the biases we bring to any group, we have to adjust for them. A balance of bias may be the best we can achieve.

Knowing the hard limits to our cognitive capacity and the huge cost of working long hours should not be an intractable problem to address. We have a century of data and a roll call of the disastrous consequences that follow those who insist that heroic hours are a proof of commitment to an employer. Companies that measure work by hours could make themselves smarter by the simple act of measuring contribution by output and rewarding those who go home.

Many people—and not a few employers—prefer to think that they can somehow stretch the cognitive limits of their minds, that doing lots of sudoku or using programs like Brain Trainer will somehow enlarge their capacity. They're out of luck. The only exercise that seems to nurture, or at least protect, our brains is aerobic exercise.[1] Yoga, toning, and stretching may make you feel good but, in fMRI scans, only aerobic exercise seemed to have a visibly positive impact on the brain. If you want to protect your own intellectual capacity, or that of your employees, the only way to do that is to go to the gym—or go home. When Gail Rebuck assumed the chairmanship of Random House UK, she inherited what she calls "an hours culture" in which everyone stayed late to please the boss. Unwilling and unable to work this way herself, she let it be known that anyone working past six P.M. was either incompetent or had a boss who didn't understand how to manage workload. The culture shifted overnight.

The sooner we associate long hours and multitasking with incompetence and carelessness, the better. The next time you hear boasts of executives pulling an all-nighter or holding conference calls in their cars, be sure to offer your condolences. It's grim being stuck in sweatshops run by managers too ignorant to understand productivity and risk. In manufacturing and engineering businesses, everyone learns that the priority is asset integrity: protecting the machinery on which the business depends. In knowledge-based economies, that machinery is the mind.

We can—and should—all learn to be extremely wary of big ideas, the grand ideologies that appear too neatly to answer all questions. But being wary isn't enough to combat blindness; we need actively to seek disconfirmation. When Alice Stewart conducted her survey on childhood cancers, she worked with a statistician named George Kneale, and their partnership is a model of how different, contentious minds can support each other.

"I couldn't have done anything without George," Alice Stewart told her biographer, Gayle Greene. "I like to think he's the power engine of our ship and that I occasionally flick the steering wheel."[2]

Fellow scientists described Kneale's work as outstanding, elegant, and exquisite, but what's most interesting is the way that Kneale himself thought about his job.

"It's my job to prove that Dr. Stewart's theories are wrong. I am, in effect, trying to disprove her. Hence the strength of our long association."[3]

In his seeking for *dis*confirmation, Stewart knew that Kneale protected her from potential blindness in her own thinking—and she was smart and confident enough to appreciate that challenge. Kneale and Stewart understood between them that the risk of losing their theory was outweighed by the danger of being blind. To paraphrase Voltaire, they understood (in ways that Marian Keech, Alan Greenspan, and Richard Doll did not) that while doubt isn't a very pleasant condition, certainty is absurd.

Theirs was an elegant and inspiring collaboration between two very different people: Stewart articulate, sociable, and energetic, Kneale withdrawn, shy, more comfortable with numbers than with people. What made them so effective was not that they were the same but that they brought different thinking styles, questions, and challenges to a problem whose solution they both sought. They tackled a common purpose with uncommon levels of challenge and debate. It was precisely because Kneale kept trying to disprove Stewart and couldn't that she was able to stand up for so many years against Richard Doll and the medical establishment. If we admire what Stewart did, we might best express that admiration by adopting her methods.

The ability to endure and even welcome debate and conflict requires practice and protection. Sometimes this can be done with humor, as when the former CEO of British Airways Sir Colin Marshall appointed Paul Birch to be the official corporate fool. Birch had license to speak up and to challenge.

"One of the roles of the jester is to declare, 'Just because you're the boss doesn't mean you know better,'" Birch said. "The jester's role is to draw attention to things that are going wrong, to stir things up."

Birch says he got the idea from *King Lear* but he used his position to get BA employees to unpack some of their conventional thinking and to approach problems in different ways. It helped, he said, to highlight customer grievances and to enable executives to see how foolish they, and the company, could be at times.

"When things go wrong," he said, "employees usually have a good idea of how to fix them. You need to create a state in which they've got the courage to do something. You want to build organizations where everyone sees provocation as one of their essential roles."[4]

Writing about groupthink, Irving Janis recommended institutionalizing dissent. He used the example of the Vatican, which used to appoint a devil's advocate to ask hard questions during the process of canonization. When Janis was writing, there was already some evidence that the role had decayed into a formality, but at least it still existed. Today, it's sad (but perhaps telling) that the post has disappeared. We would do well to resurrect it within our organizations as a means of protecting dissent and encouraging argument.

"How do you know what's going on in the company?" my CFO once asked me. It was a brilliant question because, regardless of the size of the company or the leadership, it's very hard to answer. Many executives say the numbers tell them everything, but anyone working in those organizations knows that that is wrong. In some of the organizations I've worked with, we have conducted blind audits and obedience audits, which measure just how much organizational silence, obedience, and conformity exist within an organization. The results were always startling, because they unearthed the unmentionables: the known unknowns that no one wanted to talk about. That helped us to understand what needed to be changed and, perhaps more importantly, sent a signal that silence wasn't golden, it was dangerous. When she led Guidant, CEO Ginger Graham instigated a form of radical honesty during her tenure, though hers was more confrontational.

"Each member of the senior management team would take turns sitting on a tall stool in front of the room. One by one, their peers would bring up a shortcoming they'd observed and offer suggestions for improvement. The manager on the hot seat could only listen, not comment. As you can imagine, many a manager's first impulse was to disagree or try to explain away some of these comments. But if several people in the group mentioned the same thing, the manager would begin to understand that his or her behavior truly needed to be addressed. As the members of the management team became more comfortable with this approach, they began to welcome more and more feedback."[5]

Graham acknowledged that the process sounded rather cruel but said that it achieved a level of honesty among colleagues that she hadn't achieved any other way. The fact that she too took part in it was essential and she valued it because it allowed her to see what her biases and mental habits had obscured.

"There is tremendous power in an organization when you hear the truth said out loud. The cat is out of the bag. We can see the cat. Now, are we going to just look at it or do something about it? We had changed the frame.

"You have to decide you are going to seek disconfirmation; you just can't expect it spontaneously to emerge because it won't happen," she told me. "In many meetings, we would assign someone in public to be devil's advocate, to call out challenges, disagreements, identify holes, gaps, and concerns. You need to be really clear about the role. The person taking it has to be thanked and rewarded for it. Another way to do the same thing is to ask two questions: What are all the reasons we are right? What are all the reasons we are wrong? It takes a lot of discipline to do this, and not to stack the deck."

Bringing in outsiders is one way to identify the unconscious knowledge embedded within organizations and bring it to the surface. It can be startling how a little dissent, how even a few questions, can change the tenor of a discussion. Graham used coaches in her organization a great deal, to deliver feedback to her about her own performance and to keep the dialogue within her organization open and free-flowing. Hers was an aggressive and consistent attempt to ensure she was not surrounded by ostriches, that her organization was not silent. Critical to her success was not just having one outside voice, but having a multitude of voices and perspectives. She engineered what many leaders miss: debate.

"I wish someone had challenged me," John Browne wrote when reviewing his mercurial career running BP. "I wish someone had challenged me and been brave enough to say: 'We need to ask more disagreeable questions.'"[6] Browne could have sought out more serious challenge, and he should have. That he did not says much about him and the organization that Tony Hayward inherited.

"Once you are in a leadership position, no one will ever give you the inner circle you need," says Saj-Nicole Joni. "You have to go out and find it." Joni is a professional "third opinion," the person brought in to work with leaders who, uniquely, has no agenda.

"When you are at the top of an organization, everyone has an agenda," she says. "They will either be pushing forward their agenda to please you, or their own agenda to enhance themselves. That's fine; you can recognize that and that's the first opinion you'll get. Then you'll get a second opinion from a technical expert: a lawyer, accountant, software architect, or strategist. But you need a third opinion that comes from someone who has nothing but your best interests, the company's best interests, at heart. That person is a thinking partner. Not someone who knows the answer but someone who thinks alongside with you in order to find it."[7]

What Joni is describing is that dialogue with oneself that Arendt calls thinking—except she's suggesting it doesn't have to be done alone. It is the very best leaders, she says, who recognize that they need this dialogue and who reach out and find the people with whom they can have it.

"Most leaders in big positions live in a world where every major decision is never really clearly right or wrong. They become aware of that often through some jarring event in their life—illness, some level of fear, perhaps something that happened in their childhood. And they realize that, at the level they're playing, if they don't get countervailing voices, they are personally at risk of not meeting their obligations."

Talking to her, it's clear why Joni is a third opinion. She works hard at thinking. She comes, she says, from a family in which what she was told as a child didn't fully explain what she saw. That left her with a lifelong drive to search for the full story. In conversation, her responses don't automatically echo or affirm what's been said, but challenge it, test it, take it further. Joni believes that, in order not to be blind, two things are critical: unvarnished truth and unfettered exploration. One alone won't do.

"If you just do unfettered exploration, it wastes energy. The exploration has to have impact; it has to be mission-critical and real. Same with unvarnished truth. Leaders who don't build the networks that bring them the truth will make big mistakes. Having a small network of people, who will bring you the unvarnished truth and with whom you can have unfettered exploration, they are a partial antidote to willful blindness.

"True leaders—whether they are at the top of an organization or within it—know that you cannot go into execution mode and retain peripheral vision. You can't focus both on the woods and the trees. So you need a network to watch out when you have your head down. There is tremendous value to being able to shut down and focus—but you put yourself at risk if you don't have people out there scouting the horizon, covering your back."

Joni says that part of what third opinions provide, and monitor, is dissonance. They don't look to quell it; rather they look to ensure that there is appropriate dissonance around critical issues.

"It's about having the right fight. Dissonance has value but it has to be practical. Leaders have to ask: What issues are so critical that we create end-to-end line of sight and structured dissonance around them? You can't do it on everything. You have to choose where it counts and make it work, and stop nonsense everywhere else. Using your riverbed analogy: dissonance and third opinions offer a tributary that takes you somewhere else, gives you a different perspective. It isn't so wildly different that it's irrelevant—but it stops you sinking into a place where you cannot see what's happening around you."

In his analysis of why smart executives fail, Sydney Finkelstein calls companies in which there is no dissent "zombie companies."[8] These zombie companies can still be full of energy and activity, and they may even inspire tremendous loyalty and generate a great deal of cash. But, as Pat Lewis found at Bear Stearns, that activity is blind because it can't and won't embrace the "troublemaker" who is on the lookout for unpredictable threats and challenges.

Outsiders—whether you call them Cassandras, devil's advocates, dissidents, mentors, troublemakers, fools, or coaches—are essential to any leader's ability to see. But it's impossible for outsiders to remain outsiders forever. At Harvard Business School, Max Bazerman has looked extensively at the forces of willful blindness that conspire to erode the independent perspective of auditors. They may be humorless but their role is the same as the fool's: to challenge, question, and test assumptions. The real problem, Bazerman concluded, is not that auditors are blatantly corrupted; such cases are very rare. What is more common is that, over time, the outsider's familiarity with the business biases him or her in its favor, or in favor of its ends and goals. This is entirely unconscious and he or she can't help it—which is why Bazerman recommends that auditors have fixed, limited contract periods during which they can't be fired.

"Auditors must have fixed, limited contract periods during which they cannot be terminated. All fees and other contractual details should be specified at the beginning of the contract and must be unchangeable. In addition, the client must be prohibited from rehiring the auditing firm at the end of the contract; instead, the major accounting firms would be required to rotate clients."[9]

Current legislation doesn't make these requirements; it mandates auditor rotation but this is just defined as a change in the lead partner within the firm—not a change of firm itself. And there is nothing in current regulations to prevent a client from firing an auditor. In other words, many of the incentives to turn a blind eye to accounting detail remain firmly in place.

Bazerman also argues that clients should be prohibited from hiring auditors to come and work for them. As he points out, "an auditor can't be impartial when he or she hopes to please a client in order to develop job options."

That Bazerman recommends such draconian steps isn't because he has some deep-seated suspicion of accountants. It is because he understands all too well the forces that conspire to make, and keep, such advisors blind. Bazerman's judicious insight into the problems of auditors applies to any outside advisor, because unconscious bias isn't specific to accounting but to being human. But we can't depend on outsiders alone. We need also to develop in ourselves two critical habits: critical thinking and courage.

I remember studying Hegel with Michael Tanner, a notorious and difficult philosophy professor, renowned for his leather jackets and for a record collection—mostly Wagner—that covered most of his office floor. After reading him my analysis of Hegel's *Philosophy of History*, I looked to him for praise that I'd mastered so difficult and obscure a text. No chance. "That's fine," said Tanner, unimpressed. "Now: What's wrong with Hegel?" That was the beginning of my education. What's a little worrying is that such critical thinking hadn't occurred to me until I got to college.

Being a critical thinker starts with resisting the urge to be a pleaser. Today, I'm shocked by the consistency with which my students prefer knowing the "right" answer to the process of searching for it. "Tell me what I need to know to get a good grade/pass the exam/get the degree" is the common students' refrain. They've been brought up in an educational system of multiple-choice tests, on which the point is not to think but to know—to limit knowledge, not to explore it. They've been taught, in effect, an intellectual form of obedience. In college, their idea of debate is often little more than second-guessing the instructor. When their answer is the same as mine, they believe they're right—and they stop thinking just when they most need to start. When business school leaders start wondering whether they should teach critical thinking, you have to wonder what they've been teaching heretofore—*un*critical thinking? Is that thinking at all? Or is it just a style of informed obedience that can carry on, uninterrupted, into employment?

"Jail is full of pleasers," says Justin Paperny. He's one of Walt Pavlo's protégés, another young man who made the wrong choices in financial services and ended up in jail. Today, inspired by Pavlo, he shares his experiences with college students, trying to warn them of the dangers he so blithely overlooked.

"The other day, I was doing a talk at the University of Southern

California, and I asked: How many of you are pleasers? Three quarters of the hands go up. And I said to them, 'How you are today in the classroom is how you will be at work. I was a pleaser. If you will do anything for an A, then you will do anything for your boss.'

"I wanted to please my professor. Thinking back to high school, I think of people who were not afraid to be different, to think their own way. Sometimes they were ostracized and people made fun of them—but lots of people secretly admired them! I never had their courage. I wanted to fit in and not be different. And I look at those people now and they have wonderful lives! They're their own people, living their own lives."[10]

Their own people, living their own lives: That is what we should aspire to in the schools that we build and the teaching that we deliver. Not compliant, obedient conformists but individuals who insist on thinking for themselves.

That aspiration lies at the heart of programs developed by the psychologist Philip Zimbardo. Having learned from his Stanford Prison Experiment just how powerfully the dynamics of a situation can blind us to who we are and the moral impact of our actions, Zimbardo has devoted a distinguished career to interrogating many of the behaviors which that early experiment showed him: How do we raise and educate individuals so that they will think for themselves, challenge what they see, be prepared to turn their assumptions upside down and examine them? In particular, how do we teach them to resist the influence of the situations in which they find themselves?

"One of the things we used to do," Zimbardo recalled, "was something I called 'deviant for a day.' It was just a little exercise in trying to step outside yourself, violate your own image and see what happens. Sometimes it was no more than just putting a dot on your head and walking around like that all day. The world responds to you differently—so you see the world differently."[11]

The exercise, Zimbardo told me, made the students aware of just how responsive they were to what their friends expected of them. They came to appreciate how easily and unwittingly they conformed to others' expectations of them. They got used to being pleasers because that's what everyone else was doing, too.

"Their friends want them to be their expectation, for them to behave as they're 'supposed' to behave. But at the end, they all say that the experience of bucking that expectation is so liberating—breaking these bonds. It's tremendously important to learn that you do not have to be, and you do not have to think, what everyone else expects or wants you to be or to think. That you can be your own person."

Zimbardo was creating for his students the experience that Roy Spence had had with his sister: learning how to think about what other people are seeing and what they themselves might be missing. But such critical thinking is pointless and frustrating without the courage to act on it.

That's the aim of Ervin Staub's program for teaching children how to deal with bullies: the development of interventionists who have the courage and expertise not to be passive but who gain the experience of standing up for others. The same thinking underlies Zimbardo's newest venture, the Heroic Imagination Project, which aims to find, train, and celebrate ordinary men and women who see and seize the opportunity to reach beyond their own narrow purview to become what he calls "ordinary heroes."

"We are currently pilot testing a full-scale hero curriculum for fifth graders in Michigan and Wisconsin and we want to transfer it to summer camps and clubs," Zimbardo told me. "The goal is to change people's patterns of understanding, altering their thinking from 'me' to 'we.' We do think anyone can be a hero but it's about compassion, altruism, empathy, and moral courage to empower people to take positive action during crucial moments in their lives."

When Zimbardo talked about his project to a group of some six hundred high school students, their enthusiasm was palpable. They had an instant, visceral response to the idea that they did not have to be passive, that their dissonant perspectives could be positive, constructive, even heroic. Across the country there's a proliferation of such programs (the Green Spot campaign in Kentucky is another) the goals of which are to widen our horizons, both in what we see around us and in how we see our options to intervene.

These programs all confront the fear of conflict that so often leaves us paralyzed, preferring not to see. Their emphasis on rehearsal—practicing and acting out different kinds of response—is based on the premise that this is how we can change the way our minds are comfortable behaving. Their big promise is that they teach generations of individuals not to be bystanders. Crimes like the poisoning of Libby, Montana, aren't perpetrated by a few bad people but by large numbers of individuals who don't blow the whistle, don't stand up and say no.

Changing the game can require surprisingly little: A simple question—Do we mean this? Did I understand correctly?—can turn the tide. The French sociologist Serge Moscovici found that the mere existence of a minority opinion can have a huge impact on the direction discussions take. Subsequent researchers have found that, just knowing that there is a dissenting voice is enough to induce different cognitive processes that yield better judgments.[12] Each of us needs to develop the courage to intervene when we are worried by what we see.

Context counts. Undoubtedly there are organizational constructs and cultures that create more favorable conditions for willful blindness than others. Heroic leadership styles, companies highly focused on the power and influence of a single individual, provoke the kind of second-guessing among executives that stops them thinking or analyzing what they know to be true. It is always intrinsically difficult for leaders to know what is going on in their organizations, but never more so than when their personalities or egos quash debate or dissent. That so many recent corporate and institutional failures have occurred inside organizations with strong leaders should make us all wonder whether the celebrity of magazine covers and guru status is good for anyone. Whether CEOs are celebrated for being a "Sun King," "the most aggressive CEO in America," or whiz kids, you can be sure that the more elevated their status, the less likely it is that anyone will dare to articulate an uncomfortable truth to them. Power is dangerous, a bubble and a barrier, and wise leaders would do well to see it as a handicap, not a reward—even where there is a profound level of discontinuity built into the environment already.

"In India, it is just impossible to escape contradiction," says Ajit Nayak. He's been studying the emergence of Indian businesses and business leaders over the past decade. "India, as a nation, is still under construction—so no matter how successful you are, it is impossible to keep life out. You can't escape people. You can go on the train and you're looking out the window and you can never see the landscape without people in it. So even if you're very wealthy and you're very successful, the contradictions of poverty and disease and just the sheer difficulty of getting things done—they're always right there in front of you. You cannot be cut off; you can't sanitize your experience. The contradictions are everywhere."[13]

He's particularly intrigued by Ratan Tata, who runs the largest business and is the largest employer in India. Tata lives alone in a small flat; his lifestyle is striking only for its lack of flamboyance.

"If you take someone like Ratan Tata," says Nayak, "he sits in the front of his car with his driver. He can't sit in the back and read the paper because it's too bumpy. There are so many potholes in the road that it's just physically impossible to read! So he knows when his driver's child is sick and what he needs to do because they talk. He has no choice; they have to engage."

However uncomfortable they may be, the potholes of Indian roads help to keep Tata better connected. The discontinuities of life in India, says Nayak, are so endemic that the bubble of power into which the wealthy and successful disappear in the West simply doesn't exist. At least not yet.

"It's very paradoxical because Indian companies are very hierarchical so you will be surrounded by yes men. But at the same time, the country itself is so unpredictable that you can build a company—as Sunil Mittal did, importing generators—and then have it taken away from you. So you know you just have to keep interrogating everything you see. Because the one thing you know is that you cannot control what will happen."

That a discontinuous environment might constitute a competitive advantage is an interesting thought. But Tata's motto—question the unquestionable—suggests that his perspective isn't merely passive but deliberate. Is it possible to engineer this kind of discontinuity? Perhaps. Two psychologists—one from California, one from Canada—did it just by asking their students to read an absurd short story by Franz Kafka, "The Country Doctor."[14] The story is full of contradictory or apparently senseless details. Its nonlinear untraditional story is uncomfortable; it won't fit our expectation and that, it turns out, can be quite a good challenge for our brains.

"People feel uncomfortable when their expected associations are violated," said Travis Proulx, one of the study's authors. "That creates an unconscious desire to make sense of their surroundings. That feeling of discomfort may come from a surreal story, or from contemplating their own contradictory behaviors, but either way, they're motivated to learn new patterns."

After reading the short story, Proulx's volunteers were both more motivated to look for different patterns and more successful in finding them. In other words, they could see more. Proulx was at pains to point out that merely assailing your mind with Kafka, Lewis Carroll, or a David Lynch movie won't suddenly enhance your performance; it is the unexpectedness of the experience that counts.

"What is critical here is that our participants were not expecting to encounter this bizarre story," he continued. "If you expect that you'll encounter something strange or out of the ordinary, you won't experience the same sense of alienation. You may be disturbed by it, but you won't show the same learning ability. The key to our study is that our participants were surprised by the series of unexpected events, and they had no way to make sense of them. Hence, they strived to make sense of something else."[15]

Although this is what many an offsite tries to achieve, many leaders would balk at artificially injecting discontinuity into their working environment, arguing that the economic environment is quite disturbing enough. But what Proulx's experiment aimed at—jolting us out of blinkered thinking and obedient behavior—can be achieved in less exotic ways. In her landmark book, *Mindfulness*, Harvard psychologist Ellen Langer writes about the positive impact of uncertainty. Says Langer:

> When working for confident but uncertain leaders we are less likely to feign knowledge or hide mistakes, practices that can be costly to a company. Instead, we are likely to think, "If he's not sure, I guess I don't have to be right 100 percent of the time," and risk taking becomes less risky . . . Admission of uncertainty leads to *a search for more information*, [my italics] and with more information there may be more options.

It's important that Langer does not position confidence and uncertainty as opposites: rather, she insists that true leaders may be confident that the job will get done even while remaining uncertain about how it gets done. Managers who lead in this way were found by Langer to be evaluated by their employees as more likely to allow independent judgment and a more general freedom of action. What was critical was leaving the space in which thinking—or mindfulness—could occur without fear.

If managers make clear that they see certainty as foolhardy, it is easier to ask questions based on one's own uncertainty. Questions provide a good deal of information for managers. Moreover, if managers seek out information from employees to answer these questions, both will probably become more mindful and innovative.[16]

Perplexed by the findings of his own groupthink hypothesis, Irving Janis proposed that leaderless meetings might have a similar impact freeing participants to explore a wider array of information and solutions. That bad habit of second-guessing doesn't disappear even after college; however vigilant leaders can be in suppressing their own thoughts and preferences, opinion and debate often flow more freely in their absence. Once anyone has a hint of a desired outcome—and smart people infer some hints from nothing more than a word or two—the desire to please the boss can eliminate a whole range of options.

My best memory of my management team captures a moment in the history of our company, when we needed to confront major operational issues on the east coast at the same time that I had to be on the west coast. I tried phoning in for a while but it was clear the team could either talk to me or talk to each other. The decisions they made that day without me were some of the smartest we made.

The value of my absence was that it allowed people to change position without feeling that they were losing face. One of the reasons groups become so polarized is that participants feel that, having laid out their position, changing it appears weak. That nervousness is exacerbated when the boss is present. Discussions and creative dissonance, though, aren't about defending but about exploring positions—and that's easier when no one feels that changing their mind looks indecisive.

Similarly, setting several different teams to solve the same problem sends a clear message that there are no right answers; what matters is to find as wide an array of possible answers as possible. One of the best chief executives I've ever seen in action, Carol Vallone of WebCT, used to require her department heads to change roles when debating strategy. That way, she said, they had to abandon their silos and adopt different perspectives.

History is a different perspective, albeit one that is strikingly absent from most business thinking and education. The commercial world's love affair with novelty, innovation, and revolution is so pronounced as to blind it to longer-term trends and patterns. As eager as every pundit and politician was to castigate BP during its Deepwater Hori-

zon disaster in 2010, no one wanted to know about the long track record of fatalities and accidents that characterized BP's performance
over the years. Nor was there any serious analysis of the heroic leadership of John Browne and its long-term impact on the firm he had
built. The excitement and heat around the event was focused on the
here and now, not on any of the harder, deeper lessons that might have
been derived from a longer view. It was easier to castigate Tony Hayward's poor decisions than to reflect on the origins of a company apparently unable to fix itself.

When I discussed the lack of history in the business community
with Frank Partnoy, who has himself so wryly chronicled wild examples of Wall Street malfeasance, he was pessimistic.

"Certain aspects of history just tend to disappear. We hear it but
don't want to hear it—so it goes away. And then we have to learn all
those important lessons anew. Many of my students haven't heard of
Ken Lay or Michael Milken or Ivar Kreuger. There are kids graduating now who know nothing about Enron. I sometimes think we
ought to make desk calendars to keep those memories right in front of
you: Frank Partnoy's financial fraud desk calendar!"

We talked about Alfred Chandler, who had, virtually single-
handedly, invented deep, analytic business history and had lived long
enough (until he died in 2007 at the age of eighty-eight) to remember
much of it personally. But today, Partnoy reckoned, Chandler wouldn't
even get tenure. Business schools prefer to teach the live case study,
always in the present, with no past at all. There is a special narcissim in
the belief that we, and our times, are special, that we are so smart that
we have nothing to learn from the past—even about who we are. This
extreme bias for the present leaves us blind to the patterns developing
all around us.

One of the benefits of a sense of history is that it can alert us to trends,
and sensitize us to weak signals; that's what it did for Lawrence Rockwood in Haiti. The challenge of weak signals, or near-misses, is knowing when to take them seriously and when to dismiss them. Most
people aren't seers; they can't immediately distinguish the trivial from
the serious. What they can do is watch where the weak signals accumulate. When is an accident a fluke and when is it a trend? When is the
information you're getting denied by the evidence you are *not* getting?

That was the question Herb Meyer asked himself when, in the early
1980s, he forecast the collapse of the Soviet Union. Meyer was and

remains a contentious figure. Deceptively understated, he describes himself as running a small independent publishing business in Washington State. What that doesn't tell you is that under President Ronald Reagan, Meyer served as special assistant to the director of the Central Intelligence Agency and as vice chairman of the CIA's National Intelligence Council. In that capacity, he managed the production of the U.S. National Intelligence Estimates—which meant that, in the face of derision from the political and intelligence communities, he could test his hypothesis that the Soviet Union was on the verge of collapse.

"Everyone was telling us the Soviet Union was fine. Our spies would bring us information about how many bombs, how many tanks. They would bring us all the data they'd always brought us. So we kept thinking what we'd always been thinking. Ask the same questions of the same people, of course you're going to get the same answers.[17]

"So I decided to do something different. I made a list of everything I might expect to find if my hypothesis was right. If the Soviet economy was collapsing, what would you see? If it *wasn't* collapsing, what would you see? And then—this is the critical part—I made sure all that information went to one guy. Just one guy. Then, if nothing comes in, you have your answer. If something does come in, it doesn't get lost in all the noise."

One of the pieces of information that came in, Meyer told me, was news that a weekly meat train had been hijacked and all the meat had been stolen. The Russian army had come out—but then the Politburo had told the army to back off but tell no one. Let the people have the meat.

"Well, that's not what happens when everything in the economy's just fine, is it? You don't have people stealing meat and you don't have the army letting them get away with it. So that started to tell us something. And then there was more like that. What's important is that, without the hypothesis, that piece of information would never *ever* have been picked up. That's what didn't happen in 9/11: we weren't looking for what we couldn't see."

Meyer was accumulating weak signals to see if they added up to a meaningful trend. He might have been wrong. But if he had been wrong, he would at least have known that. He wouldn't have just kept wondering. Looking for what he couldn't see, taking weak signals seriously, allowed him to see what others so confidently missed.

Doesn't all of this require a great deal of time and patience? Yes, it does. But the best decisions require testing, painful discussion, dialogue, thinking without banisters. In his memoirs, the diplomat George F. Kennan described one of the greatest and boldest government decisions, which was the creation of the Marshall Plan by the U.S. government at the end of the Second World War.

> You say: "This should not be so difficult. Why don't we tell these people to draw up a plan for the reconstruction of their economic life and we'll see whether we can support it?"
>
> Someone says, "That's no good. They are too tired to draw up a plan. We have to do it for them."
>
> Then someone says: "Maybe what we need isn't a plan at all. Maybe we just haven't given them enough in the past. If we just give them more, things will work out all right."
>
> Another then says: "That's probably true but we've got to figure out how the money is going to be spent."
>
> Then somebody says: "That's right we need a program but it would be a mistake for us to try to draw this program up all by ourselves."
>
> Then someone says: "That's absolutely right. The thing for us to do is to tell these Europeans to draw up a plan and submit it . . ."[18]

Kennan describes being driven to tears of agony and frustration by the endless critical debate and evaluation that eventually produced the plan—and yet it was he who had insisted from the outset that this kind of open debate was needed.

Essential issues aren't going to be resolved quickly. Who ever imagined global warming was going to be solved in one week? If the issue is so vital, isn't it worth spending time on it? We should remember the patience and pain that the Marshall Plan required, and be prepared to stay until we are resolved. If one of the symptoms of blindness is comfort, so one of the indicators of critical thinking may be discomfort. That's why unanimous decisions are intrinsically suspicious. Were there no options? No alternatives? Unanimous decisions are incomplete decisions, made when there was too much power in the room, too much obedience, and too much conformity. If only one solution is visible, look again.

The sheer complexity of many decisions makes blindness all the more tempting. Can't these things be simplified? Can't we leave it to the experts?

"The banking world became very siloed in part because it all looked so complicated and geeky and boring," says Gillian Tett, one of the few journalists who was willing to work through banking's complexity to see what was going on. "But there are lots of issues that are like that—like global warming and poverty and science—and these are really going to affect our lives! We can't afford to delegate knowledge of these things to experts because that's how those silos get built. And not just in businesses but in our lives, in our society."

Her point is well made. As long as we back away from subjects we find too complex or too complicated, we keep ourselves blind to them and abdicate responsibility. The banking collapse could happen, Tett argues, because we let it happen by our decision not to question financial instruments we did not understand.

"You need cultural translators—journalists, academics, thinkers who can interpret a lot of technical information," Tett concedes. "You need them to make these subjects accessible, so that we are *all* thinking about them. We have to ask ourselves: How many silos are there that I am shutting my eyes to? We need constant monitoring of those silos and a lot of checks and balances so they cannot get so isolated."[19]

In Libby, Montana, journalist Andrew Schneider was one of those cultural translators. Had he not written his story for the Seattle *Post-Intelligencer*, Libby's children might still be playing on contaminated playgrounds. But that newspaper published its last print edition on March 17, 2009. It still publishes online and Schneider now publishes his own investigative journalism online (www.coldtruth.com). But the resources—people, time, and money—needed to uncover stories like Libby are increasingly hard to find. In 2005, students of investigative reporting at Arizona State University surveyed one hundred of the largest newspapers in the United States. All eighty-six respondents were members of Investigative Reporters and Editors, the nation's foremost organization devoted to investigative reporting, but even so, only 42 percent said that their newspapers and senior editors had "a lot" of interest in investigative reporting. Sixty-one percent had no investigative projects or teams and 62 percent did not have a single editor charged with working on investigations of any kind.[20] And that's in the newspapers that are still printing. Newspaperdeathwatch.com tracks the journals closing down in America; since March 2007, twelve metropolitan dailies have vanished completely and eight have moved to online editions only.

Even more buoyant outlets like the *Wall Street Journal* struggle. When Harry Markopolos tried to warn investors about Bernard Madoff, he worked with *Wall Street Journal* reporter John Wilke for *three years* but Wilke was just too busy to cover the story. He had all the information— Markopolos had done the work—but there were always too many other stories demanding attention. Had the paper unmasked Madoff earlier they might have caught him before all his investors' money was gone. Living and working in the United Kingdom, American journalist Heather Brooke fought her Freedom of Information battle for years, trying to get public insight into the expenses of Members of Parliament. She had the help of a barrister working pro bono but no British newspaper was up for the challenge.

Investigative reporting, whether in newspapers or television, has a grand but fading tradition of asking hard questions and unveiling awkward truths. It is an expensive business, because it takes time, effort, and legal protection; and it will ultimately disappear if our desire to be entertained cripples our need to be informed.

"We need to keep having discussions about what is important to an open society," Heather Brooke argues. "The public needs to understand that, if the media are considered just to be business operations, and if they abdicate their responsibility by reading *OK!* and celebrity gossip all day, then they can't expect the government to be upstanding or to be held to account. It is up to everyone to be involved, keep an eye out and be aware of what is going on and to be outraged when their trust is abused. But if people just sit around reading *Heat* or *US* and don't stay engaged, then you have to accept a corrupt government. A corrupt banking system. And scientists who lie. If you can't be bothered to know what is going on, you have no right to complain. It comes down to whether you think of yourself as a child and a victim or as an adult who can make change."[21]

It is in this new context that new ventures, like ProPublica and WikiLeaks, take on crucial importance. Both were set up to counter the waning of investigative journalism, albeit they address the challenge in quite different ways. ProPublica focuses on stories "with moral force," aiming to produce journalism that "shines a light on the exploitation of the weak by the strong and on the failures of those with power to vindicate the trust placed in them."

We won't lobby. We won't ally with politicians or advocacy groups. We look hard at the critical functions of business and of government, the two biggest centers of power, in areas ranging from product safety to securities fraud, from flaws in our system of criminal justice to practices that undermine fair elections. But we also focus on such institutions as unions, universities, hospitals, foundations and on the media when they constitute the strong exploiting or oppressing the weak, or when they are abusing the public trust.[22]

In 2009, the Web site's first full year of publication, ProPublica won the Pulitzer Prize for Investigative Reporting, the George Polk Award for environmental reporting, the National Magazine Award for Reporting, the Selden Ring Award for "investigative reporting that has brought results" from the Annenberg School of the University of Southern California, both the Magazine Award and the Online Award from Investigative Reporters and Editors, the Overseas Press Club Online Journalism Award, the Sigma Delta Chi Award for online investigative reporting, the Edward R. Murrow Award for Media Entrepreneurship, the Dart Award for Excellence in Coverage of Trauma, and the James Aronson Award for Social Justice Journalism. Funding for the site depends entirely on charitable donations.[23]

Although also funded by donations, WikiLeaks operates a different model, providing a publishing platform for leaked information which is classified, confidential, censored, or otherwise withheld from the public and which must be deemed "of political, diplomatic, ethical, or historic significance" by its board. Since launching in December 2006, the site has posted leaked documents on everything from Somali execution plans to the Iraq War, scientology, and Russian oil field explosions. It exists explicitly as an outlet for whistleblowers whom it goes to great technical lengths to protect. Its servers are distributed over multiple international jurisdictions and the servers do not keep logs so that no records of their access can be seized. Anonymization is built into the WikiLeaks network so that no one—neither the organization itself nor any government or enforcement agency—can know who has accessed the sites. In addition, the organization provides instructions on how to submit material by post and from Internet cafes and wireless hotspots, so that, were WikiLeaks to be infiltrated by a government intelligence agency, leakers could not be traced. All of this is designed to make it safe to surface and expose the information to which others might prefer we remain blind.

In July 2010, WikiLeaks was widely criticized when it published more than ninety thousand pages of documents concerning the Iraq War. Publishing the documents, military leaders argued, put the lives of informants and collaborators at risk. But at the heart of WikiLeaks's mission is the belief, as articulated by the Supreme Court when ruling on the Pentagon Papers, that "only a free and unrestrained press can effectively expose deception in government."

According to the site, "it is easy to perceive the connection between publication and the complaints people make about publication. But this generates a perception bias, because it overlooks the vastness of the invisible. It overlooks the unintended consequences of failing to publish and it overlooks all those who are emancipated by a climate of free speech."[24]

In other words, the organization is using a combination of technology and international legal jurisdictions to try to ensure that citizens and media outlets can no longer say that they were blind, that they did not and could not know what was being done in their name. What is less clear is whether people will make the effort to look. While the public appetite for ninety thousand pages of confidential government memos may be limited, for impact, WikiLeaks still needs traditional media to make sense of it.

When you make the effort to look, to do the critical thinking, you come up with a lot of critical questions. And in the course of writing this book, several have stuck with me.

As I've watched BP wrestle with its operational issues, I've begun to wonder whether we now have organizations that are simply too complex to manage. There's a whole army of complexity consultants who seem to revel in the sheer difficulty we have created for ourselves. After John Browne left BP and the company sat down to try to analyze what had gone so horribly wrong, it became clear that one of the culprits was the BP leadership's love of complexity—a kind of intellectual hubris that, incredible as it may seem, saw the ability to manage internal complexity as a source of competitive advantage. This is Daedalus gone mad. Instead of worshipping complexity, we need to challenge it.

But BP is not unique in its love affair with complexity. Many organizations view their own impenetrability as a feat of fantastic intellectual virtuosity. In reality, it's a huge cause of blindness and explains why, when such companies get into trouble, they can't find their way out of it. Aren't we in danger of building monstrosities we can't run? Never mind too big to fail—haven't we built corporations that, in their size, complexity, and impact, are simply too dangerous?

If they are too complex to grasp, either we need to change, or they do. Gillian Tett's argument—that banking products became too complex for anyone to understand—has to provoke skepticism around complexity. That seems to be what lies behind the legislative paralysis that has followed the banking crisis. No one can quite figure out what to do, in part because the business itself is so complex that most legislators don't understand it and are easily bamboozled by lobbyists, flattery, and deliberate obfuscation. If they didn't understand derivatives, they certainly won't understand how to regulate them—and they need to find the courage to say so. Complexity persists at least in part because, as in the tale of the emperor's new clothes, no one is prepared to stand up and say: I don't understand. But there isn't anything inherently brilliant about complexity or any reason why a failure to untangle it should be mortifying.

The questions concerning the safety of banks that are too big to fail apply to any vast corporation: Are they not only too big to manage but too big to police? As a society are we comfortable with companies that put their employees' lives in danger? Isn't there a limit to the number of people any corporation can kill before it is no longer allowed to trade? In the same way that we have to acknowledge the cognitive limits of our minds, we need to accept the effective limits of organizations and, when they get too big to manage, break them up.

If we lack the legislative or regulatory muscle to control such businesses, we place ourselves in the position of being willfully blind to their actions. Inevitably we make ourselves bystanders—because there's nothing we can do about them. That means we seem prepared to treat very large complex organizations the same way that we treated banking and financial services: despair of their opacity and walk away. Their sheer size isolates them from critical dissent. But what these companies do matters too much. We cannot afford to abdicate, handing over control of them to others who may not know any better.

The model that the manufacturing company W. L. Gore has adopted—in which no business unit can be larger than one hundred people—is intriguing. Many would argue that true global industries simply can't be effective on such a scale, but we need to challenge this orthodoxy and have the debate. I'd go further and argue that complexity fails until or unless we can prove our mastery of it.

We could know, and we should know, when these businesses are simply beyond us. What we do know is that hierarchies exacerbate blindness and obedience. That means we need to find ways to either tease the obedience out of these organizations or change their structures. Every business is a community and all business communities need to become places where, as Sherron Watkins says, what you do matters.

We need to ask some hard questions too of the way we educate and train our children. To what extent are we bringing them up to be "good soldiers," compliant and well conformed? In a straitened economy, the perceived risks of being outspoken and the implied rewards of obedience are immense. Yes, I can hear a thousand teachers despairing at the prospect of more argument; but it's the silent classrooms that scare me.

The psychotherapist Pamela Stewart works with a startling array of patients, from middle-class professionals to convicted murderers. She once observed to me that there was one significant similarity among her patients: their childhoods were invariably silent. That silence, she said, was about fear—fear of conflict primarily, a fear that a debate, once started, could only end with the family's destruction. That silence becomes self-perpetuating: without conflict, everyone remains afraid and blind. The only way to break that cycle is to be willing to endure the noise.

But we also need to celebrate those that make the noise, heroes more inspiring than talent contest winners and drunken movie stars.

"We have monuments for people who have displayed physical courage in war," Lieutenant Colonel Krawchuk mused. "But where are the monuments to people who said no, we won't do this because it's a bad or wrong or unethical decision?"

It's a good question and one that pertains well beyond the military. How can we celebrate the dissenters, the debaters, the Cassandras? Where is the statue to Hugh Thompson, the U.S. Army helicopter pilot who intervened in the My Lai massacre? To Joe Darby or Maria Garzino? Their heroic dissent sets a standard for critical thinking that is more inspiring than skepticism, and richer than doubt. Generations of lawyers had their worldview informed by Atticus Finch when they read *To Kill a Mockingbird*. Journalists since 1974 have emulated Bob Woodward and Carl Bernstein, who uncovered the Watergate scandal, and around the world new voices entered politics because of Nelson Mandela. We need to celebrate the Darbys, Benefields, Rockwoods, and Thomases, the ordinary people who refused to be blind, who took action because it was the right thing to do. The most important thing to remember about Cassandras and whistleblowers is that they are ordinary people. They show us our own capacity to see and to act on what we see.

When we are willfully blind, it is in the presence of information that we could know, and should know, but don't know because it makes us feel better not to know. Neuroscience shows us how some of this occurs, offering a tangible reality to experiences that, heretofore, felt entirely abstract. But in the course of writing this book, I've started to wonder how far the science encourages us to see our brains as separate entities, grand machines of which we are the passive agents. How long will we wait, I wonder, before a murderer pleads innocent on the grounds that "my brain made me do it"? Could the science encourage us to believe that our blindness is hardwired, inevitable, inescapable— not willful at all?

The most crucial learning that has emerged from this science is the recognition that we continue to change right up to the moment we die. Every experience and encounter, each piece of new learning, each relationship or reassessment alters how our minds work. And no two experiences are the same. In his work on the human genome, the Nobel laureate Sydney Brenner reminds us that even identical twins will have different experiences in different environments and that that makes them fundamentally different beings. Identical twins develop different immune systems. Mental practice alone can change how our brains operate.[25] The plasticity and responsiveness of our minds is what makes each of us most remarkable.

In other words, however determinist the brain science may appear, we all handle our experiences in unique ways. We aren't automata serving the master computer in our heads, and our capacity for change can never be underestimated. The parents and children who emerge from abusive families full of new hope and the conventional student whose college experience exposes him to dissent have a stronger sense of their own capacity because of what they've seen and been able to overcome. Towns like Libby, Montana, are not weaker but stronger because of the power to change which they discovered in themselves. Scientists are stronger when they confront disconfirmation than when they hide from it; and companies only regain confidence and value when they stop defending the past and can conceive of a different future.

We make ourselves powerless when we choose not to know. But we give ourselves hope when we insist on looking. The very fact that willful blindness is willed, that it is a product of a rich mix of experience, knowledge, thinking, neurons, and neuroses, is what gives us the capacity to change it. Like Lear, we can learn to see better, not just because our brain changes but because we do. As all wisdom does, seeing starts with simple questions: What could I know, should I know, that I don't know? Just what am I missing here?

ACKNOWLEDGMENTS

The idea for this book derived from two plays that I wrote for the BBC about Enron; had it not been for the commissioning courage of Jeremy Howe, Clare McGinn, and Sara Davies, I would never have found myself submerged in the transcript of Ken Lay's trial. Encountering the legal doctrine of willful blindness felt like introducing a magnet to a mess of iron filings. Without Fiona Wilson, I would not have had access to that transcript; and without a timely conversation with Joelle Delbourgo, my ensuing thoughts might have gone nowhere.

One of the glories of American academic life is the openness and enthusiasm with which scholars generously share their work and insights with curious investigators. I am immensely grateful to Albert Bandura, Robert Burton, Joel Cooper, John Darley, and Daniel Simons, who gave their time generously and were always prepared to engage with my questions and challenges. If their work is imperfectly articulated, that is my fault, not theirs.

I'd also like to thank Beth Edwards for guiding me through the legal nuances of willful blindness and the attorneys Brent Coon and Eric Newell for sharing with me their years of insight into the workings of BP. They will, alas, be at work for many years to come.

I would also like to thank the people of Libby, Montana, who were open, hospitable, and generous. Their character is more impressive even than the stunning surroundings in which they live.

I also owe a great deal to Peggy Northrop, Karen Steen, Donna Banks, and Nancy Coveney, all wonderful editors whose encouragement and obsessive fact-checking has made me a more fastidious writer.

In the United Kingdom, I am especially grateful to the London Library and the library at the University of Bath without whose resources I would have been blind indeed. I've also been grateful for stimulating and provocative colleagues, especially Glynis Breakwell, Ajit Nayak, Michael Meyer, Sarah Dixon, and Svenja Tams. I'm indebted to Ian Stockley for his insights into the world of digital direct marketing and its relationship to big ideas. I would also like to thank Don Honeyman and Gitta Sereny for being prepared to share their memories of Albert Speer after all these years.

In tracking down a strange array of experts, fraudsters, and Cassandras, Isobel Eaton was fearless and determined, regardless of time zone. While crossing the United States in what sometimes felt like a tour of industrial disasters, I was hugely encouraged and energized by the hospitality, generosity, and kindness of Paul Muldoon, Jean Hanff Korelitz, Rob and Fiona Wilson, Tatiana Lanning, Cindy Solomon, David and Denise Nicholson, and Beth Weiner and Chuck Finkle. They provided sustenance in more ways than one and stopped my own blind spots from being bigger and more numerous.

I'm indebted to George Gibson and Jacqueline Johnson for their wonderful mixture of patience, punctiliousness, and enthusiasm; it's a tremendous privilege to have such quality collaborators who truly care.

If at times writing this book made me willfully blind to the needs and wants of my two children, Felix and Leonora Nicholson, I hope it's also left me more appreciative of their stamina and self-sufficiency. More impressive still has been the patience and forbearance of my husband, Lindsay Nicholson. He put up with my gross intrusions into the world of neuroscience, constantly spotted more examples of willful blindness, and demonstrated yet again his tremendous capacity for the perfect probing question. My trip into the land of willful blindness was a long one and it's good to be home.

Finally I'd like to pay tribute to my sister, Pamela Stewart, who has seen willful blindness and its costs at close quarters. Her determination to articulate difficult truths has been a model and an inspiration since childhood.

NOTES

INTRODUCTION

1. This comes from the transcript of the court case, United States of America v Kenneth L. Lay in the United States District Court for the Southern District of Texas, Houston Division, May 2006.
2. Model Penal Code Section 2.02(7) and Willful Blindness Author(s): Jonathan L. Marcus Source: The Yale Law Journal, Vol. 102, No. 8, Symposium: Economic Competitiveness and the Law (Jun., 1993), pp. 2231-2257

1: AFFINITY AND BEYOND

1. S. Luo and E. C. Klohnen (2005). "Assortative Mating and Marital Quality in Newlyweds: A Couple-Centered Approach." *Journal of Personality and Social Psychology* 88(2): 304–326. Also G. J. Hitsch, A. Hortaçsu, et al. (2009). "Matching and Sorting in Online Dating." *American Economic Review* 10(1): 130–163.
2. A *Wall Street Journal* reporter queried the statistics emerging from online dating sites match.com, PlentyofFish.com, and eHarmony.com and concluded that of these only the eHarmony statistics were convincing. See Carl Bialik, "Marriage-Maker Claims are Tied in Knots." *Wall Street Journal*, July 29, 2009.
3. J. Chandler, T. M. Griffin, et al. (2008). "In the 'I' of the Storm: Shared Initials Increase Disaster Donations." *Judgment and Decision Making* 3(5): 404–410.
4. C. M. Brendl, A. Chattopadhyay, et al. (2005). "Name Letter Branding: Valence Transfers When Product-Specific Needs are Active." *Journal of Consumer Research* 32: 405–415.
5. R. L. Moreland and R. B. Zajonc (1982). "Exposure Effects in Person Perception: Familiarity, Similarity, and Attraction." *Journal of Experimental Social Psychology* 18: 395–415.

6. See Philip Ball, *The Music Instinct: How Music Works and Why We Can't Do Without It* (London: Bodley Head, 2010).

7. Matthew 7:3.

8. E. Pronin, T. Gilovich, et al. (2004). "Objectivity in the Eye of the Beholder: Divergent Perceptions of Bias in Self Versus Others." *Psychological Review* 111(3): 781–799.

9. There are two excellent Web sites where you can find out about the different areas in which the IAT is relevant and where you can take the tests yourself: http://www.projectimplicit.net/generalinfo.php and https://implicit.harvard.edu/implicit/.

10. C. Neil Macrae, Alan B. Milne, and Galen V. Bodenhausen (1994). "Stereotypes as Energy-Saving Devices: A Peek Inside the Cognitive Toolbox." *Journal of Personality and Social Psychology* 66(1): 37–47.

11. E-mail to author from William Osborne, Friday, October 30, 2009.

12. William Osborne, "Blind Auditions and Moral Myopia: The Gender/Racial Ideologies of the Vienna Philharmonic and the Employment Practices That Allow Them to Continue." http://www.osborne-conant.org/posts/blind.htm.

13. William Osborne keeps track of these issues on his Web site, http://www.osborne-conant.org/articles.htm.

14. Bill Bishop, *The Big Sort: Why the Clustering of Like-Minded America Is Tearing Us Apart* (Boston: Houghton Mifflin, 2008), 41.

15. Ibid., 5.

16. "Who Moves? Who Stays Put? Where's Home?" Pew Research Center, December 2008.

17. Ibid., 213. Also http://www.ranchomissionviejo.com/utilities/030506.php.

18. Cass R. Sunstein, *Going to Extremes: How Like Minds Unite and Divide* (Oxford: Oxford University Press, 2009).

19. William Hart, Dolores Albarracín, Alice H. Eagly, Matthew J. Lindberg, Lisa Merril, Inge Brechan (2009). "Feeling Validated versus Being Correct: A Meta-Analysis of Selective Exposure to Information." *Psychological Bulletin* 135(4): 555.

20. M. Massing, "The News About the Internet." *New York Review of Books*, August 13, 2009.

2: LOVE IS BLIND

1. S. L. Murray, J. G. Holmes, et al. (1996). "The Self-Fulfilling Nature of Positive Illusions in Romantic Relationships: Love is Not Blind, but Prescient." *Journal of Personality and Social Psychology* 7(6): 1155–1180.

2. Daniel Kahneman, Paul Slovic, and Amos Tversky, *Judgement Under Uncertainty: Heuristics and Biases* (Cambridge: Cambridge University Press, 1982).

3. http://www.truthaboutdeception.com/site/public/sources%10references.html.

4. Harvey Araton, "Apologizing, Woods Sets No Date for Return to Golf," *New York Times*, February 20, 2010.

5. Public Health Agency of Canada. "Canadian Incidence Study of Reported Child Abuse and Neglect—2003." http://www.phac-aspc.gc.ca/cm-vee/csca-ecve/pdf/childabuse_final_e.pdf.

6. Author interview with Emily Brown, December 22, 2009.

7. V. Florian, M. Mikulincer, and Gilad Hirschberger (2002). "The Anxiety-Buffering Function of Close Relationships: Evidence that Relationship Commitment Acts as a Terror Management Mechanism." *Journal of Personality and Social Psychology* 82(4): 527–542.

8. A. Bartels and S. Zeki (2004). "The Neural Correlates of Maternal and Romantic Love." *NeuroImage* 21(3): 1155–1166.

9. Colm O'Gorman, *Beyond Belief* (London: Hodder and Stoughton, 2009).

10. Ronan McGreevy, "Most People No Longer Trust the Church, Government or Banks." *Irish Times* (Dublin), April 29, 2010.

11. Author interview with Gitta Sereny, November 16, 2009.

12. Ibid.

13. Gitta Sereny, *Albert Speer: His Battle with Truth* (London: Picador, 1996), 102–103.

14. Ibid., 106.

15. Author interview with Sereny.

16. Sereny, *Albert Speer*, 115.

17. Ibid., 368.

18. Ibid., 405.

3: DANGEROUS CONVICTIONS

1. http://www.sightline.org/research/sust_toolkit/communications-strategy/drewwestenresearch.

2. Drew Westen, *The Political Brain: The Role of Emotion in Deciding the Fate of the Nation* (New York: Public Affairs, 2007).

3. Gayle Greene, *The Woman Who Knew Too Much: Alice Stewart and the Secrets of Radiation* (Ann Arbor, Mich.: University of Michigan Press, 1999), 57.

4. Ibid., 73.

5. British Medical Journal video: http://www.youtube.com/watch?v=proyrn2AAMA.

6. Greene, *The Woman Who Knew Too Much*, 82.

7. Author interview with Anne Marshall, November 26, 2009.

8. "Cakes Under the X-ray." *The Lancet* (January 23, 1897): 289.

9. J. J. Lowe, inventor. *"Method and Means for Visually Determining the Fit of Footwear."* U.S. patent 1,614,988. Washington, D.C.: United States Patent Office, 1927.

10. Leon Festinger, H. W. Riecken, et al., *When Prophecy Fails: A Social and Psychological Study of A Modern Group that Predicted the Destruction of the World* (New York: Harper Torch Books, 1956) 56.

11. Ibid., 138.

12. Ibid., 88.

13. Ibid., 108.

14. Ibid., 110.

15. Ibid., 161.

16. Ibid., 171.

17. A. G. Greenwald (1980). "The Totalitarian Ego: Fabrication and Revision of Personal History." *American Psychologist* 35(7): 603–618.

18. Larissa MacFarquhar, "The Deflationist: How Paul Krugman Found Politics." *New Yorker*, March 1, 2010.

19. Ayn Rand Interview with Mike Wallace, 1959. www.youtube.com/watch?v=pMTDaVpBPRO.

20. Alan Greenspan, *The Age of Turbulence* (New York: Allen Lane, 2007), 51–52.

21. Testimony before Congress, The financial crisis and the role of federal regulators, Thursday, October 23, 2008. U.S. House of Representatives, Committee on Oversight and Government Reform. Washington, D.C.

22. Frank Partnoy, *Infectious Greed: How Deceit and Risk Corrupted the Financial Markets* (London: Profile Books, 2003), 114.

23. Ibid., 406.

24. Speaking at Bath Literature Festival, February 27, 2010.

25. "Prophet and Loss," *Stanford* magazine, March/April 2009, 46.

26. Michael Kirk produced "The Warning," which first aired on the PBS program *Frontline* on October 20, 2009. See also http://www.pbs.org/wgbh/pages/frontline/warning/view/.

27. U.S. Senate hearing 107-724: *An Overview of the Enron Collapse*, December 18, 2001.

28. Testimony before Congress, The financial crisis and the role of federal regulators, October 23, 2008. House of Representatives, Committee on Oversight and Government Reform. Washington, D.C., page 37.

29. Richard Doll and R. Wakeford (1997). *British Journal of Radiology* 70: 130–139.

4: THE LIMITS OF YOUR MIND

1. Quotes and descriptions are taken from author interviews, the Telos Group's report commissioned by BP before the incident, and the U.S. Chemical Safety Board's report following the incident: Telos Group, *BP Texas City Site Report of Findings: Texas City's Protection Performance, Behaviors, Culture, Management and Leadership*, January 21, 2005; and U.S. Chemical Safety and Hazard Investigation Board, *Investigation Report: Refinery Explosion and Fire (15 Killed, 180 Injured) BP Texas City, March 23, 2005*. Report No. 2005-04-I-TX,

March 2007. Available online at http://www.csb.gov/assets/document/CSB FinalReportBP.pdf.

2. From the U.S. Chemical Safety and Hazard Investigation Board's investigation report.

3. Electronic Arts 2004 Annual Report, available online at http://www.bp .com/liveassets/bp_internet/globalbp/STAGING/global_assets/down loads/B/bp_ara_2004_annual_review.pdf.

4. "EA: The Human Story" was nominated for Joel Spolsky's *Best Software Essays of 2004.*

5. The collected works of Ernst Abbe can be found via the Gutenberg Project: http://www.gutenberg.org/etext/19755.

6. If you are interested in more technical detail, there's an interesting analysis of how productivity declines throughout the day at http://www.workless party.org/timework/chapman.htm.

7. D. Tomasi, R. L. Wang, F. Telang, V. Boronikolas, M. C. Jayne, G.-J. Wang, and N. D. Volkow (2009). "Impairment of Attentional Networks After 1 Night of Sleep Deprivation." *Cerebral Cortex* 19(1): 233–40.

8. University of California at Berkeley Labor Occupational Health Program, "Human Factors Curriculum for Refinery Workers."

9. G. Belenky, M. D. "Managing Sleep and Circadian Rhythms to Sustain Operational Performance." PowerPoint presentation given to the ALPA 52nd Air Safety Forum.

10. Some researchers speculate that the epidemic of obesity in the United States and elsewhere may be related to chronic sleep loss. See B. Fryer (2006). "Sleep Deficit: The Performance Killer. A Conversation with Charles A. Czeisler." *Harvard Business Review* 84(10): 53–59.

11. Ibid. "Brain Activity Is Visibly Altered Following Sleep Deprivation." *Nature* 2002 news release. D. Tomasi, R. L. Wang, et al. (2009). "Impairment of Attentional Networks after 1 Night of Sleep Deprivation." *Cerebral Cortex* 19(1): 233–240. National Safety Foundation. "Asleep in America: Poll Highlight and Findings." Washington, D.C.: 2009.

12. Fryer. "Sleep Deficit."

13. Author interview with Dan Simons in Urbana, Illinois.

14. Christopher Chabris and Daniel Simons, *The Invisible Gorilla* (New York: Crown Publishing, 2010).

15. Jason McCarley, "Elements of Human Performance in Baggage X-Ray Screening." Paper presented at the Fourth Annual Aviation Security Technology Symposium, Washington, D.C., November 29, 2006.

16. Daniel J. Simons (2007). "Inattentional Blindness." *Scholarpedia* 2(5): 3244; W. J. Horrey, Daniel J. Simons, et al. (2006). "Assessing Interference from Mental Workload Using a Naturalistic Simulated Driving Task: A Pilot Study." *Proceedings of the Human Factors and Ergonomics Society, 50th Annual Meeting*: 2003–2006. M. S. Ambinder and Daniel J. Simons (2005). "Attention Capture: The Interplay of Expectations, Attention and Awareness." *Neurobiology of Attention* 12: 69–75.

17. David L. Strayer, Frank A. Drews, and Dennis J. Crouch (2006). "A Comparison of the Cell Phone Driver and the Drunk Driver." *Human Factors* 48(2): 381–391.

18. Matt Richtel and Ashlee Vance, "Despite Risks, Internet Creeps Onto Car Dashboards," *New York Times*, January 7, 2010.

19. Ibid.

20. Nvidia press release: http://www.nvidia.com/object/io_1262839759949 .html.

21. T. Grimes (1991). "Mild auditory-visual dissonance in television news may exceed viewer attentional capacity." *Human Communication Research* 18(2): 268–298.

22. http://www.stanford.edu/group/multitasking/memos/Bergen_Multitask ingMemo.pdf.

23. Daniel Kahneman, *Attention and Effort* (New York: Prentice Hall, 1973). See also Daniel Kahneman and Anne Treisman, "Changing Views of Attention and Automaticity." In R. Parasuraman and R. Davies, eds., *Varieties of Attention* (New York: Academic Press, 1984), 29–61.

24. D. T. Gilbert (1991). "How Mental Systems Believe." *American Psychologist* 46(2): 107–119.

25. D. T. Gilbert, R. W. Tafarodi, et al. (1993). "You Can't Not Believe Everything You Read." *Journal of Personality and Social Psychology* 65(2): 221–233.

26. Most of the leading investment banks have worked hard to ensure that their intake of new recruits is evenly balanced, 50 percent men and 50 percent women. But they mostly fail to maintain this balance because the women leave, recognizing that this kind of work schedule is not conducive to family life—or any kind of life. When I have confronted partners on this issue, they have pointed out that more employees would dilute the bonus pool.

27. Sidney Finkelstein, *Why Smart Executives Fail* (New York: Portfolio, 2003).

28. Stanley Milgram (1970). "The Experience of Living in Cities." *Science* 167.

29. Not his real name; he asked to remain anonymous.

30. Philip G. Zimbardo, *The Lucifer Effect: How Good People Turn Evil* (New York: Random House 2007), 347.

31. Zimbardo has written extensively about the Stanford Prison Experiment. Among the many accounts, perhaps the best is the most recent in his book *The Lucifer Effect*. There is also excellent video of the experiment on his Web site: http://www.prisonexp.org/.

32. Zimbardo, *The Lucifer Effect*.

5: THE OSTRICH INSTRUCTION

1. *Daily Mail* (London), October 3, 2009.

2. According to the British Association of Dermatologists Web site, launching their Sun Awareness program: http://www.bad.org.uk//site/994/default .aspx.

3. Public Health Agency of Canada data for 2008. http://www.phac-aspc.gc.ca/cd-mc/cancer/melanoma_skin_cancer-cancer_peau_melanome-eng.php.

4. American Academy of Dermatology. "What is Skin Cancer?" http://www.skincarephysicians.com/skincancernet/whatis.html.

5. Author interview with Dr. Mona Saraiya, October 8, 2009.

6. "Girl, 10, Burned at Tanning Salon," May 1, 2009. http://news.bbc.co.uk/2/hi/uk_news/wales/south_west/8028898.stm.

7. http://www.dailymail.co.uk/news/article-466395/Tanorexic-young-mother-dies-skin-cancer-seven-years-sunbeds.html#ixzz0YRAwzhRd.

8. American Academy of Dermatology, Indoor Tanning Fact Sheet.

9. L. Luborsky and B. Blinder (1965). "Looking, Recalling, and GSR as a Function of Defense." *Journal of Abnormal Psychology* 70(4): 270–280.

10. Dennis Cauchon, "Leap in U.S. Debt Hits Taxpayers with 12% More Red Ink," *USA Today*, May 29, 2009.

11. According to the National Bankruptcy Research Center.

12. John S. Hammond, Ralph L. Keeney, et al. (2006). "The Hidden Traps In Decision Making." *Harvard Business Review* 84(1): 118–126.

13. http://www.rgemonitor.com/blog/roubini/142759/.

14. Author interview, November 18, 2009.

15. Author interview, September 18, 2009; other information is from Kate Kelly, *Street Fighters: The Last 72 Hours of Bear Stearns, the Toughest Firm on Wall Street* (New York: Portfolio, 2009).

16. Frances J. Milliken, Elizabeth W. Morrison, et al. (2003). "An Exploratory Study of Employee Silence: Issues that Employees Don't Communicate Upward and Why." *The Journal of Management Studies* 40(6): 1453–1476.

17. A. Schneider and D. McCumber, *An Air That Kills: How the Asbestos Poisoning of Libby, Montana Uncovered a National Scandal* (New York: G. P. Putnam's Sons, 2004).

18. Ibid., 105.

19. Ibid., 8.

6: JUST FOLLOWING ORDERS

1. Martin E. P. Seligman, *Authentic Happiness* (London: Nicholas Brealey Books, 2003).

2. Stanley Milgram, *Obedience to Authority* (New York: Harper Perennial, 1974), xiii.

3. Ibid., 31.

4. According to John Darley in author interview at Princeton, New Jersey, September 2009.

5. Milgram, *Obedience to Authority*, 188.

6. For more detail, see *Obedience to Authority* by Stanley Milgram. Although much has been written about this experiment, there is no substitute for the firsthand account, which is lucid, accessible, and thought-provoking.

7. Charles Sheridan and Richard G. King (1972). "Obedience to Authority with an Authentic Victim." *Proceedings of the 80th Annual Convention of the American Psychological Association*: 165–166.

8. Thomas Blass (1999). "The Milgram Paradigm After 35 Years: Some Things We Now Know about Obedience to Authority." *Journal of Applied Social Psychology* 29(5): 955–978.

9. J. M. Burger (2009). "Would People Still Obey Today?" *American Psychologist* 64(1): 1–12.

10. The show was done with a live audience that shouted "Punishment! Punishment!" One participant, whose grandparents had died in the Holocaust, said she regretted having taken part; another participant, who had been raised in Romania, said that her experience under Nicolae Ceauşescu had given her the strength to say no.

11. Milgram, *Obedience to Authority*, 8.

12. C. K., Hofling, E. Brotzman, et al. (1966). "An Experimental Study in Nurse-Physician Relationships." *The Journal of Nervous and Mental Disease* 143(2): 171–180.

13. Walt J. Pavlo and Neil Weinberg, *Stolen Without a Gun* (Tampa, FL: Etika LLC, 2007).

14. Declassified evidence available at www.texascityexplosion.com.

15. U. S. Chemical Safety and Hazard Investigation Board, *Investigation Report: Refinery Explosion and Fire (15 Killed, 180 Injured) BP Texas City, March 23, 2005.* Report No. 2005-04-I-TX, March 2007: 142.

16. E-mail dated August 26, 2004.

17. Telos Group, *BP Texas City Site Report of Findings: Texas City's Protection Performance, Behaviors, Culture, Management and Leadership*, January 21, 2005: 32.

18. Errol Morris (2003). *Standard Operating Procedure*. USA, Sony Pictures: 111 minutes.

19. Eugen Tarnow, "Self Destructive Obedience in the Airplane Cockpit and the Concept of Obedience Optimization." In *Obedience to Authority: Current Perspectives on the Milgram Paradigm*, edited by Thomas Blass (Hillsdale, NJ: Erlbaum Associates, 2000).

20. J. Martin, B. Lobb, G. Chapman, and R. Spillane (1976). "Obedience Under Conditions Demanding Self-Immolation." *Human Relations* 29: 345–356.

21. Mark Osiel, *Obeying Orders: Atrocity, Military Discipline and the Law of War* (New Brunswick: Transaction Publishers, 2002), 8.

22. Ibid.

7: THE CULT OF CULTURES

1. Author interview with Walt Pavlo, Washington, D.C., September 2009. See also Pavlo, *Stolen Without a Gun*.

2. Milgram, *Obedience to Authority*, 114.

3. Solomon E. Asch (1955). "Opinions and Social Pressure." *Scientific American* 193(5): 31–35.

4. K. S. Larsen, J. S. Triplett, et al. (1979). "Collaborator Status, Subject Characteristics and Conformity in the Asch Paradigm." *The Journal of Social Psychology* 108: 259–263.

5. Ibid.

6. James Surowiecki, *The Wisdom of Crowds* (New York: Doubleday, 2004). Also B. Grofman, and S. Feld (1988). "Rousseau's General Will: A Condorcetian Perspective." *American Political Science Review* 82: 567–576.

7. "Bubbleology: Wall Street Goofed on the Last Bubble. Now It Sees New Ones Forming Everywhere." CNNMoney, June 24, 2003.

8. M. Weisbuch, S. A. Sinclair, et al. (2009). "Self-Esteem Depends on the Beholder: Effects of a Subtle Social Value Cue." *Journal of Experimental Social Psychology* 45(1): 143–149.

9. J. Panksepp, S. M. Siviy, and L. A. Normansell, "Brain Opioids and Social Emotions." In M. Reite and T. Field, eds., *The Psychobiology of Attachment and Separation* (New York: Academic Press, 1985), 3–49.

10. J. Panksepp (2003). "Neuroscience: Feeling the Pain of Social Loss." *Science* 302(5643): 237–239. Also Roy F. Baumeister and Mark R. Leary (May 1995). "The Need to Belong: Desire for Interpersonal Attachments as a Fundamental Human Motivation." *Psychological Bulletin* 117(3): 497–529.

11. T. F. Stillman, R. F. Baumeister, et al. (2009). "Alone and Without Purpose: Life Loses Meaning Following Social Exclusion." *Journal of Experimental Social Psychology* 45(4): 686–694.

12. Frank Partnoy, *F.I.A.S.C.O.: Blood in the Water on Wall Street* (New York: W.W. Norton, 1997, 2009).

13. Ibid., 95–96.

14. G. S. Berns, J. Chappelow, et al. (2005). "Neurobiological Correlates of Social Conformity and Independence During Mental Rotation." *Journal of Biological Psychiatry* 58: 245–253.

15. Ibid.

16. Irving L. Janis, *Victims of Groupthink: A Psychological Study of Foreign-Policy Decisions and Fiascoes* (Boston: Houghton Mifflin, 1972), 13.

17. Kate Kelly. *Street Fighters: The Last 72 Hours of Bear Stearns, the Toughest Firm on Wall Street* (New York: Portfolio, 2009), 152–153, 160–161.

18. Scott McClellan, *What Happened: Inside the Bush White House and Washington's Culture of Deceptions* (New York: Public Affairs, 2008).

19. Paul O'Neill, *The Price of Loyalty: George W. Bush, the White House, and the Education of Paul O'Neill* (New York: Simon & Schuster, 2004). Also McClellan, *What Happened*.

8: BYSTANDERS

1. Errol Morris (2003). *Standard Operating Procedure*. USA, Sony Pictures, 111 minutes.
2. J. Darley and B. Latané (1968). "Group Inhibition of Bystander Intervention in Emergencies." *Journal of Personality and Social Psychology* 10(3): 215–221.
3. J. Darley and B. Latané (1968). "Bystander Intervention in Emergencies: Diffusion of Responsibility." *Journal of Personality and Social Psychology* 8(4): 377–383.
4. B. Latané and S. Nida (1981). "Ten Years of Research on Group Size and Helping." *Psychological Bulletin* 89(2): 308–324.
5. Lisa Decarlo, "Murder, She Read." *New York*, May 11, 1998.
6. J. Blenkinsopp and M. S. Edwards (2008). "On Not Blowing the Whistle: Quiescent Silence as an Emotion Episode." *Research on Emotion in Organizations* 4: 181–206.
7. http://www.ellsberg.net/bio.
8. Lynn Brewer, *Confessions of an Enron Executive* (Bloomington, IN: Author House, 2004).
9. Mimi Swartz and Sherron Watkins, *Power Failure: The Inside Story of the Collapse of Enron* (New York: Doubleday, 2003).
10. U.S. Department of Justice, Office of Community Oriented Policing. Report on Bullying in Schools. www.cops.doj.gov.
11. Bullying UK, "The National Survey," http://www.thenationalsurvey.co.uk/.
12. Keith E. Stanovich and Richard F. West (2000). "Individual Differences in Reasoning: Implications for the Rationality Debate?" *Behavioral and Brain Sciences* 23: 645–666.
13. G. J. Horwitz, *In the Shadow of Death: Living Outside the Gates of Mauthausen* (London: I.B.Tauris & Co., 1991).

9: OUT OF SIGHT, OUT OF MIND

1. U.S. Chemical Safety and Hazard Investigation Board. *Investigation Report: Refinery Explosion and Fire (15 Killed, 180 Injured) BP Texas City, March 23, 2005*. Report No. 2005-04-I-TX, March 2007.
2. Telos Group, *BP Texas City Site Report of Findings: Texas City's Protection Performance, Behaviors, Culture, Management and Leadership*. January 21, 2005. See also U.S. Chemical Safety and Hazard Investigation Board, *Investigation Report: Refinery Explosion and Fire (15 Killed, 180 Injured) BP Texas City, March 23, 2005*. Report No. 2005-04-I-TX, March 2007, 193.
3. John Manzoni's deposition: http://texascityexplosion.com/etc/broadcast/files/ev5/DEPO–Manzoni,%20John.pdf.
4. Stanley Milgram, *Obedience to Authority* (New York: Harper Perennial, 1974), 38.

5. John Darley, Allan I. Teger, and Lawrence D. Lewis (1973). "Do Groups Always Inhibit Individuals' Responses to Potential Emergencies? *Journal of Personality and Social Psychology* 26(3): 395–399.

6. Norman F. Dixon, *On the Psychology of Military Incompetence* (London: Futura Publications Limited, 1976).

7. Norman F. Dixon, *Our Own Worst Enemy* (London: Jonathan Cape Ltd., 1987).

8. Stephanie A. Goodwin, Alexandra Gubin, Susan T. Fiske, and Vincent Y. Yzerbyt (2000). "Power Can Bias Impression Processes: Stereotyping Subordinates by Default and by Design," *Group Processes and Intergroup Relations* 3(3): 227–256.

9. http://i.a.cnn.net/cnn/2005/images/11/03/brown.emails.pdf.

10. My edited version of an interview of Michael Brown conducted by Ted Koppel, September 2, 2005. http://espanol.video.yahoo.com/watch/223063/786068.

11. http://i.a.cnn.net/cnn/2005/images/11/03/brown.emails.pdf, September 2, 2005.

12. One of the most remarkable examples of this is done by Rush Trucking, which trucks car components into Native American reservations in Canada, where they are assembled before being trucked out again to the United States.

13. Note made by Wilhelm Bonse as part of his internal inquiry into the Texas City explosion: Management Accountability Project, Texas City Isomerization Explosion, Final Report. June 26, 2006.

14. Testimony of Dr. David Graham, November 24, 2004, to the Senate Finance Committee. http://finance.senate.gov/hearings/testimony/2004test/111804dgtest.pdf.

15. Phillip Inman and Jill Treanor, "London Lawyers Linklaters Accused of Helping to Hide Lehman Billions," *Guardian*, March 13, 2010; and Michael J. de la Merced, "Auditor Could Face Liability in Lehman Case," *New York Times*, March 14, 2010.

16. Richard P. Feynman, *What Do You Care What Other People Think: Further Adventures of a Curious Character* (London: Norton, 1988).

17. http://lightgreenstairs.com/green-choices/sigg-not-taking-responsibility/.

18. Peter W. Singer, "Outsourcing the Fight" (Washington, D.C.: Brookings Institution, June 5, 2008). http://www.brookings.edu/opinions/2008/0605_military_contractors_singer.aspx. See also: http://www.washingtonpost.com/wp-dyn/articles/A21858-2004Jul28.html.

19. Michael Sandell, *The Reith Lectures*, transcript available: http://www.bbc.co.uk/programmes/b00kt7sh.

20. The Financial Crisis and the Role of Federal Regulators (Washington, D.C.: U.S. House of Representatives, Committee on Oversight and Government Reform, October 23, 2008). http://oversight.house.gov/images/stories/documents/20081024163819.pdf.

21. Letter to Her Majesty The Queen, July 22, 2009: http://media.ft.com/cms/3e3b6ca8-7a08-11de-b86f-00144feabdc0.pdf.

10: DE-MORALIZING WORK

1. R.S. Schwab, "Motivation in Measurements of Fatigue." In *Symposium on Fatigue*, W. Floyd and A. Welford, eds. (London: H. K. Lewis & Co, 1953), 143–148.
2. Kathleen D. Vohs (2008). "Merely Activating the Concept of Money Changes Personal and Interpersonal Behavior." *Current Directions in Psychological Science* 17(3): 208–212.
3. R. A. Adcock, A. Thangavel, et al. (2006). "Reward-Motivated Learning: Mesolimbic Activation Precedes Memory Formation." *Neuron* 50(3): 507–517.
4. M. Pessiglione, L. Schmidt, et al. (2007). "How the Brain Translates Money into Force: A Neuroimaging Study of Subliminal Motivation." *Science* 316(5826): 904–906.
5. Daniel H. Pink, *Drive: The Surprising Truth about What Motivates Us* (New York: Canongate, 2009).
6. X. Zhou, Kathleen D. Vohs, et al. (2009). "The Symbolic Power of Money: Reminders of Money Alter Social Distress and Physical Pain." *Psychological Science* 20(6): 700–706.
7. Author interview with David Ring, October 1, 2009.
8. Kathleen D. Vohs, N. L. Mead, et al. (2006). "The Psychological Consequences of Money." *Science* 314(5802): 1154–1156.
9. Kathleen D. Vohs, (2008). "Merely Activating the Concept of Money Changes Personal and Interpersonal Behavior." *Current Directions in Psychological Science* 17(3): 208–212.
10. J. Finch, "I Save Tax by Never Visiting My Family, Says Tycoon Hands." *Guardian*, February 6, 2010.
11. Paul Moore's testimony to the House of Commons Select Committee: http://ftalphaville.ft.com/blog/2009/02/11/52320/hbos-the-moore-memo/.
12. The Risk Minds Risk Managers Survey 2009: http://www.slideshare.net/kakabadse/risk-minds-2009-risk-survey-presentation.
13. S. F. Bruno (1997). "A Constitution for Knaves Crowds Out Civic Virtues." *Economic Journal* 107(443): 1043–1053.
14. B. S. Frey and F. Oberholzer-Gee (1997). "The Cost of Price Incentives: An Empirical Analysis of Motivation Crowding-Out." *American Economic Review* 87(4): 746–755.
15. U. Gneezy and A. Rustichini (2000). "A Fine Is a Price." *Journal of Legal Studies* 29(1): 1–17.
16. Samuel Bowles (2008). "Policies Designed for Self-Interested Citizens May Undermine 'The Moral Sentiments': Evidence from Economic Experiments." *Science* 320(5883): 1605–1609.

17. J. D. Greene, R. B. Sommerville, et al. (2001). "An fMRI Investigation of Emotional Engagement in Moral Judgment." *Science* 293(5537): 2105–2108. See also D. Robertson, J. Snarey, et al. (2007). "The Neural Processing of Moral Sensitivity to Issues of Justice and Care." *Neuropsychologia* 45(4): 755–766.

18. Michael Lewis, *The Big Short: Inside the Doomsday Machine* (New York: W.W. Norton, 2010).

19. Court document. Viewable here: http://www.thedailybeast.com/blogs-and-stories/2010-05-25/shocking-bp-memo-and-the-oil-spill-in-the-gulf/full/.

20. Author interview, September 17, 2009. See also Albert Bandura (1999). "Moral Disengagement in the Perpetuation of Inhumanities." *Personality and Social Psychology Review* 3: 193–209.

21. Newt Gingrich, *To Renew America* (New York: HarperCollins, 1995).

22. Albert Bandura, "Impeding Ecological Sustainability Through Selective Moral Disengagement." *International Journal of Innovation and Sustainable Development* 2(1): 2007.

11: CASSANDRA

1. M. P. Miceli and J. P. Near (2005). "Standing Up or Standing By: What Predicts Blowing the Whistle on Organizational Wrongdoing?" *Research in Personnel and Human Resources Management* 24: 93–136.

 2. Written testimony of Harry Markopolos, CFA, CFE, before the U.S. Senate Banking, Housing and Urban Affairs Committee, September 10, 2009.

 3. Author interview with Sherron Watkins, October 23, 2008.

 4. J. Hansen et al. (1981). "Climate Impact of Increasing Atmospheric Carbon Dioxide." *Science* 213: 957–966.

 5. Ryan Lizza, "The Contrarian," *New Yorker*, July 6 and 13, 2009.

 6. Author interview with Aaron Krowne, September 3, 2009.

 7. "On the Money," a profile of Gillian Tett, *Guardian*, October 31, 2008.

 8. Bath Literary Festival, February 27, 2010.

 9. Gillian Tett, *Fool's Gold: How Unrestrained Greed Corrupted a Dream, Shattered Global Markets and Unleashed a Catastrophe* (London: Little Brown, 2009), 299.

10. A twelve-year study published in the June 2007 issue of the journal *Epidemiology and Health* clearly demonstrated that the risk of suicide among male U.S. veterans is more than two times greater than that of the general population after adjusting for a host of potentially compounding factors, including age, time of service, and health status. A report released in May 2010 by the inspector general of the Veterans Administration noted that "veterans returning from Iraq and Afghanistan are at increased risk for suicide because not all VA clinics have 24-hour mental care available . . . and many lack properly trained workers."

Media reports of suicide deaths and suicide attempts among active-duty Operation Enduring Freedom and Operation Iraqi Freedom soldiers and veterans began to surface back in 2003 after a spate of suicides in Iraq during the first months of the war. Since then, both the military and the VA have stumbled and fumbled in their attempts to answer questions about the severity of this malady. For example, while all the military services maintain suicide prevention programs, the Army in its August 2007 Army Suicide Event Report acknowledged that soldiers committed suicide last year at the highest rate in twenty-six years, and more than a quarter did so while serving in Iraq and Afghanistan. The report noted "a significant relationship between suicide attempts and number of days deployed in Iraq, Afghanistan or nearby countries where troops are participating in the war effort." The report added that there also "was limited evidence to support the view that multiple deployments are a risk factor for suicide behaviors." It might be noted here that this report was released only after a request was made under the Freedom of Information Act. From the Vietnam Veterans of America: http://www.vva.org/who.html.

11. Author interview with Lawrence Rockwood, February 3, 2010.
12. Author interview with Maria Garzino, February 3, 2010.
13. www.osc.gov.
14. GQ magazine, September 2006. http://www.gq.com/news-politics/news makers/200608/joe-darby-abu-ghraib?currentPage=2.
15. C. F. Alford, *Whistleblowers: Broken Lives and Organizational Power* (Ithaca, NY: Cornell University Press, 2001).
16. CBS *Sixty Minutes*, January 25, 2007. http://www.cbsnews.com/video/watch/?id=2972689n&tag=related;photovideo.
17. Author interview with Sherron Watkins, October 22, 2008, Houston, Texas.

12: SEE BETTER

1. C. H. Hillman, K. I. Erickson, et al. (2008). "Be Smart, Exercise Your Heart: Exercise Effects on Brain and Cognition." *Nature Reviews Neuroscience* 9: 58–65.
2. Gayle Greene, *The Woman Who Knew Too Much: Alice Stewart and the Secrets of Radiation* (Ann Arbor, MI: University of Michigan Press, 1999), 223.
3. Ibid., 244.
4. Curtis Sittenfeld, "He's No Fool (But He Plays One inside Companies)," *Fast Company*, October 31, 1998. http://www.fastcompany.com/magazine/19/nofool.html.
5. Author interview with Ginger Graham, February 2, 2010.
6. John Browne, *Beyond Business* (London: Weidenfeld and Nicholson, 2010), 211.
7. Author interview with Saj-Nicole Joni, October 25, 2009.

8. Sydney Finkelstein, *Why Smart Executives Fail: And What You Can Learn From Their Mistakes* (New York: Portfolio, 2003).

9. Max H. Bazerman, G. Loewenstein, et al. (2002). "Why Good Accountants Do Bad Audits." *Harvard Business Review* 80(11): 96–102.

10. Author interview with Justin Paperny, November 12, 2009.

11. Author interview with Philip Zimbardo, November 12, 2009.

12. Charles Nemeth et al. (1990). "Exposure to Dissent and Recall of Information." *Journal of Personality and Social Psychology* 58(3): 429–437.

13. Author interview with Ajit Nayak, February 26, 2010.

14. Travis Proulx and Steven J. Heine (2009). "Connections From Kafka: Exposure to Meaning Threats Improves Implicit Learning of an Artificial Grammar." *Psychological Science* 20(9): 1125–1131.

15. http://biblioklept.org/2009/09/16/reading-kafka-and-watching-lynch-will-make-you-smarter/.

16. Langer, Ellen J., *Mindfulness* (Cambridge, MA: Perseus Books, 1989).

17. Author interview with Herb Meyer, May 10, 2010.

18. George F. Kennan, *Memoirs 1925–1950* (New York: Pantheon, 1983).

19. Gillian Tett at Bath Literary Festival, February 27, 2010.

20. Chelsea Ide and Kanupriya Vashisht, "Today's investigative reporters lack resources," May 28, 2006, www.azcentral.com/specials/special01/0528bolles-stateofreporting.html.

21. Author interview with Heather Brookes, March 5, 2010.

22. www.propublica.org

23. In 2010, ProPublica collaborated with PBS on an in-depth study of BP, *Frontline: The Spill*, broadcast October 26, 2010.

24. www.wikileaks.org

25. A. Pascual-Leone, N. Dang, et al. (1995). "Modulation of Muscle Responses Evoked by Transcranial Magnetic Stimulation During the Acquisition of New Fine Motor Skills." *Journal of Neurophysiology* 74(3): 1037–1045.

BIBLIOGRAPHY

Abagnale, Frank. *Catch Me If You Can: The Amazing True Story of the Most Extraordinary Liar in the History of Fun and Profit*. New York: Broadway Books, 1980.

Adcock, R. Alison, Arul Thangavel, Susan Whitfield-Gabriel, Brian Knutson, and John D. E. Gabriele. "Reward-Motivated Learning: Mesolimbic Activation Precedes Memory Formation." *Neuron* 50, no. 3 (2006) 507–517.

Addley, Esther. "How Britain Fell in Love with the Tan." *Guardian*, August 1, 2009.

Akerlof, George A., and Robert J. Shiller. *Animal-Spirits: How Human Psychology Drives the Economy, and Why It Matters for Global Capitalism*. Princeton, NJ: Princeton University Press, 2009.

Aleccia, JoNel. "Hospital Bullies Take a Toll on Patient Safety," *www.MSNBC.com/* July 9, 2008.

Alford, C. Fred. *Whistleblowers: Broken Lives and Organizational Power*. Ithaca, NY: Cornell University Press, 2001.

Ambinder, Michael S., and Daniel J. Simons. "Attention Capture: The Interplay of Expectations, Attention and Awareness." *Neurobiology of Attention* 12 (2005) 69–75.

American Academy of Dermatology. "What is Skin Cancer?" http://www.skincarephysicians.com/skincancernet/whatis.html.

———. "Indoor Tanning Fact Sheet."
http://www.aad.org/media/background/factsheets/fact_indoortanning.html.

Anderson, Cameron, and Jennifer L. Berdahl. "The Experience of Power: Examining the Effects of Power on Approach and Inhibition Tendencies." *Journal of Personality and Social Psychology* 83, no. 6 (2002) 1362–1377.

Anderson, Cameron, and Adam D. Galinsky. "Power, Optimism and Risk Taking." *European Journal of Social Psychology* 36 (2006) 511–536.

Arendt, Hannah. "Personal Responsibility under Dictatorship." In *Responsibility and Judgment*, edited by Jerome Kohn. New York: Schocken Books, 2003.

————. *The Jewish Writings*. New York: Schocken Books, 2007.

Ariely, Dan. *Predictably Irrational: The Hidden Forces That Shape Our Decisions*. New York: HarperCollins, 2008.

Aron, Arthur, Elaine N. Aron, Michael Tudor, and Greg Nelson. "Close Relationships as Including Other in the Self." *Journal of Personality and Social Psychology* 60, no. 2 (1991) 241–253.

Aronson, Elliott. "Back to the Future: Retrospective Review of Leon Festinger's *A Theory of Cognitive Dissonance*." *American Journal of Psychology* 110, no. 1 (1997) 127–157.

Asch, Solomon E. "Opinions and Social Pressure." *Scientific American* 193, no. 5 (1955) 31–35.

Asthana, Anushka. "Report Reveals How Britons Were Lured into Spiral of Debt." *Observer* (London), February 7, 2010.

Auletta, Ken. *Three Blind Mice: How the TV Networks Lost Their Way*. New York: Vintage Books, 1991.

Baars, Bernard J., William P. Banks, and James B. Newman, eds. *Essential Sources in the Scientific Study of Consciousness*. Cambridge, MA: MIT Press, 2003.

Banaji, Mahzarin R. "The Moral Obligation to Be Intelligent." In *Beyond Common Sense: Psychological Science in the Courtroom*, edited by Eugene Borgida and Susan T. Fiske. Malden, MA: Wiley-Blackwell, 2007.

Banaji, Mahzarin R., Max H. Bazerman, and Dolly Chugh. "How (Un)Ethical Are You?" *Harvard Business Review* (December 2003) 56–64.

Banaji, Mahzarin R., Curtis Hardin, and Alexander J. Rothman. "Implicit Stereotyping in Person Judgment." *Journal of Personality and Social Psychology* 65, no. 2 (1993) 272–281.

Bandura, Albert. "Social Cognitive Theory of Moral Thought and Action." In *Handbook of Moral Behavior and Development*, edited by William M. Kurtines and Jacob L. Gewirtz. Hillsdale, NJ: Lawrence Erlbaum Associates, 1991.

————. "Moral Disengagement in the Perpetration of Inhumanities." *Personality and Social Psychology Review* 3 (1999) 193–209.

————. "Impeding Ecological Sustainability Through Selective Moral Disengagement." *International Journal of Innovation and Sustainable Development* 2, no. 1 (2007) 8–32.

————. "The Reconstrual of 'Free Will' From the Agentic Perspective of Social Cognitive Theory." In *Are We Free? Psychology and Freewill,* edited by J. Baer, J. G. Kaufman, and R. F. Baumeister. Oxford: Oxford University Press, 2008.

————. "Social Cognitive Theory Goes Global." *British Psychological Society* 22, no. 6 (2009) 504–506.

Bandura, Albert, Gian-Vittorio Caprara, and Laszlo Zsolnai. "Corporate Transgressions Through Moral Disengagement." *Journal of Human Values* 6, no. 1 (2000) 57–64.

Barnes, Brooks. "Studios' Quest for Life after DVDs." *New York Times*, October 25, 2009.

Bartels, Andreas, and Semir Zeki. "The Neural Correlates of Maternal and Romantic Love." *NeuroImage* 21, no. 3 (2004) 1155–1166.

Barton, Laura. "On the Money." *Guardian*, October 31, 2008.

Baumeister, Roy, C. Nathan DeWall, Nicole Mead, and Kathleen Vohs. "Social Rejection Can Reduce Pain and Increase Spending: Further Evidence That Money, Pain, and Belongingness Are Interrelated." *Psychological Inquiry* 19, no. 3–4 (2008) 145–147.

Baumeister, Roy F., and Kenneth J. Cairns. "Repression and Self-Presentation: When Audiences Interfere with Self-Deceptive Strategies." *Journal of Personality and Social Psychology* 62, no. 5 (1992) 851–862.

Baumeister, Roy F., and Mark R. Leary. "The Need to Belong: Desire for Interpersonal Attachments as a Fundamental Human Motivation." *Psychological Bulletin* 117, no. 3 (1995) 497–529.

Baumgardner, Ann H. "To Know Oneself Is to Like Oneself: Self-Certainty and Self-Affect." *Journal of Personality and Social Psychology* 58, no. 6 (1990) 1062–1072.

Bazerman, Max H. *Negotiating Rationally*. New York: Free Press, 1993.

———. *Judgment in Managerial Decision-Making*. New York: Wiley, 2002.

Bazerman, Max H., and Mahzarin R. Banaji. "The Social Psychology of Ordinary Ethical Failures." *Social Justice Research* 17, no. 2 (2004) 111–115.

Bazerman, Max, H., and Dolly Chugh. "Decisions Without Blinders." *Harvard Business Review* 84, no. 1 (2006) 88–97.

Bazerman, Max, H., George Loewenstein, and A. Moore Don. "Why Good Accountants Do Bad Audits." *Harvard Business Review* 80, no. 11 (2002) 96–102.

bbc.co.uk. "Girl, 10, Burned at Tanning Salon," May 1, 2009. http://news.bbc.co.uk/2/hi/uk_news/wales/south_west/8028898.stm.

Begley, Sharon. "Adventures in Good and Evil." *Newsweek* 153, no. 18 (2009) 46–49.

Belenky, Gregory M. D. "Managing Sleep and Circadian Rhythms to Sustain Operational Performance." PowerPoint presentation to the ALPA 52nd Air Safety Forum, July 2006.

Berns, Gregory S., Jonathan Chappelow, Caroline F. Zink, Giuseppe Pagnoni, Megan E. Martin-Skursk, and Jim Richards. "Neurobiological Correlates of Social Conformity and Independence During Mental Rotation." *Journal of Biological Psychiatry* 58 (2005) 245–253.

Bishop, Bill. *The Big Sort: Why the Clustering of Like-Minded America Is Tearing Us Apart*. Boston: Houghton Mifflin, 2008.

Blakeslee, Sandra. "What Other People Say May Change What You See." *New York Times*, June 28, 2005.

Blanchflower, David. "My Time at Threadneedle Street Certainly Wasn't Boring." *Guardian*, June 8, 2009.

Blanford, Nicholas. "The Admiral Ordered 'Turn' and the Ships Collided." *Times* (London), September 2, 2004.

Blass, Thomas. "The Milgram Paradigm After 35 Years: Some Things We Now Know About Obedience to Authority." *Journal of Applied Social Psychology* 29, no. 5 (1999) 955–978.

Blass, Thomas, ed. *Obedience to Authority: Current Perspectives on the Milgram Paradigm.* Hillsdale, NJ: Lawrence Erlbaum, 2000.

Blenkinsopp, John, and Marissa S. Edwards. "On Not Blowing the Whistle: Quiescent Silence as an Emotion Episode." *Research on Emotion in Organizations* 4 (2008) 181–206.

Bolsin, Stephen N., Tom Faunce, and Mark Colson. "Using Portable Digital Technology for Clinical Care and Critical Incidents: A New Model." *Australian Health Review* 29, no. 3 (2005) 297–305.

Bowen, Frances, and Kate Blackmon. "Spirals of Silence: The Dynamic Effects of Diversity on Organizational Voice." *Journal of Management Studies* 40, no. 6 (2003) 1393–1417.

Bowles, Samuel. "Policies Designed for Self-Interested Citizens May Undermine 'The Moral Sentiments': Evidence from Economic Experiments." *Science* 320, no. 5883 (2008) 1605–1609.

BP. "Cost Benefit Analysis of the Three Little Pigs." PowerPoint slide produced in evidence by BP, date unknown.

Brendl, C. Miguel, Amitaa Chattopadhyay, Brett W. Pelham, and Mauricio Carvallo. "Name Letter Branding: Valence Transfers When Product Specific Needs Are Active." *Journal of Consumer Research* 32 (2005) 405–415.

Brewer, Lynn. *Confessions of an Enron Executive.* Bloomington, IN: Author House, 2004.

Brooke, Heather. "Promises of More Open Government Have Been Made Before." *Times* (London), June 11, 2009.

———. "Unsung Hero." *Guardian*, May 15, 2009.

Brown, David K. *Warrior to Dreadnought: Warship Development 1860–1905.* Barnsley, England: Chatham Publishing, 1997.

Brown, Jim. "New Federal Whistleblower Office Off to Slow Start in First Year on the Job." *Canadian Press* (Toronto), May 20, 2008.

Browne, John. *Beyond Business: An Inspirational Memoir from a Visionary Leader.* London: Weidenfeld & Nicholson, 2009.

Bruno, S. Frey. "A Constitution for Knaves Crowds Out Civic Virtues." *Economic Journal* 107, no. 443 (1997) 1043–1053.

Bullying UK. "The National Survey." http://www.thenationalsurvey.co.uk/.

Burger, Jerry M. "Would People Still Obey Today?" *American Psychologist* 64, no. 1 (2009) 1–12.

Burkin, Kevin, and Brian H. Kleiner. "Protecting the Whistleblower: Preventing Retaliation Following a Report of Patient Abuse in Health-Care Institutions." *Health Manpower Management* 24, no. 3 (1998) 119–124.

Burton, Robert A. *On Being Certain: Believing You Are Right Even When You're Not.* New York: St. Martin's Press, 2008.

"Bystanders Can Stop Bullying." http://myhighplains.com/fulltext?nxd_id=64841.

Cacioppo, John T., Richard E. Petty, and Mary E. Losch. "Attributions of Responsibility for Helping and Doing Harm: Evidence for Confusion of Responsibility." *Journal of Personality and Social Psychology* 50, no. 1 (1986) 100–105.

Canada Safety Council. "Don't Just Stand There—Do Something," 2004.

Cannon, M. D., and A. C. Edmondson. "Failing to Learn and Learning to Fail (Intelligently)." *Long Range Planning* 38, no. 3 (2005) 299–319.

Carey, John. "The Unwisdom of Crowds." *BusinessWeek*, May 7, 2009.

Carozza, Dick. "Chasing Madoff: An Interview with Harry Markopolos." *Fraud* 23, no. 3 (2009).

Carr, Drury Gunn, and Doug Hawes-Davis. "Libby, Montana." A film produced by High Plains Films and distributed by Typecast Releasing, 2006.

Carville, James, and Mary Matalin. *All's Fair: Love, War and Running for President*. New York: Random House, 1994.

Cassidy, John. "After the Blowup." *New Yorker*, January 11, 2010, 28–33.

Chandler, Jesse, Tiffany M. Griffin, and Nicholas Sorensen. "Improving Decision Making by Means of Dissent." *Journal of Applied Social Psychology* 31 (2001) 48–58.

———. "In the 'I' of the Storm: Shared Initials Increase Disaster Donations." *Judgment and Decision Making* 3, no. 5 (2008) 404–410.

Channel 4 Television (UK) 4, "Would You Save a Stranger," April 12, 2009. Available online at http://channel4.com/programmes/would-you-save-a-stranger.

Chugh, Dolly, and Max H. Bazerman. "Bounded Awareness: What You Fail to See Can Hurt You." *Mind and Society* 6, no. 1 (2007) 1–18.

Chugh, Dolly, Max H. Bazerman, and Mahzarin R. Banaji. "Bounded Ethicality as a Psychological Barrier to Recognizing Conflicts of Interest." To appear in D. Moore, D. Cain, G. Loewenstein, and M. H. Bazerman, eds., *Conflicts of Interest: Problems and Solutions from Law, Medicine and Organizational Settings*. London: Cambridge University Press.

Cohen, Stanley. *States of Denial: Knowing About Atrocities and Suffering*. London: Polity, 2001.

Cornblatt, Johannah. "Bystanders No More: Teaching Kids to Respond to Violent Crime." *Newsweek*, October 30, 2009.

Creed, W. E. Douglas. "Voice Lessons: Tempered Radicalism and the Use of Voice and Silence." *Journal of Management Studies* 40, no. 6 (2003) 1503–1536.

"Criminal Law: Willful Blindness: Ninth Circuit Holds That Motive Is Not an Element of Willful Blindness." *Harvard Law Review* 121, no. 4 (2008) 1245–1253.

Crozier, W. Ray. *Shyness and Embarrassment: Perspectives from Social Psychology*. Cambridge: Cambridge University Press, 1990.

Darley, John, and B. Latané. "Bystander Intervention in Emergencies: Diffusion of Responsibility." *Journal of Personality and Social Psychology* 8, no. 4 (1968) 377–383.

Darley, John M. "Social Organization for the Production of Evil." *Psychological Inquiry* 3, no. 2 (1992) 199–218.

Darley, John M., and C. Daniel Batson. "'From Jerusalem to Jericho': A Study of Situational and Dispositional Variables in Helping Behavior." *Journal of Personality and Social Psychology* 27, no. 1 (1973) 100–108.

Darley, John, Allan Teger, and Lawrence D. Lewis. "Do Groups Always Inhibit Individuals' Responses to Potential Emergencies?" *Journal of Personality and Social Psychology* 26, no. 3 (1973) 395–399.

DiMaggio, Paul. "Culture and Cognition." *Annual Review of Sociology* (1997).

Dixon, Norman F. *On the Psychology of Military Incompetence.* London: Futura Publications, 1976.

———. *Our Own Worst Enemy.* London: Jonathan Cape, 1987.

Dorsey, David. *The Force.* New York: Random House, 1994.

Eastwick, Paul W., Jennifer A. Richeson, Deborah Son, and Eli J. Finkely. "Is Love Colorblind? Political Orientation and Interracial Romantic Desire." *Personality and Social Psychology Bulletin* 35, no. 9 (2009) 1258–1268.

Edelman, Aida. "A Double Agent, That's What I Was." *Guardian*, November 14, 2009.

Edmondson, Amy C. "Speaking Up in the Operating Room: How Team Leaders Promote Learning in Interdisciplinary Action Teams." *Journal of Management Studies* 40, no. 6 (2003) 1419–1452.

Edmondson, Vickie Cox, and George Munchus. "Managing the Unwanted Truth: A Framework for Dissent Strategy." *Journal of Organizational Change Management* 20, no. 6 (2007) 747–760.

Ehrlinger, Joyce, Thomas Gilovich, and Lee Ross. "Peering into the Bias Blind Spot: People's Assessments of Bias in Themselves and Others." *Personality and Social Psychology Bulletin* 31, no. 5 (2005) 680–692.

Eichenwald, Kurt. *Serpent on the Rock.* New York: Broadway Books, 1995.

Engelmann, Jan B., C. Monica Capra, Charles Noussair, and Gregory S. Berns. "Expert Financial Advice Neurobiologically 'Offloads' Financial Decision-Making under Risk." *Public Library of Science* (2009).

Epley, Nicholas, and Thomas Gilovich. "Just Going Along: Nonconscious Priming and Conformity to Social Pressure." *Journal of Experimental Social Psychology* 35, no. 6 (1999) 578–589.

Evans, Rob. "The Lonely Life of a Construction Industry Whistleblower." *Guardian*, May 15, 2009.

Felblinger, Dianne M. "Incivility and Bullying in the Workplace and Nurses' Shame Responses." *Journal of Obstetric, Gynecologic and Neonatal Nursing* 37 (2008) 234–242.

Festinger, Leon, and James M. Carlsmith. "Cognitive Consequences of Forced Compliance." *Journal of Abnormal and Social Psychology* 58 (1959) 203–210.

Festinger, Leon, and Nathan Maccoby. "On Resistance to Persuasive Communications." *Journal of Abnormal and Social Psychology* 68, no. 4 (1964) 359–366.

Festinger, Leon, Henry W. Riecken, and Stanley Schachter. *When Prophecy*

Fails: A Social and Psychological Study of a Modern Group that Predicted the Destruction of the World. New York: Harper Torch Books, 1956.

Feynman, Richard P. *What Do You Care What Other People Think? Further Adventures of a Curious Character.* London: Unwin Paperbacks, 1988.

Finch, Julia. "I Save Tax by Never Visiting My Family, Says Tycoon Hands." *Guardian*, February 6, 2010.

Fincher, Richard D. "Mediating Whistleblow Disputes." *Dispute Resolution Journal* (February/April 2009).

Fine, Cordelia. *A Mind of Its Own: How Your Brain Distorts and Deceives.* New York: W. W. Norton, 2006.

Finkelstein, Sydney. *Why Smart Executives Fail.* New York: Portfolio, 2003.

Fitzgerald, C. C. Penrose. *The Life of Vice-Admiral Sir George Tryon K.C.B.* Edinburgh: William Blackwood and Sons, 1897.

Florian, Victor, Mario Mikulincer, and Gilad Hirschberger. "The Anxiety-Buffering Function of Close Relationships: Evidence That Relationship Commitment Acts as a Terror Management Mechanism." *Journal of Personality and Social Psychology* 82, no. 4 (2002) 527–542.

Fohrman, Donald W. "Champaign Couple Heartened by Pending Texting Law." http://www.illinoispersonalinjurylawyerblog.com/2009/08/champaign_couple_heartened_by.html (2009).

Forster, Sophie, and Nilli Lavie. "Harnessing the Wandering Mind: The Role of Perceptual Load." *Cognition* 111 (2009) 345–355.

Freedman, Jonathan L., and Scott C. Fraser. "Compliance Without Pressure: The Foot-in-the-Door Technique." *Journal of Personality and Social Psychology* 4, no. 2 (1966) 195–202.

Frey, Bruno S., and Felix Oberholzer-Gee. "The Cost of Price Incentives: An Empirical Analysis of Motivation Crowding-Out." *American Economic Review* 87, no. 4 (1997) 746–755.

Fryer, Bronwyn. "Sleep Deficit: The Performance Killer." *Harvard Business Review* 84, no. 10 (2006) 53–59.

Gabor, Thomas. *Everybody Does It! Crime by the Public.* Toronto: University of Toronto Press, 1994.

Garcia, Stephen M., Kim Weaver, Gordon B. Moskowitz, and John M. Darley. "Crowded Minds: The Implicit Bystander Effect." *Journal of Personality and Social Psychology* 83, no. 4 (2002) 843–853.

Gentile, Mary. "Giving Voice to Values." *Aspen Institute.* http://caseplace.org/d.asp?d=3371.

Gerstein, Marc. *Flirting with Disaster.* New York: Union Square Press, 2008.

Gerstein, Marc S., and Robert B. Shaw. "Organizational Bystanders." *People & Strategy* 31, no. 1 (2008) 47–54.

Gibb, Frances. "Joint Enterprise Law Means Even Bystanders May Get Life." *Times* (London), 2009.

Gilbert, Daniel T. "How Mental Systems Believe." *American Psychologist* 46, no. 2 (1991) 107–119.

Gilbert, Daniel T., and Randall E. Osborne. "Thinking Backward: Some Curable and Incurable Consequences of Cognitive Busyness." *Journal of Personality and Social Psychology* 57, no. 6 (1989) 940–949.

Gilbert, Daniel T., Brett W. Pelham, and Douglas S. Krull. "On Cognitive Busyness: When Person Perceivers Meet Persons Perceived." *Journal of Personality and Social Psychology* 54, no. 5 (1998) 733–740.

Gilbert, Daniel T., Romin W. Tafarodi, and Patrick S. Malone. "You Can't Not Believe Everything You Read." *Journal of Personality and Social Psychology* 65, no. 2 (1993) 221–233.

Gilovich, Thomas. *How We Know What Isn't So: The Fallibility of Human Reason in Everyday Life.* New York: Free Press, 1991.

Glazer, Myron Peretz, and Penina Migdal Glazer. *Whistleblowers: Exposing Corruption in Government and Industry.* New York: Basic Books, 1989.

Gneezy, Uri, and Aldo Rustichini. "A Fine Is a Price." *Journal of Legal Studies* 29, no. 1 (2000) 1–17.

Goldfarb, Zachary A. "Staffer at SEC Had Warned of Madoff." *Washington Post,* July 2, 2009.

Goldie, John, Lisa Schwartz, Alex McConachie, and Jillian Morrison. "Students' Attitudes and Potential Behaviour with Regard to Whistle Blowing as They Pass Through a Modern Medical Curriculum." *Medical Education* 37 (2003) 368–375.

Goleman, Daniel. *Vital Lies, Simple Truths: The Psychology of Self-Deception.* New York: Simon & Schuster, 1985.

Goodman, Michael J., Julie A. Barker, and Christopher A. Monk. "A Bibliography of Research Related to the Use of Wireless Communications Devices from Vehicles." *National Highway Traffic Safety Administration* (2005).

Goodwin, Stephanie A., Alexandra Gubin, Susan T. Fiske, and Vincent Y. Qzerbt. "Power Can Bias Impression Processes: Stereotyping Subordinates by Default and by Design." *Group Processes and Intergroup Relations* 3, no. 3 (2000) 227–256.

Gordon, Andrew. *The Rules of the Game: Jutland and British Naval Command.* Annapolis: Naval Institute Press, 2000.

Government Accountability Project. "Internal World Bank Report Finds Staff Fear Reprisal; Corruption Inadequately Addressed," April 22, 2009. www .whistleblower.org.

Gray, Judy H., and Iain L. Densten. "How Leaders Woo Followers in the Romance of Leadership." *Applied Psychology: An International Review* 56, no. 4 (2007) 558–581.

Green, Stephen. *Good Value: Reflections on Money, Morality and an Uncertain World.* London: Allen Lane, 2009.

Greene, Gayle. *The Woman Who Knew Too Much: Alice Stewart and the Secrets of Radiation.* Ann Arbor, MI: University of Michigan Press, 1999.

Greene, Joshua D., R. Brian Sommerville, Leigh E. Nystrom, John M. Darley, and Jonathan D. Cohen. "An fMRI Investigation of Emotional Engagement in Moral Judgment." *Science* 293, no. 5537 (2001) 2105–2108.

Greenspan, Alan. *The Age of Turbulence.* New York: Allen Lane, 2007.

Greenwald, Anthony G. "The Totalitarian Ego: Fabrication and Revision of Personal History." *American Psychologist* 35, no. 7 (1980) 603–618.

Greenwald, Anthony G., and Mahzarin R. Banaji. "Implicit Social Cognition: Attitudes, Self-Esteem and Stereotypes." *Psychological Review* 102, no. 1 (1995) 4–27.

Groopman, Jerome. "Diagnosis: What Doctors Are Missing." *New York Review of Books,* November 5, 2009.

Grover, Steven L., and Chun Hui. "How Job Pressures and Extrinsic Rewards Affect Lying Behavior." *International Journal of Conflict Management* 16, no. 3 (2005) 287–300.

Gruenfeld, Deborah H. "Status, Ideology and Integrative Complexity on the Supreme Court: Rethinking the Politics of Political Decision Making." *Journal of Personality and Social Psychology* 68, no. 1 (1995) 5–20.

Hammond John S., L. Keeney Ralph, and Howard Raiffa. "The Hidden Traps in Decision Making." *Harvard Business Review* 84, no. 1 (2006) 118–126.

Hansen, J., D. Johnson, A. Lacis, S. Lebedeff, P. Lee, D. Rind, and G. Russell. "Climate Impact of Increasing Atmospheric Carbon Dioxide." *Science* 213, no. 4511 (1981) 957–966.

Harris, Gardiner. "Prosecutors Plan Crackdown on Doctors Who Accept Kickback." *New York Times,* March 4, 2009.

Hawkins, Peter. "Organizational Culture: Sailing Between Evangelism and Complexity." *Human Relations* 50, no. 4 (1997) 417–440.

Henriksen, Kerm, and Elizabeth Dayton. "Organizational Silence and Hidden Threats to Patient Safety." *Health Services Research* 41, no. 4p2 (2006) 1539–1554.

Hester, Robert, and Hugh Garavan. "Working Memory and Executive Function: The Influence of Content and Load on the Control of Attention." *Memory & Cognition* 33, no. 2 (2005) 221–233.

Heyman, James, and Dan Ariely. "Effort for Payment." *Psychological Science* 15, no. 11 (2004) 787–793.

Hilberg, Raul. *Perpetrators, Victims, Bystanders: The Jewish Catastrophe 1933–1945.* New York: HarperCollins, 1992.

Hillman, Charles H., Kirk I. Erickson, and Arthur F. Kramer. "Be Smart, Exercise Your Heart: Exercise Effects on Brain and Cognition." *Nature Reviews Neuroscience* 9 (2008) 58–65.

Hills, Stuart L., ed. *Corporate Violence: Injury and Death for Profit.* Lanham, MD: Rowman and Littlefield, 1987.

Hitsch, Gunter J., Ali Hortaçsu, and Dan Ariely. "Matching and Sorting in Online Dating." *American Economic Review* 10, no. 1 (2009) 130–163.

Hofling, Charles K., Eveline Brotzman, Sarah Dalrymple, Nancy Graves, and Chester M. Pierce. "An Experimental Study in Nurse-Physician Relationships." *Journal of Nervous and Mental Disease* 143, no. 2 (1966) 171–180.

Hogan, Linda. "Confronting the Truth: Conscience in the Catholic Tradition." Mahwah, NJ: Paulist Press, 2000.

Horrey, William J., Daniel J. Simons, Evan G. Buschmann, and Kevin M. Zinter. "Assessing Interference from Mental Workload Using a Naturalistic Simulated Driving Task: A Pilot Study." *Proceedings of the Human Factors and Ergonomics Society, 48th Annual Meeting*, 2003–2006 (2006).

Horwitz, Gordon J. *In the Shadow of Death: Living Outside the Gates of Mauthausen*. London: I. B. Tauris & Co., 1991.

Hough, Richard. *Admirals in Collision*. London: Hamish Hamilton, 1959.

Howard, John W., and Myron Rothbard. "Social Categorization and Memory for In-Group and Out-Group Behavior." *Journal of Personality and Social Psychology* 38, no. 2 (1980) 301–310.

"Info Overload Can Kill." *Star-Ledger News*, October 1, 2006.

Jackson, Maggie. *Distracted: The Erosion of Attention and the Coming Dark Age*. Amherst, NY: Prometheus Books, 2008.

Janis, Irving L. *Victims of Groupthink: A Psychological Study of Foreign-Policy Decisions and Fiascoes*. Boston: Houghton Mifflin, 1972.

———. *Crucial Decisions: Leadership in Policymaking and Crisis Management*. New York: Free Press, 1989.

Janis, Irving L., and Robert F. Terwilliger. "An Experimental Study of Psychological Resistances to Fear Arousing Communications." *Journal of Abnormal and Social Psychology* 65, no. 6 (1962) 403–410.

Joint Commission. "Behaviors that Undermine a Culture of Safety." Joint Commission, teleconference, July 9, 2008. http://jointcommission.org/NR/rdonlyres/CE6FE184-1.

Kahneman, Daniel, Paul Slovic, and Amos Tversky. *Judgement Under Uncertainty: Heuristics and Biases*. Cambridge: Cambridge University Press, 1982.

Kahneman, Daniel, Alan B. Krueger, David Schkade, Norbert Schwarz, and Arthur A. Stone. "Would You Be Happier If You Were Richer? A Focusing Illusion." *Science* 312, no. 5782 (2006) 1908–1910.

Karabell, Zachary. "The One Who Saw It Coming." *Newsweek*, January 19, 2009.

Kegan, Robert, and Lisa Laskow Lahey. "The Real Reason People Won't Change." *Harvard Business Review* (2001) 85–92.

———. *Immunity to Change: How to Overcome It and Unlock Potential in Yourself and Your Organization*. Harvard Business School Press, 2009.

Kelly, Kate. *Street Fighters: The Last 72 Hours of Bear Stearns, the Toughest Firm on Wall Street*. New York: Portfolio, 2009.

Kerber, Ross. "The Whistleblower: Dogged Pursuer of Madoff Wary of Fame." *Boston.com*, January 8, 2009. http://www.boston.com/business/articles/2009/01/08/the_whistleblower/.

Kida, Thomas. *Don't Believe Everything You Think: The 6 Basic Mistakes We Make in Thinking*. Amherst, NY: Prometheus Books, 2006.

Knutson, Brian, Andrew Westdorp, Erica Kaiser, and Daniel Hommer. "FMRI Visualization of Brain Activity During a Monetary Incentive Delay Task." *NeuroImage* 12 (2000) 20–27.

Kohn, Nicholas W., and Steven M. Smith. "Collaborative Fixation: Effects of

Others" Ideas on Brainstorming." *Applied Cognitive Psychology,* http://www3
.interscience.wiley.com/cgi-bin/fulltext/123329584/PDFSTART.

Kolb, Bryan, and Ian Q. Whishaw. "Brain Plasticity and Behavior." *Annual Review of Psychology* 49 (1998) 43–64.

Kolbert, Elizabeth. "The Catastrophist." *New Yorker,* June 29, 2009.

Krackow, Annamarie, and Thomas Blass. "When Nurses Obey or Defy Inappropriate Physician Orders: Attributional Differences." *Journal of Social Behavior and Personality* 10, no. 3 (1995) 585–594.

Krugman, Paul. "How Did Economists Get It So Wrong?" *New York Times,* September 6, 2009.

Kunda, Ziva. "The Case for Motivated Reasoning." *Psychological Bulletin* 108, no. 3 (1990) 480–498.

Kunst-Wilson, William Raft, and R. B. Zajonc. "Affective Discrimination of Stimuli that Cannot Be Recognized." *Science* 207 no. 4430 (1980) 557–558.

Larsen, Knud S., Jeff S. Triplett, William D. Brant, and Don Langenberg. "Collaborator Status, Subject Characteristics and Conformity in the Asch Paradigm." *Journal of Social Psychology* 108 (1979) 259–263.

Latané, Bibb, and Steve Nida. "Ten Years of Research on Group Size and Helping." *Psychological Bulletin* 89, no. 2 (1981) 308–324.

Latané, Bibb, and J. Rodin. "A Lady in Distress: Inhibiting Effects of Friends and Strangers on Bystander Intervention." *Journal of Experimental Social Psychology* 5, no. 2 (1969) 189–202.

Latané, Bibb, and John Darley. "Group Inhibition of Bystander Intervention in Emergencies." *Journal of Personality and Social Psychology* 10, no. 3 (1968) 215–221.

———. "Apathy." *American Scientist* 57 (1969) 244–268.

Layton, Deborah. *Seductive Poison: A Jonestown Survivor's Story of Life and Death in the People's Temple.* London: Aurum Press, 1999.

Lazear, Edward P. "Performance Pay and Productivity." *American Economic Review* 90, no. 5 (2000) 1346–1361.

Lea, Stephen E. G., and Paul Webley. "Money as Tool, Money as Drug: The Biological Psychology of a Strong Incentive." *Behavioral and Brain Sciences* 29 (2006) 161–209.

Lee Hamilton, V., and Joseph Sanders. "Personality and Social Psychology Review." *Personality and Social Psychology Review* 3 (1999) 222–233.

Liu, James H., and Bibb Latané. "Extremization of Attitudes: Does Thought- and Discussion-Induced Polarization Cumulate?" *Basic and Applied Social Psychology* 20, no. 2 (1998) 103–110.

Lizza, Ryan. "The Contrarian." *New Yorker,* July 6 and 13, 2009.

London School of Economics. "Letter to the Queen in Response to Her Question: Why Had Nobody Noticed That the Credit Crunch Was on Its Way?" 2009.

Long, Jennifer. "Testimony at the Oversight Hearing on the Internal Revenue Service." U.S. Senate Committee on Finance, 1997.

Luborsky, Lester, and Barton Blinder. "Looking, Recalling, and GSR as a Function of Defense." *Journal of Abnormal Psychology* 70, no. 4 (1965) 270–280.

Lundberg, George D. "How Will Changes in Physician Payment by Medicare Influence Laboratory Testing?" *Journal of the American Medical Association* 258 no. 6 (1987) 803–809.

Luo, Shanhong, and Eva C. Klohnen. "Assortative Mating and Marital Quality in Newlyweds: A Couple-Centered Approach." *Journal of Personality and Social Psychology* 88, no. 2 (2005) 304–326.

Mack, Arien. "Inattentional Blindness: Looking Without Seeing." *Current Directions in Psychological Science* 12, no. 5 (2003) 180–184.

Macrae, C. Neil, Alan B. Milne, and Galen V. Bodenhausen. "Stereotypes as Energy-Saving Devices: A Peek Inside the Cognitive Toolbox." *Journal of Personality and Social Psychology* 66, no. 1 (1994) 37–47.

Manz, Charles C., Vikas Anand, Mahendra Joshi, and Karen P. Manz. "Emerging Paradoxes in Executive Leadership: A Theoretical Interpretation Between Corruption and Virtuous Values." *Leadership Quarterly* 19 (2008) 385–392.

Marcus, Jonathan L. "Model Penal Code Section 2.02(7) and Willful Blindness." *Yale Law Journal* 102, no. 8 (1993) 2231–2257.

Markey, P. M. "Bystander Intervention in Computer-Mediated Communication." *Computers in Human Behavior* 16, no. 2 (2000) 183–188.

Markopolos, Harry. *No One Would Listen: A True Financial Thriller.* Hoboken, NJ: Wiley & Sons, 2010.

Marsh, Jason. "We Are All Bystanders." *Greater Good*, Fall/Winter 2006.

Marsh, Stefanie, and Bojan Pancevski. *The Crimes of Josef Fritzl: Uncovering the Truth.* London: Harper Element, 2009.

Martz, John M., Julie Verette, Ximena B. Arriaga, Linda F. Slovik, Chante L. Cox, and Caryl Rusbult. "Positive Illusion in Close Relationships." *Personal Relationships* 5 (1998) 159–181.

Maslach, Christina, and Michael P. Leiter. *The Truth About Burnout: How Organizations Cause Personal Stress and What to Do About It.* San Francisco, CA: Jossey-Bass, 1997.

Massing, Michael. "The News About the Internet." *New York Review of Books*, August 13, 2009, 29–32.

McClellan, Scott. *What Happened: Inside the Bush White House and Washington's Culture of Deceptions.* New York: Public Affairs, 2008.

McLaughlin, Brian P., and Amelie Oksenberg Rorty, eds. *Perspectives on Self-Deception.* Berkeley: University of California Press, 1988.

McTague, Jim. "Looking at Greenspan's Long-Lost Thesis." *Barron's*, 2008.

Mead, Nicole L., Roy F. Baumeister, Francesca Gino, Maurice E. Schweitzer, and Dan Ariely. "Too Tired to Tell the Truth: Self-Control Resource Depletion and Dishonesty." *Journal of Experimental Social Psychology* 45, no. 3 (2009) 594–597.

Mele, Alfred R. *Self-Deception Unmasked.* Princeton, NJ: Princeton University Press, 2001.

Mendelson, Sarah E., and Theodore P. Gerber. "Failing the Stalin Test." *Foreign Affairs* 85, no. 1 (2006).

Mesmer-Magnus, Jessica, Chockalingam Viswesvaran, Jacob Joseph, and Satish P. Deshpande. "The Role of Emotional Intelligence in Integrity and Ethics Perceptions." *Emotions, Ethics and Decision-Making: Research on Emotion in Organization* 4 (2008) 225–239.

Miceli, Marcia P., and Janet P. Near. "Standing Up or Standing By: What Predicts Blowing the Whistle on Organizational Wrongdoing?" *Research in Personnel and Human Resources Management* 24 (2005) 93–136.

Milgram, Stanley. "The Experience of Living in Cities." *Science* 167 (1970) 1461.

———. *Obedience to Authority*. New York: Harper Perennial, 1974.

Milkman, Katherine, L., Dolly Chugh, and Max H. Bazerman. "How Can Decision Making Be Improved?" *Perspectives on Psychological Science* 4, no. 4 (2009) 379–383.

Miller, Dale T., and Cathy McFarland. "Pluralistic Ignorance: When Similarity Is Interpreted as Dissimilarity." *Journal of Personality and Social Psychology* 53, no. 2 (1987) 298–305.

Miller, Rowland S. *Embarrassment: Poise and Peril in Everyday Life*. New York: Guilford Press, 1996.

Milliken, Charles S., Jennifer L. Auchterlonie, and Charles W. Hoge. "Longitudinal Assessment of Mental Health Problems Among Active and Reserve Component Soldiers Returning from the Iraq War." *Journal of the American Medical Association* 298, no. 18 (2007) 2141–2148.

Milliken, Frances J., and Elizabeth Wolfe Morrison. "Shades of Silence: Emerging Themes and Future Directions for Research on Silence in Organizations." *Journal of Management Studies* 40, no. 6 (2003) 1563–1568.

Milliken, Frances J., Elizabeth W. Morrison, and Patricia F. Hewlin. "An Exploratory Study of Employee Silence: Issues that Employees Don't Communicate Upward and Why." *Journal of Management Studies* 40, no. 6 (2003) 1453–1476.

Moll, Jorge, Frank Krueger, Roland Zahn, Matteo Pardini, Ricardo de Oliveira-Souza, and Jordan Grafman. "Human Fronto-Mesolimbic Networks Guide Decisions About Charitable Donation." *Proceedings of the National Academy of Sciences* 103, no. 42 (2006) 15623–15628.

Moore, Don A., and George Loewenstein. "Self-Interest, Automaticity, and the Psychology of Conflict of Interest." *Social Justice Research* 17, no. 2 (2004) 189–202.

Moreland, Richard L., and Robert B. Zajonc. "Exposure Effects in Person Perception: Familiarity, Similarity, and Attraction." *Journal of Experimental Social Psychology* 18 (1982) 395–415.

Morewedge, Carey K., Daniel T. Gilbert, and Timothy D. Wilson. "The Least Likely of Times: How Remembering the Past Biases Forecasts of the Future." *Psychological Science* 16, no. 8 (2005) 626–630.

Morris, Errol. *Standard Operating Procedure*. Sony Pictures, 2003.

Morrison, Elizabeth W., Sara L. Wheeler-Smith, and Dishan Kamdar. "Speaking Up in Groups: A Cross-Level Study of Group Voice Climate." *Journal of Applied Psychology* (read under review), 2009.

Moscovici, Serge, and Marisa Zavalloni. "The Group as a Polarizer of Attitudes." *Journal of Personality and Social Psychology* 12, no. 2 (1969) 125–135.

Murray, Sandra L, John G. Holmes, Gina Bellavia, Dale W. Griffin, and Dan Dolderman. "Kindred Spirits? The Benefits of Egocentrism in Close Relationships." *Journal of Personality and Social Psychology* 82, no. 4 (2002).

Murray, Sandra L., John G. Holmes, and Dale W. Griffin. "The Self-Fulfilling Nature of Positive Illusions in Romantic Relationships: Love Is Not Blind, But Prescient." *Journal of Personality and Social Psychology* 7, no. 6 (1996) 1155–1180.

National Safety Council. "National Safety Council Calls for Nationwide Ban on Cell Phone Use While Driving." Press Release. January 12, 2009.

National Sleep Foundation. "Asleep in America: Poll Highlight and Findings." March 2, 2009.

Nedd, Council A. II. "When the Solution Is the Problem: A Brief History of the Shoe Fluoroscope." *American Journal of Roentgenology* 158 (1992) 1270.

Newrx.com. "Women Whistleblowers Suffer More Discrimination INFORMS-Published Study Suggests." May 28, 2009. www.soeken.lawsonline.net/articles/508WomenWSuffer.htm.

Nobuyuki, Chikudate. "Collective Myopia and Disciplinary Power Behind the Scenes of Unethical Practices: A Diagnostic Theory on Japanese Organization." *Journal of Management Studies* 39, no. 3 (2002) 289–307.

Norton, Michael I., Benoit Monin, Joel Cooper, and Michael A. Hogg. "Vicarious Dissonance: Attitude Change from the Inconsistency of Others." *Journal of Personality and Social Psychology* 85, no. 1 (2003) 47–62.

Norton, Michael I., Jeana H. Frost, and Dan Ariely. "Less Is More: The Lure of Ambiguity, or Why Familiarity Breeds Contempt." *Journal of Personality and Social Psychology* 92, no. 1 (2007) 97–105.

O'Gorman, Colm. *Beyond Belief*. London: Hodder and Stoughton, 2009.

Osborne, William. "Blind Auditions and Moral Myopia: The Gender/Racial Ideologies of the Vienna Philharmonic and the Employment Practices that Allow Them to Continue." http://www.osborne-conant.org/posts/blind.htm.

Osiel, Mark J. *Obeying Orders: Atrocity, Military Discipline and the Law of War*. New Brunswick, NJ: Transaction Publishers, 2002.

Panksepp, Jaak. "Neuroscience: Feeling the Pain of Social Loss." *Science* 302, no. 5643 (2003) 237–239.

———. *Affective Neuroscience: The Foundations of Human and Animal Emotions*. Oxford: Oxford University Press, 1998.

Paperny, Justin M. *Lessons from Prison: Bear Stearns, UBS Stockbroker Muses on Ethics and Provides a Guide through the Criminal Justice System*. APS Publishing, 2009.

Parker-Pope, Tara. "A Problem of the Brain, Not the Hands: Group Urges Phone Ban for Drivers." *New York Times*, January 13, 2009.

Partnoy, Frank. *F.I.A.S.C.O.: Blood in the Water on Wall Street.* London: W.W. Norton, 1997, 2009.

———. *Infectious Greed: How Deceit and Risk Corrupted the Financial Markets.* London: Profile Books, 2003.

———. "The Case Against Alan Greenspan." *Euromoney* 36, no. 437 (2005) 90–96.

Pascual-Leonoe, Alvaro, Nguyet Dang, Leonardo G. Cohen, Joaquim P. Brasil-Neto, Angel Cammarota, and Mark Hallett. "Modulation of Muscle Responses Evoked by Transcranial Magnetic Stimulation During the Acquisition of New Fine Motor Skills." *Journal of Neurophysiology* 74, no. 3 (1995) 1037–1045.

Pavlo, Walter Jr., and Neil Weinberg. *Stolen Without a Gun.* Tampa, FL: Etika LLC, 2007.

PBS *Frontline.* "The Warning." Produced by Michael Kirk, first aired October 20, 2009.

Pelham, Brett W., Matthew C. Mirenberg, and John T. Jones. "Why Susie Sells Seashells by the Seashore: Implicit Egotism and Major Life Decisions." *Journal of Personality and Social Psychology* 82, no. 4 (2002) 469–487.

Pennebaker, Ruth. "The Mediocre Multitasker." *New York Times*, August 30, 2009.

Perry, David L. "Why Hearts and Minds Matter." *Armed Forces Journal*, September 2006. http://www.afji.com/2006/09/2002037.

Pessiglione, Mathias, Liane Schmidt, Bogdan Draganski, Raffael Kalisch, Hakwan Lau, Ray J. Dolan, and Chris D. Frith. "How the Brain Translates Money into Force: A Neuroimaging Study of Subliminal Motivation." *Science* 316, no. 5826 (2007) 904–906.

Petty, Richard E., Gary L. Wells, and Timothy C. Brock. "Distraction Can Enhance or Reduce Yielding to Propaganda: Thought Disruption Versus Effort Justification." *Journal of Personality and Social Psychology* 34, no. 5 (1976) 874–884.

Phillips, Katherine W., and Robert B. Lount Jr. "The Affective Consequences of Diversity and Homogeneity in Groups." *Affect and Groups: Research on Managing Groups and Teams* 10 (2007) 1–20.

Piderit, Sandy Kristin, and Susan J. Ashford. "Breaking Silence: Tactical Choices Women Managers Make in Speaking Up About Gender-Equity Issues." *Journal of Management Studies* 40, no. 6 (2003) 1477–1502.

Premeaux, Sonya Fontenot, and Arthur G. Bedeian. "Breaking the Silence: The Moderating Effects of Self-Monitoring in Predicting Speaking Up in the Workplace." *Journal of Management Studies* 40, no. 6 (2003) 1537–1562.

Prentice, Deborah A., and Dale T. Miller. "Pluralistic Ignorance and Alcohol Use on Campus: Some Consequences of Misperceiving the Social Norm." *Journal of Personality and Social Psychology* 64, no. 2, (1993) 243–256.

Proctor, Robert N., and London Schiebinger, eds. *Agnotology: The Making and Unmaking of Ignorance.* Stanford, CA: Stanford University Press, 2008.

Pronin, Emily, Thomas Gilovich, and Lee Ross. "Objectivity in the Eye of the Beholder: Divergent Perceptions of Bias in Self Versus Others." *Psychological Review* 111, no. 3 (2004) 781–799.

Proulx, Travis, and Steven J. Heine. "Connections from Kafka: Exposure to Meaning Threats Improves Implicit Learning of an Artificial Grammar." *Psychological Science* 20, no. 9 (2009) 1125–1131.

Public Health Agency of Canada. "Canadian Incidence Study of Reported Child Abuse and Neglect." 2003. http://www.phac-aspc.gc.ca/cm-vee/csca-ecve/pdf/childabuse_final_e.pdf.

———. "Melanoma Skin Cancer." http://www.phac-aspc.gc.ca/cd-mc/cancer/melanoma_skin_cancer-cancer_peau_melanome-eng.php.

Reite, M., and T. Field, eds. *The Psychobiology of Attachment and Separation.* New York: Academic Press, 1985.

Richtel, Matt. "U.S. Withheld Data on Risks of Distracted Driving." *New York Times,* July 21, 2009.

Robertson, Diana, John Snarey, Opal Ousley, Keith Harenski, F. DuBois Bowman, Rick Gilkey, and Clinton Kilts. "The Neural Processing of Moral Sensitivity to Issues of Justice and Care." *Neuropsychologia* 45, no. 4 (2007) 755–766.

Robinson, Evan. "Why Crunch Mode Doesn't Work: 6 Lessons." *International Game Developers Association,* 2005.

Rosenhan, D. L. "On Being Sane in Insane Places." *Science* 179, no. 4070 (1973) 250–258.

Rosin, Hanna. "When Joseph Comes Marching Home: In a Western Maryland Town, Ambivalence About the Son Who Blew the Whistle at Abu Ghraib." *Washington Post,* May 17, 2004.

Rost, Peter. *The Whistleblower: Confessions of a Healthcare Hitman.* New York: Soft Skull Press, 2006.

Rothschild, Jeffrey M., Carol A. Keohane, Selwyn Rogers, and Charles A. Czeisler. "Risks of Complications by Attending Physicians after Performing Nighttime Procedure." *Journal of the American Medical Association* 302, no. 14 (2009) 1565–1572.

Roubini, Nouriel. "The Biggest Slip in US Housing in the Last 40 Years . . . or 53 Years?" *RGE monitor,* 2006. www.roubini.com/roubini-monitor/142759/the_biggest_slump_in_US_housing_in_the_last_40_years_or_53_years.

Rowe, Mary. "Dealing with—or Reporting—'Unacceptable' Behavior (with Additional Thoughts About the 'Bystander Effect.'" *Journal of the International Ombudsman Association* 2, no. 1 (2009).

Sanders, William Gerard, and Donald C. Hambrick. "The Effects of CEO Incentive Compensation on Subsequent Firm Investments and Performance." Unpublished.

Sands, Phillipe. "Polished, Assured . . . But Was He Persuasive? No." *Guardian,* January 28, 2010.

Schmit, Rick. "Prophet and Loss." *Stanford* magazine, March/April 2009.

Schneider, Andrew, and David McCumber. *An Air That Kills: How the Asbestos Poisoning of Libby, Montana Uncovered a National Scandal.* New York: G. P. Putnam's Sons, 2004.

Schwartz, Barry. "Incentives, Choice, Education and Well-Being." *Oxford Review of Education* 35, no. 3 (2009) 391–403.

Seager, Ashley. "Method of Inflation Targeting Was Wrong." *Guardian*, April 6, 2009.

Seligman, Martin E. P. *Authentic Happiness.* London: Nicholas Brealey Publishing, 2003.

Sereny, Gitta. *Albert Speer: His Battle with Truth.* London: Picador, 1996.

———. *The German Trauma: Experiences and Reflections 1938–2001.* London: Penguin Books, 2001.

Sheridan, Charles L., and Richard G. King. "Obedience to Authority with an Authentic Victim." *Proceedings, 80th Annual Convention,* American Psychological Association (1972) 165–166.

Shermer, Michael. "The Political Brain." *Scientific American,* June 26, 2006. www .scientificamerican.com/article.cfm?id=the-political-brain.

Simons, Daniel J. "Inattentional Blindness." *Scholarpedia* 2, no. 5 (2007) 3244.

Simons, Daniel J., and Christopher F. Chabris. "Gorillas in Our Midst: Sustained Inattentional Blindness for Dynamic Events." *Perception* 28 (1999) 1059–1074.

Smith, J. Walker, Ann Clurman, and Craig Wood. *Coming to Concurrence: Addressable Attitudes and the New Model for Marketing Productivity.* Evanston, IL: Racom Communications, 2005.

Sophocles. *The Theban Plays.* London: Penguin Classics, 1947.

Sorkin, Andrew Ross. *Too Big to Fail: Inside the Battle to Save Wall Street.* London: Allen Lane, 2010.

Stanovich, Keith E., and Richard F. West. "Individual Differences in Reasoning: Implications for the Rationality Debate?" *Behavioral and Brain Sciences* 23 (2000) 645–726.

Staub, Ervin. "The Roots of Evil: Social Conditions, Culture, Personality, and Basic Human Needs." *Personality and Social Psychology Review* 3 (1999) 179–192.

Staub, Ervin. *The Psychology of Good and Evil: Why Children, Adults, and Groups Help and Harm Others.* Cambridge: Cambridge University Press, 2003.

Stephanie, A. Goodwin, Don Operario, and Susan T. Fiske. "Empirical Approaches to Understanding Intergroup Conflict Situational Power and Interpersonal Dominance Facilitate Bias and Inequality." *Journal of Social Issues* 54, no. 4 (1998) 677–698.

Stewart, Alice, Josefine Webb, and David Hewitt. "A Survey of Childhood Malignancies." *British Medical Journal* (1958) 1495–1508.

Stillman, T. F., R. F. Baumeister, N. M. Lambert, A. W. Crescioni, C. N. DeWall, and F. D. Fincham. "Alone and Without Purpose: Life Loses Meaning Following Social Exclusion." *Journal of Experimental Social Psychology* 45, no. 4 (2009) 686–694.

Stone, Jeff, and Joel Cooper. "A Self-Standards Model of Cognitive Disso-
    nance." *Journal of Experimental Social Psychology* 37 (2001) 228–243.
Strayer, David L., Frank A. Drews, and Dennis J. Crouch. "A Comparison of the
    Cell Phone Driver and the Drunk Driver." *Human Factors* 48, no. 2 (2006)
    381–391.
Sunstein, Cass R. *Going to Extremes: How Like Minds Unite and Divide.* New
    York: Oxford University Press, 2009.
Swartz, Mimi, and Sherron Watkins. *Power Failure: The Inside Story of the Col-
    lapse of Enron.* New York: Doubleday, 2003.
Taleb, Nassim Nicholas. "David, You're Right." *Observer,* August 16, 2009.
Tangirala, Subrahmaniam, and Rangaraj Ramanujam. "Employee Silence on
    Critical Work Issues: The Cross Level Effects of Procedural Justice Cli-
    mate." *Personnel Psychology* 61 (2008) 37–68.
Tangney, June Price. *Self-Conscious Emotions: The Psychology of Shame, Guilt,
    Embarrassment and Pride.* New York: Guilford Press, 1995.
Tavris, Carol, and Elliot Aronson. *Mistakes Were Made (but Not by Me): Why We
    Justify Foolish Beliefs, Bad Decisions and Hurtful Acts.* London: Pinter & Mar-
    tin, 2008.
Tedlow, Richard S. "Leaders in Denial." *Harvard Business Review* 86, no. 7–8
    (2008) 18–19.
Tedlow, Richard S., and David Ruben. "The Dangers of Wishful Thinking."
    The American (2008) 86–90.
Tenbrunsel, Ann E., Kristina A. Diekmann, Kimberly A. Wade-Benzoni, and
    Max H. Bazerman. "The Ethical Mirage: A Temporal Explanation as to
    Why We Aren't as Ethical as We Think We Are." *Harvard Business School*
    working paper 08-012, 2007.
Tenbrunsel, Ann E., and David M. Messick. "Ethical Fading: The Role of Self-
    Deception in Unethical Behavior." *Social Justice Research* 17, no. 2 (2004)
    223–236.
Tett, Gillian. *Fool's Gold: How Unrestrained Greed Corrupted a Dream, Shattered
    Global Markets and Unleashed a Catastrophe.* London: Little, Brown, 2009.
Thaler, Richard H. "From Homo Economicus to Homo Sapiens." *Journal of
    Economic Perspectives* 14, no. 1 (2000) 133–141.
Thompson, Courtenay. "Willful Blindness." *Internal Auditor* (June 2003) 71–73.
Thornberg, Robert. "A Classmate in Distress: Schoolchildren as Bystanders and
    Their Reasons for How They Act." *Social Psychology of Education* 10 (2007)
    5–28.
Tierney, John. "How to Concentrate in a World of Distractions." *New York Times,*
    May 31, 2009.
Tomasi, D., R. L. Wang, F. Telang, V. Boronikolas, M. C. Jayne, G.-J. Wang, J.
    S. Fowler, and N. D. Volkow. "Impairment of Attentional Networks after
    1 Night of Sleep Deprivation." *Cerebral Cortex* 19, no. 1 (2009) 233–240.
Treanor, Jill. "Bankers Admit They Got It Wrong." *Guardian* (Manchester),
    February 11, 2009.

————. "Shown the Door: Brown's Banker Falls Victim to the Whistleblower." *Guardian*, February 12, 2009.

Van Dyne, Linn, Soon Ang, and Isabel C. Botero. "Conceptualizing Employee Silence and Employee Voice as Multidimensional Constructs." *Journal of Management Studies* 40, no. 6 (2003) 1359–1392.

Van Straaten, Ischa, Rutger C. M. E. Engels, Catrin Finkenauer, and Rob W. Holland. "Meeting Your Match: How Attractiveness Similarity Affects Approach Behavior in Mixed-Sex Dyads." *Personality & Social Psychology Bulletin.* 35, no. 6 (2000) 685–697.

Van Veen, Vincent, Marie K. Krug, Jonathan W. Schooler, and Cameron S. Carter. "Neural Activity Predicts Attitude Change in Cognitive Dissonance." *Nature Neuroscience* 12, no. 11 (2009) 1469–1474.

Vermeulen, Freek. "Why Stock Options Are a Bad Option." *Harvard Business Review* online, April 21, 2009. http://blogs.hbr.org/vermeulen/2009/04/why-stock-options-are-a-bad-op.html.

Vohs, Kathleen D. "Merely Activating the Concept of Money Changes Personal and Interpersonal Behavior." *Current Directions in Psychological Science* 17, no. 3 (2008) 208–212.

Vohs, Kathleen D., Nicole L. Mead, and Miranda R. Goode. "The Psychological Consequences of Money." *Science* 314, no. 5802 (2006) 1154–1156.

Walker, Sir David. *A Review of Corporate Governance in UK Banks and Other Industry Entities, July 16, 2009, Annex 4: Psychological and Behavioural Elements in Board Performance.* http://www.hm-treasury.gov.uk/walker_review_information.htm.

Webb, Tim. "Sun King Reveals His Darker Side." *Guardian*, February 9, 2010.

Webb, Tim, Robert Booth, Justin McCurry, and Paul Harris. "How World's Biggest Car Maker Managed to Veer So Far Off Course." *Observer*, February 7, 2010.

Weinberger, Joel, and Drew Westen. "Rats, We Should Have Used Clinton: Subliminal Priming in Political Campaigns." *Political Psychology* 29, no. 5 (2008) 631–651.

Weisbuch, Max, Stacey A. Sinclair, and Jeanine L. Skorinko. "Self-Esteem Depends on the Beholder: Effects of a Subtle Social Value Cue." *Journal of Experimental Social Psychology* 45, no. 1 (2009) 143–149.

Werner, Anna. "Oakland Bank's Lending Sparks Ex-Employee Lawsuit." *CBS.com*, May 21, 2008. http://cbs5.com/investigates/lawsuit.world.savings.2.729925.html.

Wertz, Adam T., Joseph M. Ronda, and Charles A. Czeisler. "Effects of Sleep Inertia on Cognition." *Journal of the American Medical Association* 295, no. 2 (2006).

Westen, Drew. *The Political Brain: The Role of Emotion in Deciding the Fate of the Nation.* New York: Public Affairs, 2007.

Westen, Drew, Pavel S. Blagov, Keith Harenski, Clint Kilts, and Stephan Hamann. "Neural Bases of Motivated Reasoning: An fMRI Study of

Emotional Constraints on Partisan Political Judgment in the 2004 U.S. Presidential Election." *Journal of Cognitive Neuroscience* 18, no. 11 (2006) 1947–1958.

White, Jenny, Albert Bandura, and Lisa A. Bero. "Moral Disengagement in the Corporate World." *Accountability in Research* 16, no. 1 (2009) 41–74.

Wispe, Lauren. *Altruism, Sympathy and Helping: Psychological and Sociological Principles.* London: Academic Press, 1978.

Woodward, Bob. *Maestro: Greenspan's Fed and the American Boom.* New York: Simon & Schuster, 2000.

———. *State of Denial: Bush at War, Part III,* New York: Simon & Schuster, 2006.

Young-Bruehl, Elisabeth. *Hannah Arendt: For Love of the World.* New Haven, CT: Yale University Press, 1982.

Zerubavel, Eviatar. *The Elephant in the Room: Silence and Denial in Everyday Life.* Oxford: Oxford University Press, 2006.

Zhou, Xinyue, Cong Feng, Lingnan He, and Ding-Guo Gao. "Toward an Integrated Understanding of Love and Money: Intrinsic and Extrinsic Pain Management Mechanisms." *Psychological Inquiry* 19 (2008) 208–220.

Zhou, Xinyue, Kathleen D. Vohs, and Roy F. Baumeister. "The Symbolic Power of Money: Reminders of Money Alter Social Distress and Physical Pain." *Psychological Science* 20, no. 6 (2009) 700–706.

Zimbardo, Philip G. "The Heroic Imagination Project." Planning documents, 2009.

———. *The Lucifer Effect: How Good People Turn Evil.* New York: Random House, 2007.

———. "Discontinuity Theory: Cognitive and Social Searches for Rationality and Normality May Lead to Madness." *Advances in Experimental Social Psychology* 31 (1999) 345–413.

INDEX

A NOTE ON THE AUTHOR

Margaret Heffernan was born in Texas, raised in Holland, and educated at Cambridge University. A former producer for the BBC, she also is an entrepreneur and former CEO of several multimedia companies. Heffernan is author of *The Naked Truth: A Working Woman's Manifesto on Business and What Really Matters* and *How She Does It: How Women Entrepreneurs Are Changing the Rules of Business Success*, and a regular contributor to *Real Business*, *Fast Company* magazine, the *Huffington Post*, and BNET.com. Visit her Web site at www.willful-blindness.com.